AF539595

SHIFTING GROUNDS

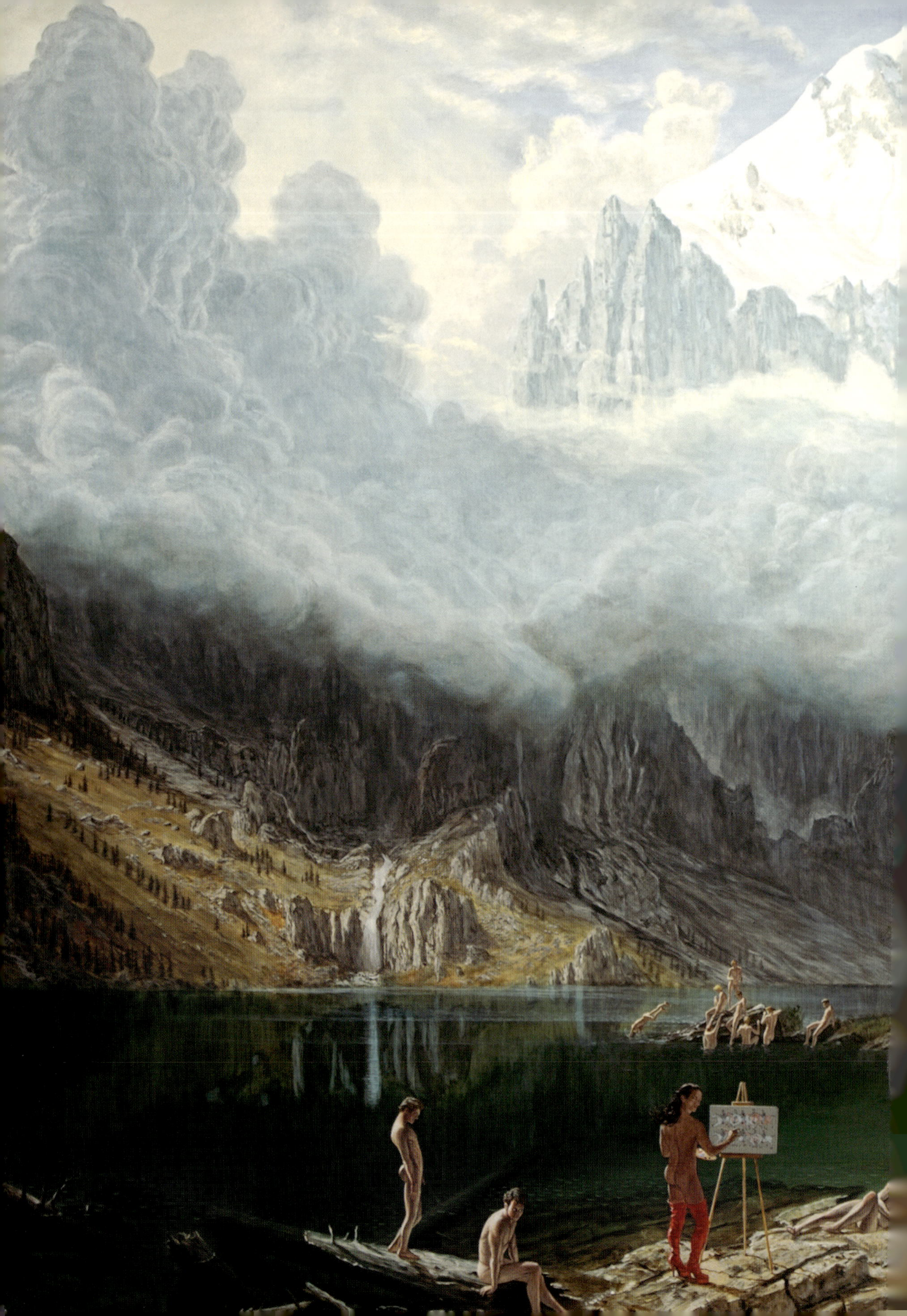

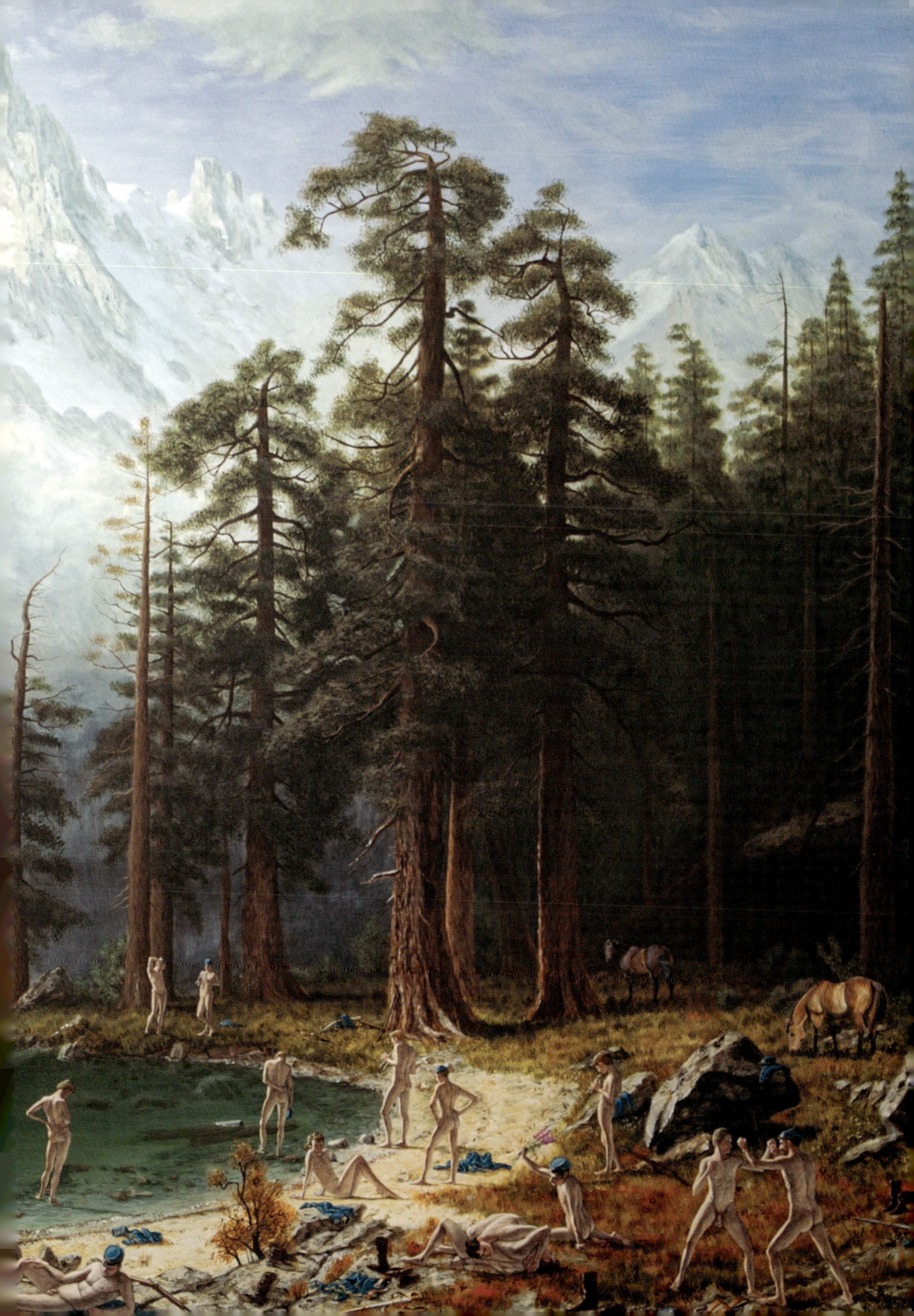

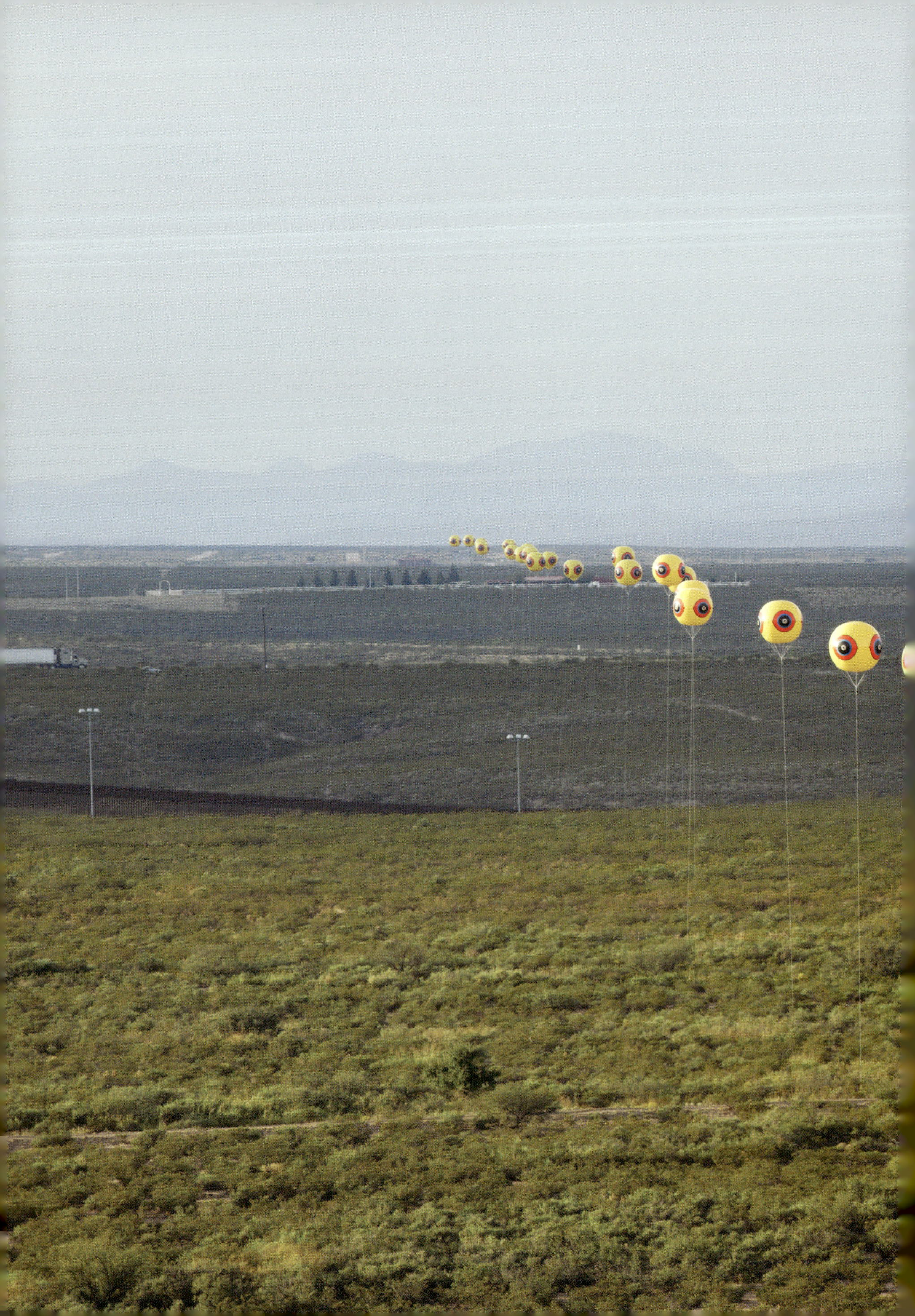

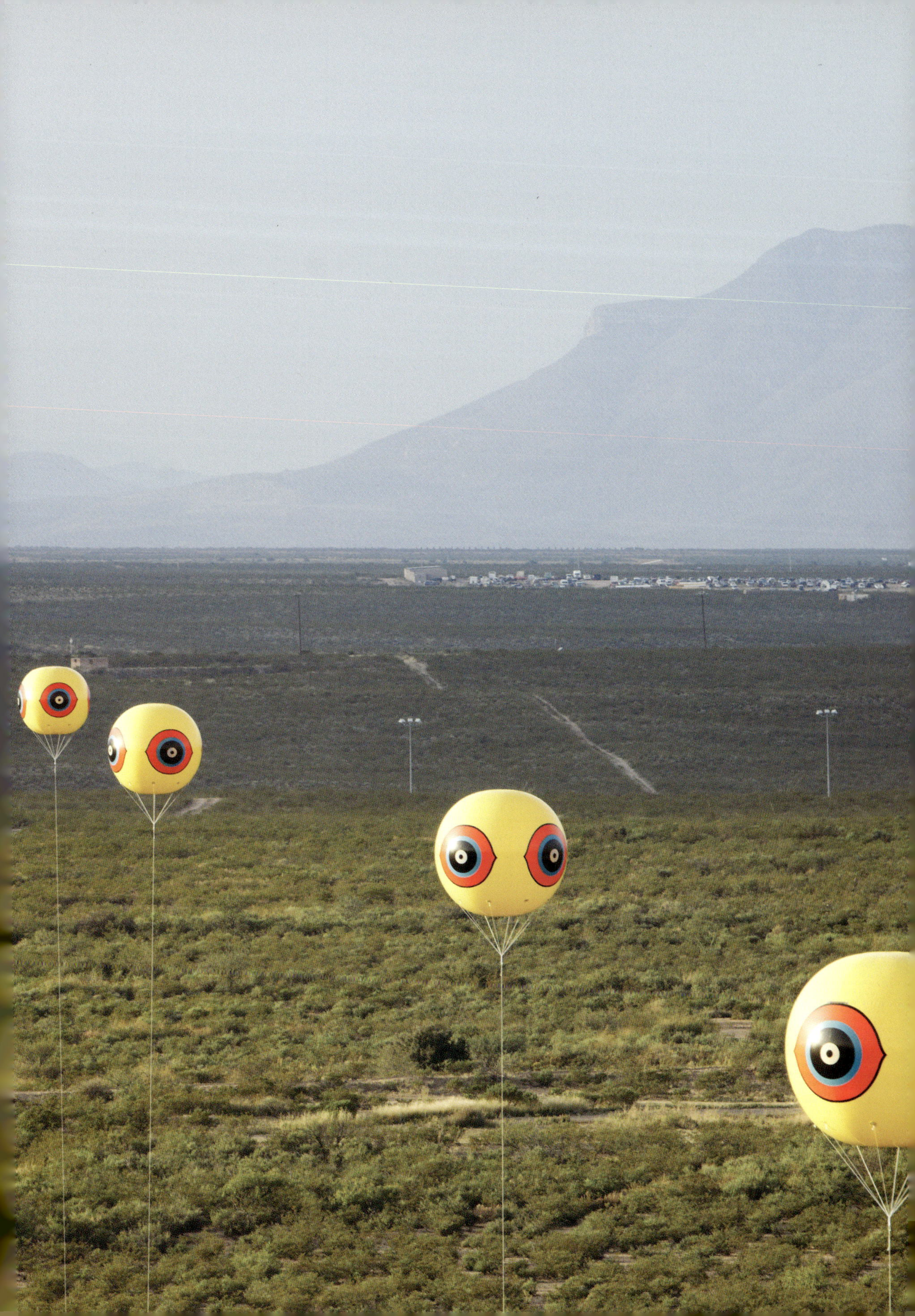

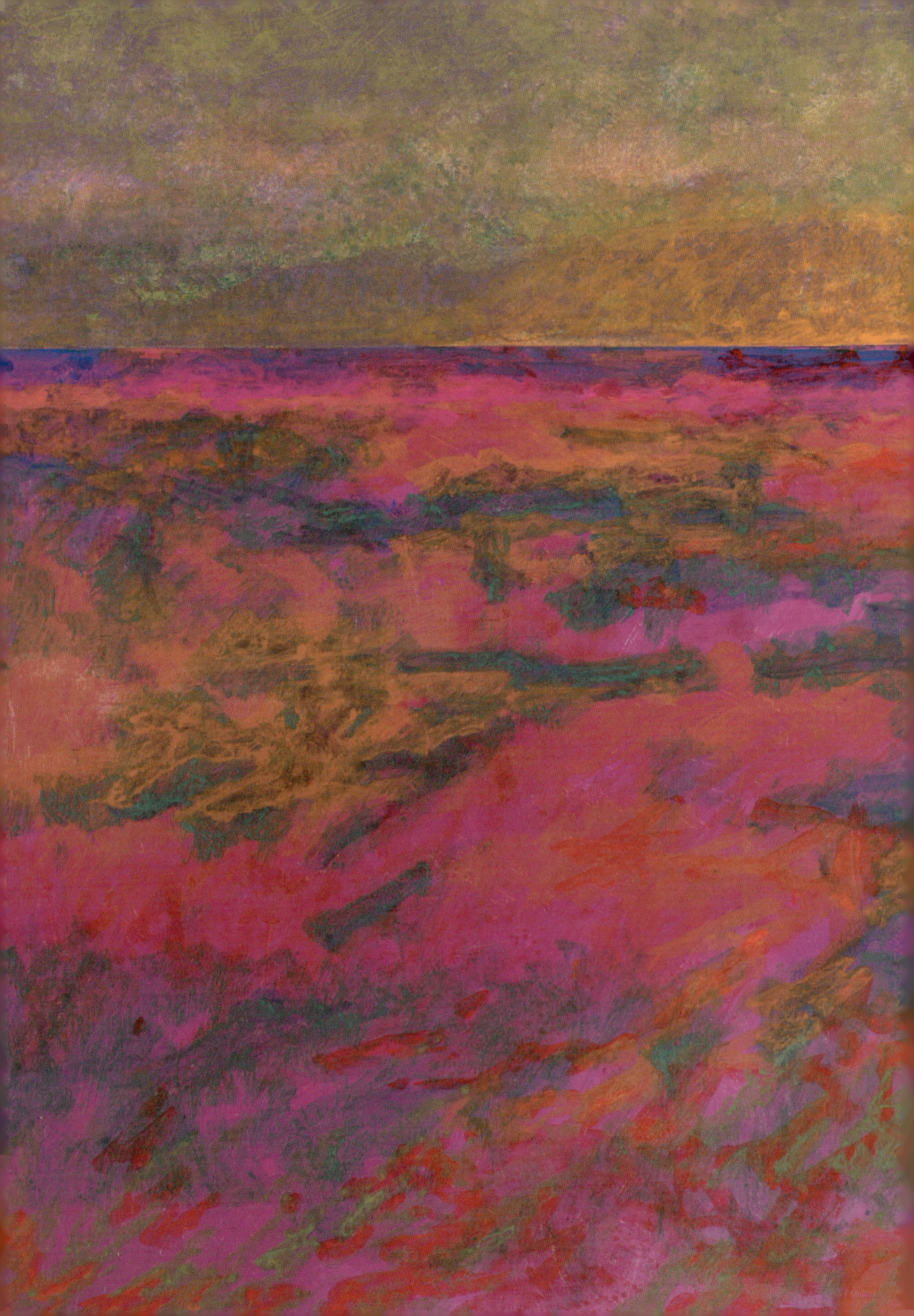

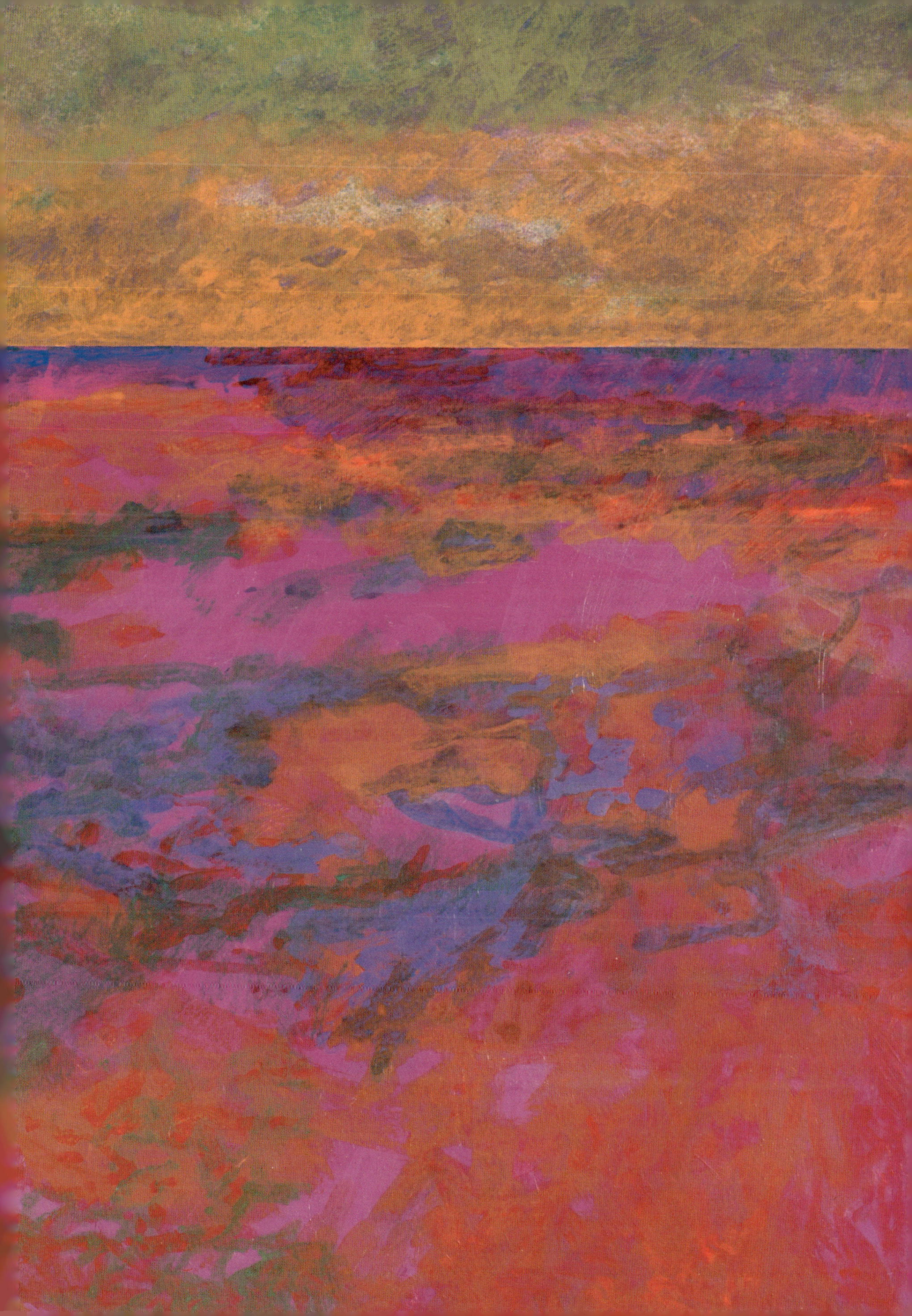

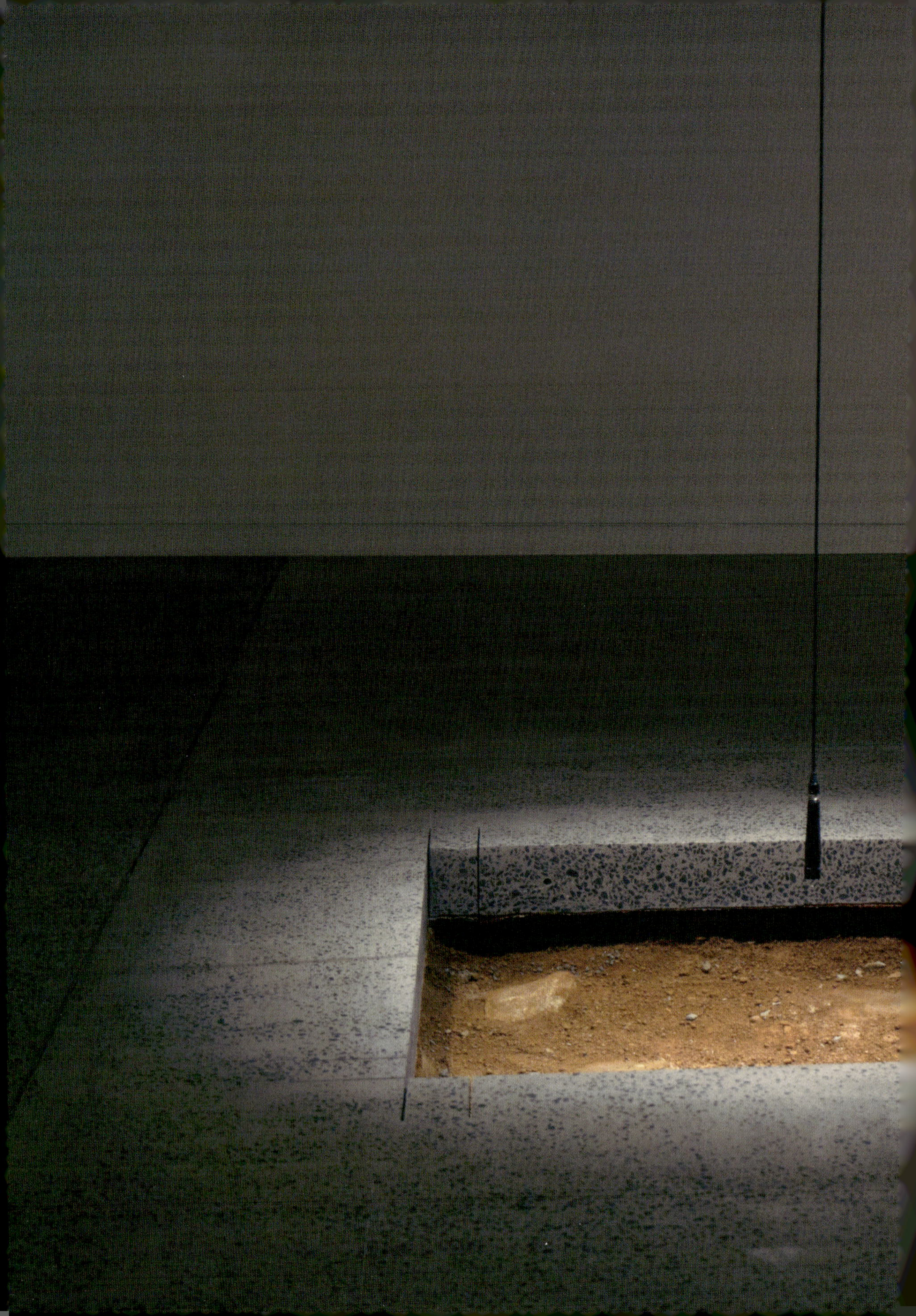

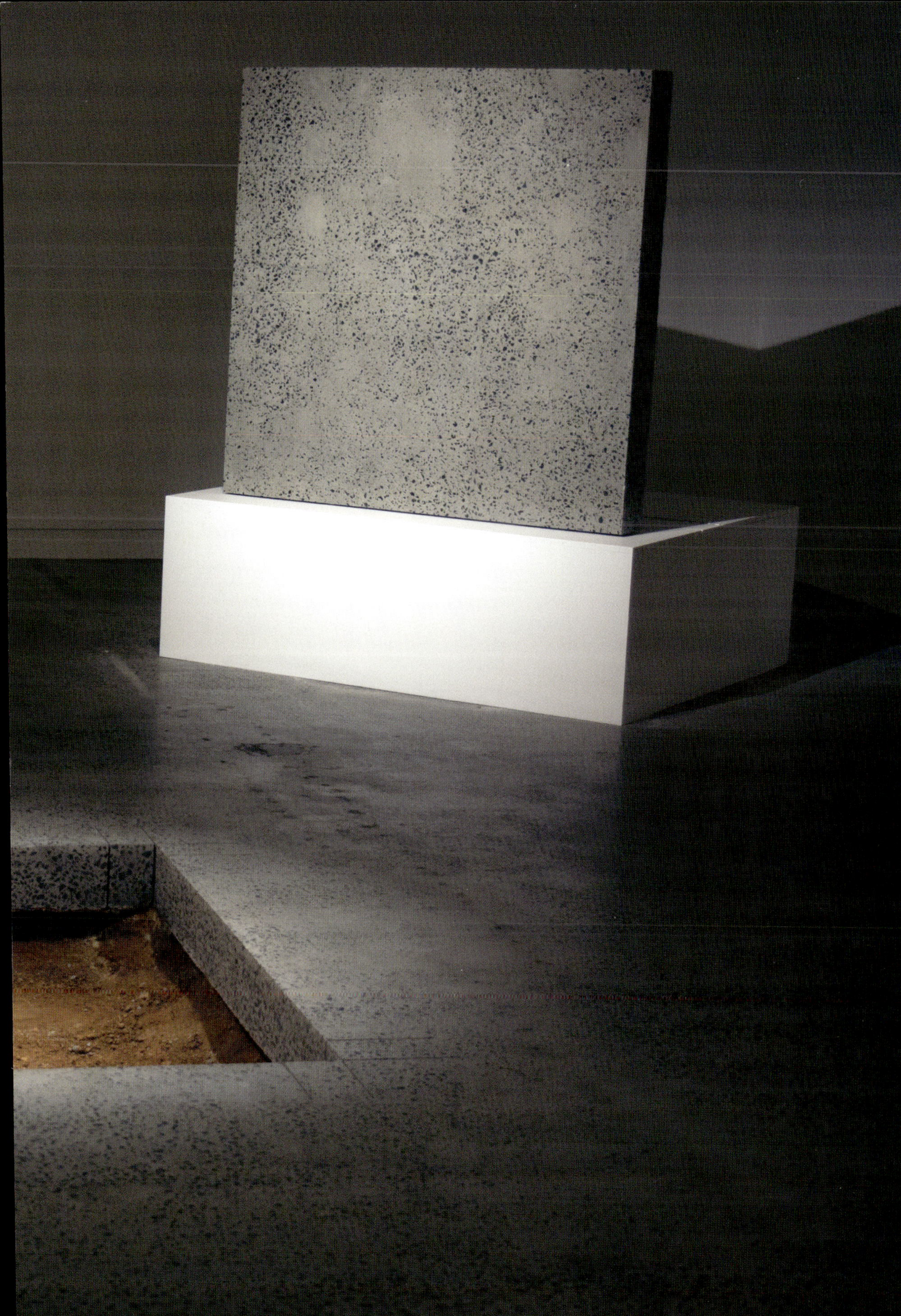

SHIFTING

GROUNDS

Landscape in Contemporary Native American Art

KATE MORRIS

UNIVERSITY OF WASHINGTON PRESS *Seattle*

Helen Marie Ryan Wyman was intelligent, curious, and gregarious; she took great stock in books and reading, and books abounded in her life. The Wyman family is proud to sponsor this book in Native American and Indigenous studies in her name.

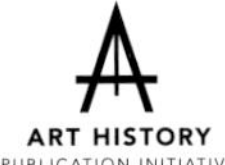

Shifting Grounds was made possible by a collaborative grant from the Andrew W. Mellon Foundation.

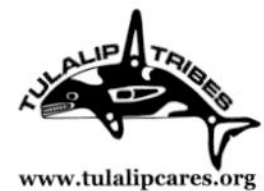

This book was supported by the Tulalip Tribes Charitable Fund, which provides the opportunity for a sustainable and healthy community for all.

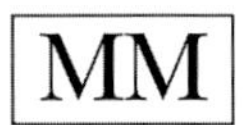

Publication of this book was aided by a grant from the Millard Meiss Publication Fund of the College Art Association.

The Office of the Provost and Office of the Dean of the College of Arts and Sciences at Santa Clara University provided additional support for this book.

Printed and bound in South Korea
Design by M. Wright
Composed in Swift, typeface designed by Gerard Unger
23 22 21 20 19 5 4 3 2 1

UNIVERSITY OF WASHINGTON PRESS
www.washington.edu/uwpress

FRONTISPIECES: Kent Monkman, *History Is Painted by the Victors* (2013), acrylic on canvas, 72 × 113 in., Courtesy of Denver Art Museum (full credit at fig. 5.7, p. 135); Postcommodity, *Repellent Fence* (2015), earth, cinder block, paracord, PVC spheres, helium, installation length 2 mi., US–Mexico border (full credit at fig. 4.11, p. 103); George Morrison, *Spirit Path, New Day, Red Rock Variation: Lake Superior Landscape* (1990), acrylic and pastel on paper, 22½ × 30⅛ in., Collection of the Minnesota Museum of American Art (full credit at fig. 3.1, p. 59); Postcommodity, *Do You Remember When?* (2012), cut concrete, exposed earth, light, sound, Art Gallery of New South Wales, Sydney (full credit at fig. 4.1, p. 82)

LIBRARY OF CONGRESS
CATALOGING-IN-PUBLICATION DATA
LC record available at https://lccn.loc.gov/2018046900

ISBN 978-0-295-74536-7 (hardcover)
ISBN 978-0-295-74482-7 (ebook)

The paper used in this publication is acid free and meets the minimum requirements of American National Standard for Information Sciences — Permanence of Paper for Printed Library Materials, ANSI Z39.48–1984.∞

For Jean

so how do
we remember
together
truthfully
above water
with our land
between us
as the primary
agent of reckoning

From Postcommodity artist pages,
Art in America 105, no. 9 (October 2017)

CONTENTS

Acknowledgments | *xvii*

Introduction | 1

1 The Lay of the Land | 9

2 The Emergent Tradition of Native American Landscape Painting | 27

3 Beyond the Horizon: Postmodern Perspectives on the Native Landscape | 57

4 Centering: Site-Specific and Land-Based Art Practices | 81

5 The Embodied Landscape | 115

Notes | 149

Bibliography | 171

Index | 181

ACKNOWLEDGMENTS

IT IS A PLEASURE TO THANK THOSE WHO HAVE CONTRIBUTED IN MANY AND various ways to this book. Numerous friends and colleagues generously read drafts, offered valuable advice, and suggested sources that have enriched this study immensely. I am especially grateful to Kathleen Ash-Milby for introducing me to many of the artists and artworks discussed here and for her wise council at many stages in this project.

I owe thanks to the provost and dean of Arts and Sciences at Santa Clara University for providing research and image reproduction support. Special thanks to my colleagues in the Department of Art and Art History, especially my writing partner Kathleen Maxwell, and to Debbie Tahmassebi and my colleagues in the dean's office for their patience when my attentions got stretched a little too thin. I am grateful to my students for their energy, enthusiasm, and keen insights over the years and to my research assistant Olivia Glaser, who came to my rescue late in the game.

The research for this book was supported in part by a Georgia O'Keeffe Research Center Fellowship, and costs of publication were underwritten by the Mellon Foundation's Art History Publication Initiative. I wish to thank my editors at the University of Washington Press, including Regan Huff, Catherine Cocks, and Julie Van Pelt. I also wish to thank the artists Kay WalkingStick, James Lavadour, Alan Michelson, Jeffrey Gibson, Kent Monkman, Postcommodity, and the many others who graciously agreed to lend their images to the project.

This book is dedicated to the scholars, artists, and curators who have made the Native American Art Studies Association my intellectual home for the past twenty-five years. I am indebted to my mentors Janet Berlo, Aldona Jonaitis,

W. Jackson Rushing, and Charlotte Townsend-Gault, and to Bill Anthes, Rebecca Dobkins, Carolyn Kastner, Karen Kramer, Henrietta Lidchi, and Amy Lonetree for their feedback on my work over the years. Their enthusiasm for contemporary Native American art has been a constant inspiration to me.

I could not have written this book without the endless support of my friends and family. My mother, Professor Linda Morris, leads by example: she is my best critic and editor, and her gentle humor both inspires and sustains me. Virginia Palmer, Kay Ellyard, Elizabeth Miller, Judy Johnston, Laura Stokes, Helen Zia, and Lia Shigemura have provided tireless encouragement and love throughout this project. I owe endless gratitude to Nancy Wadsworth for her firm writing advice, boundless energy, and unfailing friendship. To Judith Peraino, who taught me to listen to paint and accompanied me to more museums than she wishes to count, I am forever indebted. Finally, I thank Marilyn Jean Johnston for helping me find home.

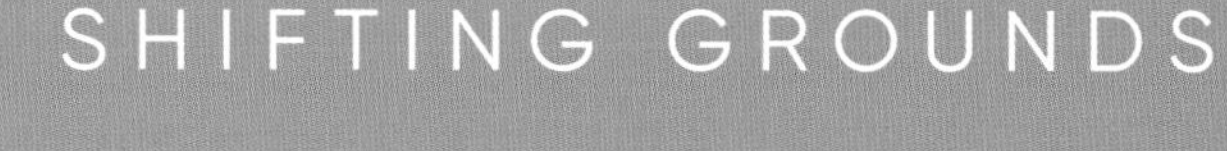
SHIFTING GROUNDS

Introduction

ON A BRIGHT COLD DAY IN DECEMBER 2016, A DRONE CAMERA FLYING OVER THE confluence of the Cannonball and Missouri Rivers in North Dakota recorded a dazzling sight: an undulating current of light rippling across the landscape. This was neither a natural occurrence nor even a supernatural one but a staged act of resistance. On this day more than 150 protestors holding "mirror shields" (16-by-48-inch reflective boards) above their heads processed in loose formation across the snowy ground of the Oceti Sakowin camp near the Standing Rock Sioux reservation to dramatize their opposition to the construction of the Dakota Access oil pipeline (DAPL).[1] The collective performance, *Mirror Shield Project: Water Serpent Action* (figure I.1), was conceived and orchestrated by artists Cannupa Hanska Luger (Mandan/Hidatsa/Arikara/Lakota) and Rory Wakemup (Ojibwe), who joined the standoff against pipeline security forces and local law enforcement at Standing Rock, the reservation on which Luger was born.[2] According to Luger, the *Mirror Shield Project: Water Serpent Action* was inspired by images of Ukrainian revolutionaries using mirrors to reflect back the images of Russian government forces amassed against them.[3] Wakemup and Luger's version advances the nonviolent spirit of the demonstration staged in Ukraine to encompass an even broader scope of sovereign political action and artistic expression; the work is, like all other forms of organized resistance to DAPL, fundamentally an assertion of Indigenous sovereignty.[4] As a site-specific performance echoing the flow of the nearby river and gesturing to both what is above (a reflected sky, an unmanned camera) and below (the "river" of oil), *Mirror Shield Project: Water Serpent Action* is also, I contend, firmly situated within an emerging and distinctly Indigenous idiom of contemporary landscape representation.[5]

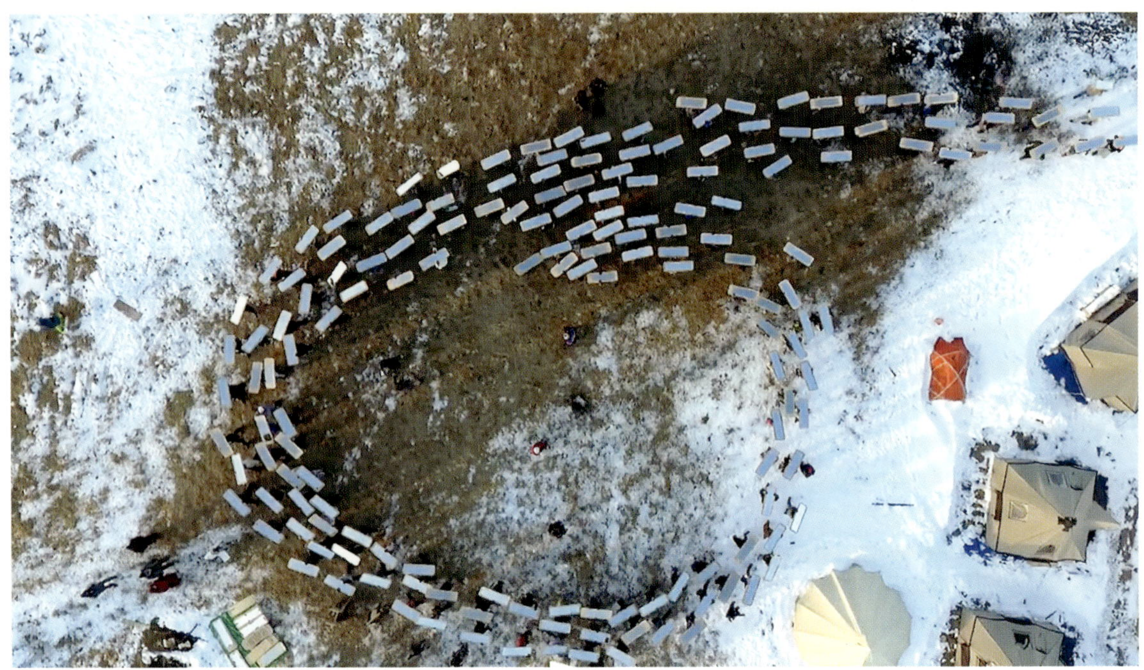

I.1 Cannupa Hanska Luger (Mandan/Hidatsa/Arikara/Lakota, b. 1979)
Mirror Shield Project: Water Serpent Action (2016)
Collective performance, Oceti Sakowin camp, North Dakota
Copyright Cannupa Hanska Luger. Drone image still by Rory Wakemup.
Courtesy of the artists

If drone footage of a group of protestors walking in the snow can be considered a landscape, it may seem that the term has all but lost its valence, that the designation has ceased to function as the coherent category of art that it once was, especially as originally constituted as a genre of European painting. In that well-established tradition, the term generally referred to views of a landscape as "captured" in the eye and depicted in paint through the use of a single-point perspective that positioned the artist and viewer as if looking out to the horizon. This basic definition of the term "landscape" in art held for hundreds of years, until the mid-twentieth century, when abstract expressionism dispensed altogether with mimesis and the illusionistic depiction of space on a painted surface.

By the 1960s the term "landscape" was more likely to be encountered in reference to sculptural forms and nascent installation and performance practices. When land art—including installation-based geological constructions such as Robert Smithson's *Spiral Jetty* (1970)—came into being as a bewildering amalgam of architecture and minimalist sculpture, it caused a category crisis in virtually every established artistic discipline. This crisis provided the impetus for one of the most widely influential documents of contemporary art criticism: Rosalind Krauss's 1978 essay, "Sculpture in the Expanded Field." In the opening passage of the essay, Krauss described standing in an actual field on Long Island, looking down into a subterranean earthwork construction by Mary Miss. She wrote, "Over the last ten years rather surprising things have come to be called sculpture: narrow corridors with TV monitors at the ends; large photographs documenting country hikes; mirrors placed at strange angles in ordinary rooms; temporary lines cut into the floor of the desert. Nothing, it would seem, could possibly give to such a motley of effort the right to lay claim to whatever one might mean by the category of sculpture. Unless, that is, the category can be made to become almost infinitely malleable."[6]

Krauss went on to describe the efforts made by critics to construct a historical genealogy for such works, one that stretched from Stonehenge through Russian constructivism right through to Long Island, reifying the category of sculpture along the way. "But in doing all of this," she continued, "the very term we had thought we were saving—*sculpture*—has begun to be somewhat obscured. We had thought to use a universal category to authenticate a group of particulars, but the category has now been forced to cover such a heterogeneity that it is, itself, in danger of collapsing. And so we stare at the pit in the earth and think we both do and don't know what sculpture is."[7]

A similar thought may occur to us today as we watch the video of *Mirror Shield Project: Water Serpent Action*, confront the torn and mended canvases of Nadia Myre's *Scar Project* (2006–13), or stare at the slab of concrete excised from an art gallery floor in Postcommodity's *Do You Remember When?* (2012) and try to make sense of them as *landscapes*. Yet if in "Sculpture in the Expanded Field," Krauss was able to assert that "we know very well what sculpture is" and follow that with an exposé of the "internal logic" of sculpture as a form of monument, so too can we begin to explore the "logic" of contemporary Indigenous landscape representation.

I stress the word "Indigenous" here to call attention to the fact that while much of the logic that undergirds the forms of representation discussed in this study—drawn from a range of contemporary media, including painting, sculpture, site-specific installation, video, and performance—may be congruent with more broadly mainstream postmodern art practices, the logic I am interested in is a particularly Indigenous logic or epistemology. In the pages that follow, I explore themes of presence and absence, connection and dislocation, survival, survivance,[8] memory, commemoration, vulnerability, power, and resistance that surface again and again in reference to the Native landscape, and I situate these within a larger discourse of Indigenous visual sovereignty.[9] In the broadest terms, Indigenous visual sovereignty describes the visual expression of Indigenous knowledge, and I am particularly attentive to what Tuscarora artist and theorist Jolene Rickard refers to as "place-based knowledge."[10]

My conception of contemporary Indigenous landscape representation is to some extent also informed by an understanding of what landscape art was (and meant) before the field expanded into the multiple dimensions and media of the postmodern era. In other words, just as Krauss had to return to the logic of the monument to discern the logic of contemporary sculpture, so I begin this study with a brief return to the history of landscape art in an era when that term was still restricted to painting—back to when "the landscape" was easier to define and easier to read. Landscape historian W. J. T. Mitchell is instructive here: in his revealing history of the genre, *Landscape and Power*, published in 1994 and substantially revised in 2002, Mitchell asked not just what landscape *is* but what it *does*. Taken together, the essays assembled in Mitchell's volume demonstrated that the formal characteristics of European landscape painting (e.g., the illusion of recession into space, and the constant reiteration of pictorial tropes such as deforested lands and roads leading from the foreground to the background) reflected an ideology of habitation, occupation, and domestication. Moreover, Mitchell posited the intriguing notion that all of the world's "originating movements in landscape painting—China, Japan, Rome, seventeenth-century Holland and France, eighteenth- and nineteenth-century Britain"—coincided with periods of imperialism, the literal expansion of empire.[11]

That Mitchell discerned a causal relationship between colonialist ideologies and landscape painting traditions bears directly on interpretations of Indigenous landscape art, which refuses to reproduce the "invitational" tropes of the European landscape tradition. Contemporary Indigenous landscape art is largely *anti-invitational* in character, in the sense that even the most seemingly representational paintings by Native American artists such as James Lavadour and Kay WalkingStick employ devices to block the imaginary entrance of a viewer into a scene, and sculptural works such as *Do You Remember When?* tend to insert themselves into the space of the viewer rather than the other way around.[12] Performance-based art practices are especially adept at achieving an anti-invitational stance, as the body of the artist literally intervenes between the spectator and the land: Mandan/Hidatsa/Arikara photographer Zig Jackson's series *Entering Zig's Indian Reservation* (1997) demonstrates just how effectively the presence of the Indigenous artist can decolonize the landscape.

While the sea change in national politics in the United States has lent new urgency to strategies, acts, and discourses of resistance, the NoDAPL protests and Idle No More treaty rights movement (as well as the Occupy and Black Lives Matter movements) and all of the works in this study that were produced before the 2016 elections should remind us that for Indigenous people in the United States and Canada, the colonial era has never ended. The coercive power of the settler state is as persistent as the Indigenous resistance to it.[13]

Nevertheless, these forms of artistic expression should not be considered exclusively oppositional; to define them only in reference to the European landscape tradition or the politics of decolonialism would deny the richly generative and vitally compelling aspects of Indigenous landscape representation. This is a crucial distinction, considering that even Mitchell concluded in 1994 that the European landscape tradition was an "'exhausted' medium."[14]

By the time Mitchell revisited *Landscape and Power* in 2002, his thinking on this matter had shifted perceptibly. While downgrading the power of the landscape from a more coercive form of real power to a softer, subtler form of persuasion or affect, he nonetheless observed, "Whatever the power of landscape might be . . . it is surely the medium in which we live, and move, and have our being, and where we are destined, ultimately, to return."[15] What accounts for this change of heart? Several possible answers to this question are discussed in chapter 1, but the most germane proposes that as Mitchell's attention turned toward ever more contemporary—and not, incidentally, non-Western—forms of landscape representation, his approach to the subject gravitated away from ideological discourse toward phenomenology, a philosophical approach that considers how individuals experience space in a more fully embodied, multisensory way.

The works of art that form the basis of this study—evocations of the landscape created in the last thirty years by Indigenous artists from North America—are rarely if ever primarily visual representations. Rather, they evoke all five senses: from the overt sensuality of Kay WalkingStick's tactile paintings to the eerie soundscapes of Alan Michelson's videos and Postcommodity's installations to the immersive environments of Kent Monkman's dioramas, all of these landscapes resonate with a fully embodied, one might even say *embedded*, subjectivity. Ideology is not replaced but joined in these works in an expression of what Stó:lō sound and performance scholar Dylan Robinson has termed "sensate sovereignty."[16] All of this is on display in *Mirror Shield Project: Water Serpent Action*, a work of art that emanates from, takes place on, and moves through the Native landscape, proclaiming, like all of the works in this book, the ongoing presence—and vigilance—of Indigenous peoples on an ever-shifting ground.

This volume is not by interest or necessity an exhaustive survey of the innumerable works by Native American artists that evoke a sense of space and place; it is instead an exploration of contemporary art as a vehicle for the expression of place-based knowledge. Loosely organized by medium, the first three chapters of this book are primarily concerned with painting, not only as the genre most closely associated with landscape representation, but also as a material process. The discussion centers on the work of two of the most prolific Native American painters of the contemporary period, James Lavadour and Kay WalkingStick, who have both been deeply engaged with landscape imagery for nearly four decades. Both artists' innovative approach to the physical process of painting precipitated the emergence of landscape on their canvases. While this approach is not specific to Indigenous painters (including George Morrison and Jaune Quick-to-See Smith, who are also discussed here), the repositioning of the artist as an insider—a conduit for a subjective experience of landscape rather than a disembodied spectator—joins the discourse of decolonialism in destabilizing forms of representation that traditionally figured both the artist and the viewer as potential "investors" in the landscape.

The final two chapters of this book consider a wider range of postmodern media and art practices, including site-specific sculpture, installation, video, and performance art. The three-dimensionality and literal emplacement of these artistic media present unique possibilities for shaping space and marking place, and many of the works discussed here assume a kind of monumental stature, asserting Indigenous presence in culturally contested landscapes from blighted urban centers to highly charged border zones. Because these media directly involve or invoke the body, themes of vulnerability and trauma are also addressed—especially the trauma of dislocation and dispossession. Again, the discussion centers on a few well-established artists who have turned (and frequently *re*turned) to the land in their work, including Alan Michelson, Kent Monkman, Rebecca Belmore, and Postcommodity. What binds all of the works in this study is the sustained engagement of the artists not only with land and landscape but also with the history of representation itself. Their efforts to reclaim history and establish connection to place *on Indigenous terms* constitutes a powerful rejoinder to the invitational tropes of the European landscape tradition.

CHAPTER ONE

The Lay of the Land

Like life, landscape is boring; we must not say so.

W. J. T. MITCHELL

IN THE SUMMER OF 2000, WALLA WALLA PAINTER JAMES LAVADOUR HAD AN epiphany. Two strains of his work that had for some time run parallel suddenly converged with tectonic force. The first strain, which has been described as Lavadour's "signature" style,[1] is exemplified by works such as *Salamander* (1997; figure 1.1): built up of hundreds of layers of oil on wood, these paintings depict primal landscapes shrouded in haze or consumed by fire, arranged in multipaneled compositions that resonate as whirling vortices of energy.[2] The second strain, which emerged more recently in Lavadour's practice, is far more abstract, characterized by pronounced drips and flows of paint and overlays of opaque washes. The material itself is more viscous than in the signature panels, so much more so that in works like *Untitled* (2000), Lavadour employed a squeegee to create broad gestural wipes of fluid paint. These later works were inspired in part by Lavadour's experimentation with printmaking processes, through which he learned to "separate the stages of an individual painting and conceive of [it] as being formed of many successive layers, like a print."[3]

Both of these strains of Lavadour's painting are inspired by the landscape, the forces of nature, and the physical properties of paint. As Lavadour puts it, "In paint there is hydrology, erosion, mass, gravity, mineral deposits"; his intent is to "display the occurrence of landscape inherent in the act of painting."[4] While these forces course through all of Lavadour's work, the artist perceives the variants described above as distinct enough to refer to the more imagistic paintings as "landscapes" and to the more abstract forms as "architectural abstractions," "structures," or "interiors."[5] It is tempting to interpret Lavadour's two forms of imagery—and his early hesitation to let the two

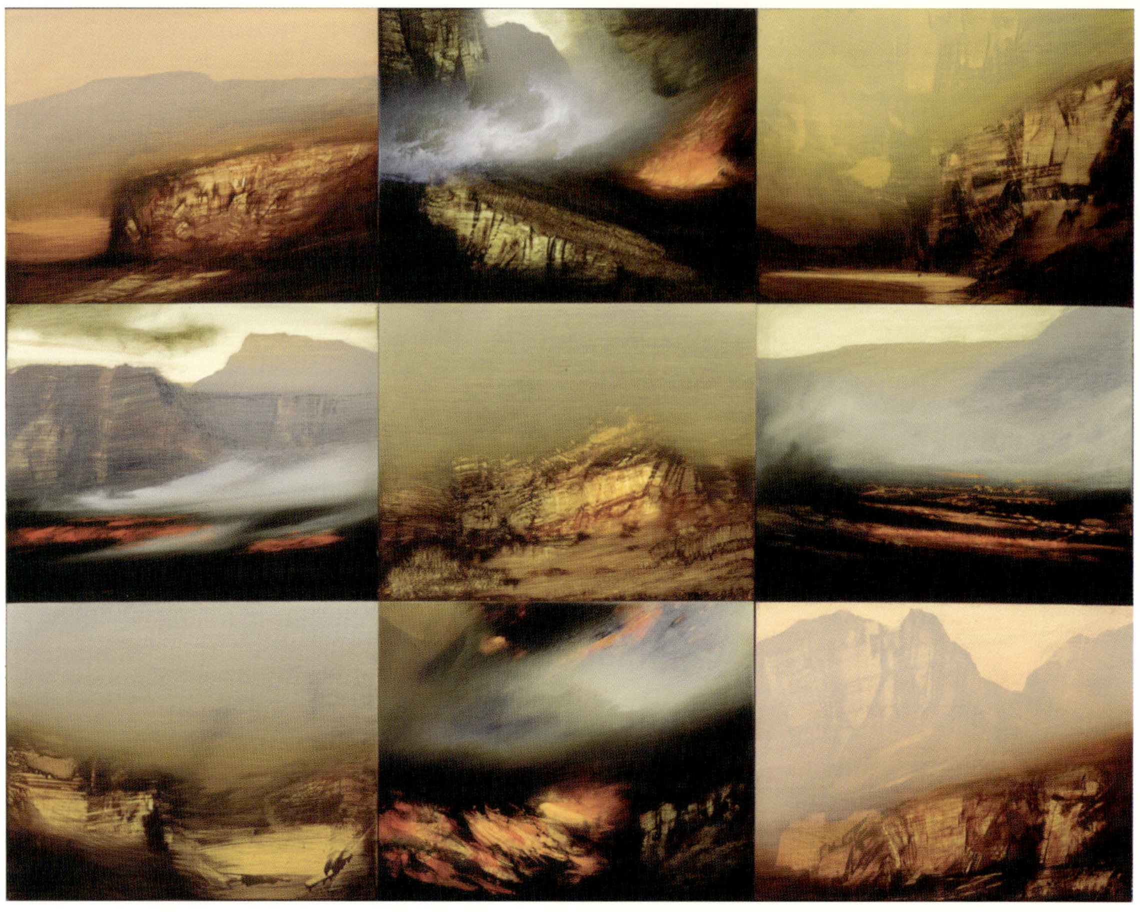

1.1 James Lavadour (Walla Walla, b. 1951)
Salamander (1997)
Oil on board, 48 ½ × 60 inches
Copyright James Lavadour. Courtesy of the artist.
Portland Art Museum

streams merge—as connoting a shift in his vision, from a more outward and objective view of the landscape to a more expressionist, even visceral perspective. Yet Lavadour maintains that none of his paintings are truly objective views of the landscape; instead his paintings are records of fully *kinetic* experiences, of walking in the mountains of the Umatilla Reservation, where he lives in eastern Oregon, and paying close attention to the "elemental aspects of the world" he encounters there. "I realized that what I was looking at and what I was doing were the same thing. . . . As a physical being, I was an event of nature myself. I could become a conduit for making art, a conduit of nature, a conduit of the extraordinary event."[6]

The intention of this book is to draw on the language that Lavadour and other Indigenous artists use to describe their art and their experience of place to build an inclusive theory of contemporary Indigenous landscape representation—one that can account for both strains of Lavadour's work and especially for the convergence of the two forms of perception that they seem to represent. In this chapter and the two that follow, I will revisit Mitchell's question of what a landscape painting *is* and what it *does*; however, while Mitchell sought answers in the European landscape tradition, I adopt key concepts regarding land and Indigeneity from sources well outside the realm of art history. I have already indicated that the broader discourse of Indigenous sovereignty heavily informs this study. In this chapter I trace the migration of the legal concept of sovereignty first into Indigenous cultural studies, then more specifically into visual culture theory. I also take into consideration the United Nations Declaration on the Rights of Indigenous Peoples (UNDRIP), which provides ample evidence for the centrality of land in Indigenous culture and self-governance. The language of the UNDRIP codifies an Indigenous view of land that encompasses much more than physical territory—a view that was echoed by George Longfish and Joan Randall in their influential 1983 essay, "Contradictions in Indian Territory," where they defined "landbase" as "the interwoven aspects of place, history, culture, philosophy, a people and their sense of themselves and their spirituality, and how the characteristics of [a] place are all part of a fabric."[7] Taken together, the language of Indigenous visual sovereignty and the UNDRIP provide new insight into the question of what a landscape painting is, what it does, and even what it pictures. In its contemporary and Indigenous form, a landscape painting is an assertion of Indigenous presence, a transmission of place-based knowledge, a depiction of *landbase*. It is a chronicle of what Lavadour terms the "extraordinary event."

CONVERGENCE

It was Lavadour's relentless pursuit of the extraordinary event that led him to interweave the two strains of his imagery in 2000. Recognizing that each form had a unique expressive power and inspired in part by the improvisational techniques of jazz music, Lavadour began to juxtapose his panels in multipaneled compositions. The process began tentatively at first: in *Flag 2* (2001) and *Scaffold* (2000), for example, five "landscapes" and four "structures" are woven into unified compositions, yet the individual panels remain basically true to type. In the latter example, however, a few panels edge toward a hybrid form in which structural drips or wipes are laid over the surface of a landscape.[8] One of these hybrid forms centers the composition of *Deep Moon* (2004; figure 1.2): the hazy, atmospheric landscape of the central panel is transformed by the addition of streaks of vibrant color in the middle ground. After *Deep Moon* Lavadour embraced the energy of the new forms, and gradually the distinction between the landscapes and architectural abstractions ceased to apply. Landscape and structural elements are fully integrated in each panel of *Blanket* (2005), *Wash* (2007), *Cache* (2007), *Straight Ahead* (2010), *Tiicham* (2013), and innumerable individual panels produced in the past decade. In these works, it is the convergence of the two strains of imagery, like the fusion of separately charged particles, that Lavadour credits with generating an explosion of energy.[9] To some extent, Lavadour's epiphany in 2000 was an extension of earlier innovations, such as his arrangement of individual panels into larger compositions. He likened this action to composing a poem: "I realized that like poetry, you put one against the other and they enhance one another and they do something larger than the individual pieces do."[10]

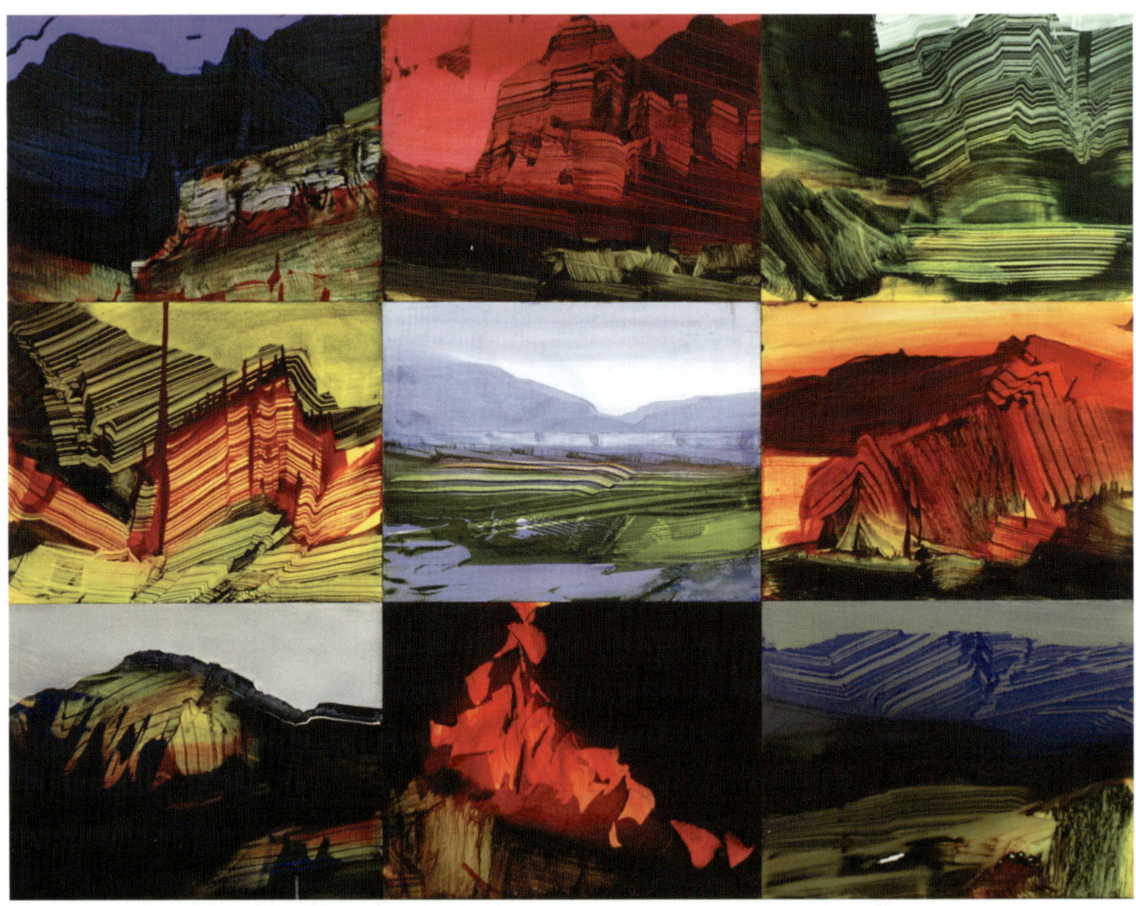

1.2 James Lavadour (Walla Walla, b. 1951)
Deep Moon (2004)
Oil on wood, 72 × 90 inches
Copyright James Lavadour. Courtesy of the artist.
Private collection

The kind of resonance that Lavadour's compound compositions produce is also felt in the multipaneled paintings of Cherokee artist Kay WalkingStick. For more than thirty years, WalkingStick has worked in diptych format, pairing what she calls "imagistic landscapes" with "pure abstractions"—forms that are analogous to the two strains of imagery that converged in Lavadour's work in 2000.[11] Describing the two types of panels that make up diptychs such as *On the Edge* (1989; figure 1.3) and *The Abyss* (1994), WalkingStick echoes Lavadour in asserting that "one is not the abstraction of the other, one is the extension of the other. I want the two portions to resonate with one another like the stanzas of a poem."[12]

In WalkingStick's case, the impetus to pair canvases came as a way to mitigate the specificity of the landscape imagery, which emerged gradually and unintentionally as a by-product of her working method. For years WalkingStick had been painting with layers of saponified wax and acrylic, laying down the material with her bare hands and scratching through successive layers to reveal the colors in the layers below. Though her imagery was resolutely abstract, employing a minimalist vocabulary of lines and arcing forms, she found that the thick layers of material were increasingly suggestive of the landscape. As she explained to interviewer Lawrence Abbott in 1991: "The paintings became more and more about the earth, the landscape, and they looked, many of them, like seeing the earth in the geological diagrams one sees of the different-layered remains of the various eons of the history of the earth. The paintings had this feeling of accruing the way the earth has accrued with layers of rock and sediment."[13] As the association with landscapes in her work became more prevalent—evolving by 1985 into "imagistic landscapes"—WalkingStick recalls that she was reluctant to abandon abstraction. Instead, she began to pair the landscape panels with purely abstract counterparts, and she found "a kind of symbiosis there that was quite remarkable, that [she] would not have predicted."[14]

Perhaps the two canvases of WalkingStick's diptychs resonate with one another because they both stem from the same source, namely the artist's love of paint's material properties and her search for archetypal or universal imagery. Rather than negating the qualities that WalkingStick strongly associated with abstraction, the pairing of abstract images with imagistic landscapes enabled her paintings to "encompass more of the visual world."[15] Nevertheless, it was important to WalkingStick that the balance in her diptychs remained weighted slightly toward the abstract side. Simply put, she did not want the viewer to regard the landscape imagery as representational in the sense of describing a specific place because that kind of particularity ran counter to her more metaphysical approach to painting. In her view, "They are paintings that are about landscapes, they are about land. The subject is the land, the earthscape, but [these are] not pictures of a place."[16] Thus, the

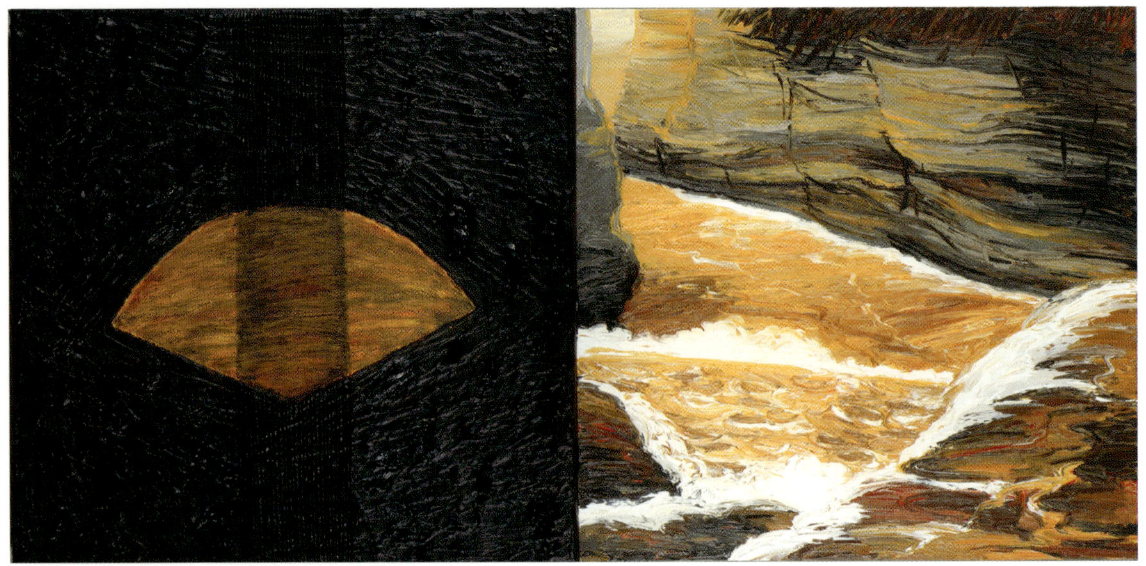

1.3 Kay WalkingStick (Cherokee, b. 1935)
On the Edge (1989)
Acrylic, saponified wax, oil, and oil stick on canvas, 32 × 64 inches
Copyright Kay WalkingStick. Courtesy of the artist.
Private collection

joining of images in WalkingStick's diptychs both enhances and mitigates the properties of the individual canvases, allowing her work to speak of one subject in two different idioms. Over time, WalkingStick has articulated how each of the two types of images contributes to expressing "two kinds of perceptions of the earth."[17] She feels the imagistic landscapes are inspired by the visual world and rooted in the present, albeit in a fleeting moment. The abstractions on the other hand are everlasting, referring to "both the past and the future."[18] In WalkingStick's view, the diptychs "represent a balance between the spiritual and the temporal—between our inner and outer selves."[19]

WalkingStick's bridging of the threshold between physical and metaphysical realms in her paintings is strongly reminiscent of Lavadour's integration of landscapes and structures, which art historian W. Jackson Rushing has characterized as a "determined fusion of internal and external realities."[20] The relative ease with which artists and critics came to reconcile these differences between strictly visual and more broadly phenomenological forms of perception in the early 2000s is reflective of the ways that landscape theory had shifted in the previous decade from regarding landscapes primarily as social hieroglyphs or textual systems to something much more subjective and integral to the individual human experience. To better understand the significance of this paradigm shift, we return to Mitchell's groundbreaking study of *Landscape and Power*.

SETTLER LANDSCAPES

In the first edition of *Landscape and Power*, Mitchell articulated the thesis that landscapes—and landscape paintings, though this distinction is not always as clear as it could be—are not simply objects of contemplation but also "a process by which social and subjective identities are formed."[21] This argument assumes the a priori position that landscape paintings have always been a "subjective formation" (rather than an unmediated visual encounter) and that the subjectivity in question extends from the paintings to the individuals and communities that create and consume them. Mitchell advanced Denis Cosgrove's work of a decade earlier, which established that landscape is "an ideological concept. It represents a way in which certain classes of people have signified themselves and their world through their imagined relationship with nature, and through which they have underlined and communicated their own social role and that of others with respect to external nature."[22]

Mitchell espoused an essentially postmodernist view: a "semiotic and hermeneutic approach" that regards landscape representation as not only steeped in ideology but also open to interpretation as text. He contrasted this view with what he characterized as the modernist attempt to "narrativize" the history of landscape painting "as a progressive movement toward purification of the visual field."[23] Whether one favors modernism's contemplative approach or postmodernism's interpretive version, the assumption is that landscapes convey meaning, that they signify. This raised two questions that Mitchell and the authors who followed him in the volume sought to illuminate: *What* do landscapes signify? And, importantly, *how* do they signify?

In her essay "System, Order, and Abstraction: The Politics of English Landscape Drawing around 1795," Ann Bermingham made a concerted effort to map the ways that landscapes might signify, not only through allegory and symbolism (what is pictured), but also through their formal properties (how it is pictured). Earlier in her career, Bermingham had established that spatial strategies of composition and perspective were key components of landscape representation. She argued that landscape paintings were essentially invitational: "Traditionally, when viewing a landscape painting, we expect the organization of light and color to highlight what is important and to lead the eye in stages into the distance. We also expect objects to be arranged in a way that facilitates this movement."[24] Though Bermingham's field of study is the English landscape tradition, her observations apply equally well to paintings of the Hudson River School, which imported many of the ideals of the English rustic tradition to American painting in the early nineteenth century. Thomas Cole's *View of Fort Putnam* (1825), for example, uses light to "lead the eye in stages into the distance" and even provides a road to facilitate travel from the foreground into the deeper recesses of the scene.[25] In her contribution to *Landscape and Power*, Bermingham explicitly linked these formal devices to the politics of the Age of Revolution, arguing that the imaginative ability of the viewer to move freely into the spaces of a composition was expressive of the larger discourse of political liberty in the wake of the American and French revolutions.[26] In such paintings, she wrote, "liberty is precisely the liberty of the beholder's eye to 'range abroad' to command a view of the landscape, to subject it to one's vision and imagination. Thus the viewer's experience of nature's expansiveness is in fact an experience of subjecting this expansiveness to visual control."[27]

It is significant that in this passage, Bermingham's concept of liberty encompassed both the freedom to experience a view and to command one; she acknowledged the degree to which European landscapes privilege the spectator's position. Moreover, Bermingham's description and a passage that follows it referencing "panoptic control" revealed her indebtedness to Michel Foucault, who firmly established a relationship between power and looking in his study of the disciplinary apparatus known as the panopticon.[28] Foucault's influence can be felt in Mitchell's introduction to *Landscape and Power* as well. It is evident in his assertion that "landscape . . . doesn't merely signify or symbolize power relations; it is an instrument of cultural power, perhaps even an agent of power."[29] Mitchell's certainty that landscape representation exerted real influence drove him to inquire "not just what landscape 'is' or 'means' but what it *does*, how it works as a cultural practice."[30]

All of the essays in *Landscape and Power* strived to demonstrate that what landscape *does*, fundamentally, is create social cohesion in European societies. Ann Jensen Adams, for example, argued in her essay on seventeenth-century Dutch landscape representation that even paintings without apparent literary or textual referents (those that were produced primarily for visual pleasure) served an important ideological purpose in helping to naturalize significant changes in the geography and demographics of an emerging nation-state. Noting that landscape was by far the most popular genre of Dutch painting, collected avidly across all classes and segments of the population, Adams concluded that a landscape "can, through the associations it engenders, create in the viewer a sense of affiliation with or difference from others, an individual identity in relation to a variety of communally held identities."[31] Just as Adams detailed the process of identity formation at the level of distinct communities that ultimately cohered on a nationalist level in Holland, other contributors to the volume addressed similar processes of nation building in England, South Africa, New Zealand, and the United States in the eighteenth and nineteenth centuries. Though these case studies move beyond the boundaries of Europe, the focus is always on European communities. David Bunn's article on South African landscapes, for example, begins with the statement that the author is concerned with "the way landscape . . . is exported from metropolitan Britain to the imperial periphery"; the study focuses on a population of Scots settlers who emigrated to South Africa in 1820.[32]

Of the essays in *Landscape and Power*, Mitchell's own study, "Imperial Landscape," was perhaps the widest-ranging in scope, commencing as it did with an itemized list of nine "Theses on Landscape" that purport to address landscape expression both inside and outside the European community. In short order, Mitchell both proposed and dismantled a number of commonly held notions about landscape, including the myth of its "Western-ness," its modernity (by which he means the seventeenth to nineteenth centuries), and its association with "a new way of seeing" (roughly an aesthetics of natural beauty). In the place of these myths, Mitchell offered some alternative truths—for example, "Thesis 1: Landscape is not a genre of art but a medium. . . . Thesis 5: Landscape is a medium found in all cultures,"[33]—and a reminder that landscape is a commodity as much as it is a site of social formation. Of all of Mitchell's contributions to our understanding of landscape, however, none is more important than his willingness to look beyond nationalism to a more global phenomenon and to name it: imperialism.[34] Having mobilized the example of classical Chinese landscape painting to dispense with the notion of a Western hegemony of landscape representation, Mitchell was moved to offer the following observation: "Is it possible that landscape, understood as the historical 'invention' of a new visual/pictorial medium, is integrally connected with imperialism? Certainly the roll call of major 'originating' movements in landscape painting—China, Japan, Rome, seventeenth-century Holland and France, eighteenth- and nineteenth-century Britain—makes the question hard to avoid. At a minimum we need to explore the possibility that the representation of landscape is not only a matter of internal politics and national or class ideology but also an international, global phenomenon, intimately bound up with the discourses of imperialism."[35] This is a crucial turn in Mitchell's thinking, for it raised the stakes of examining landscape's function as ideology to the highest level and justified his rather surprising insertion of the term "power" into a study of landscape representation. If landscape can be shown to be not only *complicit* with the ideologies of imperialism but to have had *agency* in shaping global politics, then it is powerful indeed.

In addition to amplifying the rhetoric of landscape studies in general, Mitchell's move toward the global produced two subtle shifts in his argument. First, it abandoned consideration of single individuals, be they painters or viewers, to move irrevocably to the level of collective identity, further complicating the issue of what exactly constitutes subjectivity.[36] Second, in associating landscape firmly with the politics of imperialism, Mitchell found himself in the curious position of having to admit the "death" of landscape in the postcolonial or decolonial era. Logically, though not convincingly, Mitchell was left to conclude that "landscape in the form of the picturesque European tradition may well be an 'exhausted' medium, at least for the purposes of serious art or self-critical representation."[37] Given how firmly invested the essays in the first edition of *Landscape and Power* were in the art of the seventeenth through the nineteenth centuries, this seems rather a foregone conclusion. Only the final essay in the collection, Charles Harrison's "The Effects of Landscape," steered the conversation toward the early twentieth century. Harrison insisted that the practice of modern art "allows for a degree of resistance to the protocols of vision" established in earlier periods; in fact he went so far as to pronounce that "no interpretation can be adequate if it does not recognize what [a] painting significantly *withholds* from vision."[38] Harrison's view ran so much against the grain of the collection that Mitchell characterized the essay as taking an "antithetical approach" to his own position.[39] This is no small matter, and Harrison's inference that modernist practices provide an avenue of resistance to ideological systems must be carefully considered in light of the omission it exposed in *Landscape and Power*. Despite Mitchell's admission in his own chapter that imperialism is "not a 'one-way' phenomenon but a complicated process of exchange, mutual transformation, and ambivalence," the essays in the volume failed to credit landscape strategies that have effectively *opposed* colonialist processes and coercive practices of identity formation.[40] Had any of these authors directed their attention to the landscapes being painted by Native American artists in 1994, they may well have recognized the anti-invitational strategies of that emerging tradition.

The preparation of the second edition of *Landscape and Power* in 2002 afforded Mitchell the opportunity to reconsider the strengths and weaknesses of this landmark study and its impact on the field in the intervening decade. One of the significant modifications made to the second edition is the inclusion of four new essays, some of which consider contemporary landscape representation and new media. The most compelling addition to the second edition, however, is Mitchell's six-page preface, subtitled "Space, Place, and Landscape." This short rumination on the status of landscape studies in the new millennium reveals a radical transformation of Mitchell's thinking, one that amounts to a near total refutation of his original premise that landscape is a potent instrument of political ideology. He writes, "If one wanted to continue to insist on power as the key to the significance of landscape, one would have to acknowledge that it is a relatively weak power compared to that of armies, police forces, governments, and corporations. Landscape exerts a subtle power over people, eliciting a broad range of emotions and meanings that may be difficult to specify. This indeterminacy of affect seems, in fact, to be a crucial feature of whatever force landscape can have."[41] What are we to make of this disavowal of power as a primary force in landscape studies, a disavowal so sweeping that Mitchell admits that he would excise the word "power" from the title if given the chance? On the one hand, Mitchell may have been adhering to an even more Foucauldian conception of power as something that is distributed among multiple points in a system, rather than concentrated in any singular position or expression.[42] On the other hand, his statement also reveals a growing appreciation for landscape's capacity to inspire a range of responses in a range of beholders. It is this shift—a return to focus on individuals and perhaps also to a narrower form of subjectivity—that distinguishes Mitchell's revisionist impulse in 2002, though that is not immediately evident in his newly privileged terms, "space" and "place."

These are curious terms to stress, given that they are nearly interchangeable with one another and with the third term in the revised title, "landscape." Mitchell grants that landscape paintings are basically just depictions of spaces or views of places; however, he argues that these distinctions are important and that the effort to parse them holds open the possibility of seeing landscape in a new light. Mitchell's optimism in this respect is inspired by key texts in the philosophy of perception. He notes that "in both the phenomenological and historical materialist traditions of this subject, space and place are the crucial terms" that generate radical new ideas about how we experience and order our world.[43] Mitchell notes that space and place are usually conceived of as binaries, the particulars of which are strangely reminiscent of the dichotomies that plagued interpretations of Lavadour's and WalkingStick's paintings at the beginning of this chapter: "A place . . . is basically the same thing as 'a' definite, bounded space, while space as such, without the definite article, becomes abstract and absolute."[44] Remarking that "space has connotations of abstraction and geometry, while place resonates with particularity and qualitative density," Mitchell fairly echoes WalkingStick's description of her diptychs as expressing "two kinds of perceptions of the earth"—the imagistic landscapes that are inspired by the visual world and rooted in the present (i.e., place) and the abstractions that are more timeless and eternal (i.e., space).[45] Unlike Mitchell, who is less than direct in associating space and place with forms of perception, let alone with the subjective experience of the individual, WalkingStick is explicit in this regard, asserting that the binary landscapes of her diptychs represent a balance between inner and outer selves.

Lavadour is more reluctant to characterize the two strains of his imagery as internal and external or to position the two types as binaries. Nevertheless, both he and WalkingStick have acknowledged that the pairing of disparate forms of imagery produces unforeseeable and occasionally astounding results. As Lavadour put it, the multipaneled compositions "do something larger than the individual pieces do." In the same way that Lavadour and WalkingStick embrace the tendency of juxtaposed forms to move beyond binaries, to create something unexpected, Mitchell strives to compound the "dialectical opposition" of the terms "space" and "place" with the addition of the third term:

"landscape." He writes that by employing a "dialectical triad" he hopes to engender a "more capacious and differentiated theoretical field."[46]

In summary, then, the paradigm shift in Mitchell's thinking from the first to second editions of *Landscape and Power* is from a focus on ideology (on the highest level, that of global politics) to an emphasis on philosophies of perception that privilege individual experience, especially those that contemplate a subject's perception of physical space and place. In gravitating away from a strictly historicizing impulse, Mitchell also grants landscape a wider range of both affect and effect in the present, and this leads him to conclude his preface to the second edition with a rather astonishing emendation to his earlier lament for landscape's decline. He writes, "Whatever the power of landscape might be . . . it is surely the medium in which we live, and move, and have our being, and where we are destined, ultimately, to return."[47]

Whether Mitchell can be credited with leading or following a larger trend in landscape studies between the mid-1990s and the mid-2000s, many prominent theorists moved toward a "more capacious" view of the field during this period. An Art Seminar roundtable on the topic of landscape that was convened in 2006 by art historians James Elkins and Rachael Ziady DeLue took as its initial premise that ideology may be the *starting point* for understanding what landscape is or does but that it is neither a definitive nor exhaustive approach to the subject.[48] DeLue challenged the seminar participants to consider the questions that Mitchell seems also to have asked himself: Are there "other ways of thinking about the interpretation and meaning of landscape than thinking about it as *always* and *only* ideology? . . . What do we miss when we don't allow ourselves to see anything but ideology?"[49] The consensus in the seminar was that something of the *experience* of landscape—what Mitchell called the "range of emotions" or "indeterminacy of affect"—had been occluded, and again participants looked to philosophies of perception to fill this void. Critical theorist Jessica Dubow remarked that "landscape experience . . . is not just how a given view comes to be represented, but how its viewer stakes a claim to perception and presence. It's not just about an optical sight or its symbolic mediation, but all those more hidden sensory and affective processes that allow a view to 'come into being' for the subject, all those embodied practices which, prior to representation, allow for its realization, its actualization."[50] I am sympathetic to this theoretical perspective that not only moves from a privileging of vision and visuality toward a greater awareness of the other bodily senses but also promotes a blurring of the "lines drawn between self and society, inside and outside."[51] In refusing categorical partitioning, phenomenology holds out the possibility of reconciling the internal and external events that surface in both Lavadour's and WalkingStick's paintings.

Perhaps another question DeLue should have posed, however, in addition to "what do we miss when we see only ideology?" is "what are the possible consequences of turning away from ideology toward phenomenology?" As several contributors to *Landscape Theory* warned, by denying landscape's "semiotic, political, or moral determinations," this new rhetoric invites the return of previously discredited assumptions regarding landscape's benign or apolitical aesthetics.[52] They are right to be concerned: if the complicity of the European landscape tradition in colonialist processes can be denied, then so too is the power of Indigenous landscape representation as a decolonial strategy undermined. Still, few would argue that phenomenology is any more capable than semiotic, structuralist, psychoanalytic, or even ideology theory is in accounting for landscape's multivalent and enduring power. Even as the seminar closed in 2006, it was clear that, while still elusive, the persuasive capacity of landscape has not diminished. Elkins conceded that "like the body, landscape is something we all feel ourselves to be inside. It's our subject, but we're also part of it: we help make it; we live in it."[53]

SOVEREIGN LANDSCAPES

It is encouraging to find landscape studies opening into a space of increasing complexity and inclusiveness; however, it is important to remain mindful of the ways in which the field has—and continues to—turn a blind eye to Indigenous perceptions of the land. Just as the European landscape tradition has tended to depict the landscape as if it were empty of its aboriginal inhabitants, so too has landscape theory tended to ignore the degree to which the Indigenous landscape has been fully conceptually realized. Mitchell's canonical essay on imperial landscapes, for example, not only failed to acknowledge landscape strategies that have effectively opposed colonialist processes, but it also failed to consider the view from *within* the Indigenous territories that made up the colonial peripheries. The aim of this study is not to correct these oversights or even to expose the weaknesses and biases of landscape theory per se; on the contrary, the field of landscape studies provides many tools for looking "deeply and well" at Native landscapes, and not only as an articulation of difference.[54] Nevertheless, many aspects of contemporary Native American art trouble or complicate the assumptions made when only European forms are considered, and some discourses that are less pertinent to the study of European landscapes are absolutely crucial to understanding Native articulations, such as the emerging discourse of Indigenous visual sovereignty.

The era of the early 1990s to the 2010s—the time span in which the artworks in this book were produced—was a time of rapid change in cultural studies, as the effects of postcolonial theory were felt in nearly every humanistic discipline. In the art world, postmodernism held sway, ushering artistic populations and practices that were previously marginalized into the very center. For contemporary Native American artists in particular, the year 1992 proved a pivotal moment, as the five-hundredth anniversary of Columbus's "discovery" of the New World brought a surge of public interest in Indigenous cultures past and present. In both the United States and Canada, uncritical celebrations of the Columbian quincentennial were countered by efforts to inspire meaningful reflection on the legacies of colonialism, including the mounting of group exhibitions of contemporary Native American art such as *Submuloc Show/Columbus Wohs: A Visual Commentary on the Columbus Quincentennial from the Perspective of America's First People* (multiple venues in the United States, 1992); *Our Land/Ourselves: American Indian Contemporary Artists* (multiple venues in the United States, 1991–93); *The Post-Colonial Landscape: A Billboard Exhibition* (Saskatoon, Canada, 1993); *Indigena: Contemporary Native Perspectives in Canadian Art* (Quebec, Canada, 1992); and *Land, Spirit, Power: First Nations at the National Gallery of Canada* (Ottawa, Canada, 1992).

In focusing on the experiences of Indigenous peoples in North America, these exhibitions were in their very conception decolonial projects. They were also postmodernist in the sense that they purposefully transgressed the boundaries between the art world's centers and peripheries, and they seamlessly incorporated artworks in a broad range of media, including video, performance, and installation art.[55] By and large, the intent of the quincentennial response exhibitions was to affirm and celebrate the survival of Indigenous cultures while acknowledging the devastating effects of more than five hundred years of colonialism. According to curators Gerald McMaster and Lee-Ann Martin, for example, the works of art selected for *Indigena: Contemporary Native Perspectives in Canadian Art* examined the "tangled complex of history, language, feelings, identity, concepts, preconceived notions and contemporary realities that define Aboriginal cultures today."[56]

Chief among all of the concerns addressed in these exhibitions was regard for the land itself. The curators of *Land Spirit Power: First Nations at the National Gallery of Canada* put this succinctly: "As the ongoing struggle of the aboriginal people of North America for their ancestral lands reveals, the land has social meanings that are profoundly spiritual and intensely political in their implications. To other North Americans it is becoming clearer, in part through an awareness of the environmental crisis, that survival depends on recognizing that notions of the land as an empty, alien place, or a frontier to be conquered, are not only inadequate, but destructive."[57] While this preface established a universal concern for land and the environment, it nevertheless underscored the unique centrality of land in the matrix of aboriginal culture. After all, a people's occupation of and connection to the land is the defining aspect of the words "Indigenous," "aboriginal," and "Native." Moreover, as many of the Native artists and curators who participated in the quincentennial response shows stressed, the relationship of Native peoples to the land is intimate in ways that do not apply to settler cultures. Jaune Quick-to-See Smith explained: "Euro-Americans often wonder why the American Indian is so attached to the land. Even after Indians have lived in an urban environment for two generations, they still refer to tribal land as home. . . . Each tribe's total culture is immersed in its specific area. Traditional foods, ceremonies and art come from the indigenous plants and animals as well as the land itself. The anthropomorphism of the land spawns the stories and myths. These things are the stuff of culture which keeps identity intact."[58] For Ho-chunk sculptor Truman Lowe and for Lavadour too, the land and its features "run through the body."[59] As Lavadour put it: "Whatever is in the earth is in me and whatever is in me is what I make art out of."[60]

Underscoring these more personal reflections on Native landscapes in 1992 was an increasingly vocal political discourse on Indigenous self-determination. At that time, the term "Indigenous visual sovereignty" was not yet in use; however, the language and tenets of political self-determination were becoming ever more refined due to the efforts of the United Nations to adopt an international Declaration on the Rights of Indigenous Peoples. Beginning in 1982, the UN Working Group on Indigenous Populations held hearings and gathered copious testimony in support of the Draft Declaration on the Rights of Indigenous Peoples, which they submitted to the UN in July of 1993.[61] The final declaration, which contains proclamations on an exhaustive array of concerns, from protections against forced relocation to the right to speak and preserve Indigenous languages, was not ratified by the UN General Assembly until 2007, but in the fourteen-year interim its contents were widely distributed, influencing public policy in both domestic and international arenas.[62]

On the subject of land, the UNDRIP is unequivocal. It states that "Indigenous peoples have the right to own, use, develop and control the lands, territories and resources that they possess by reason of traditional ownership or other traditional occupation or use, as well as those which they have otherwise acquired."[63] In addition to affirming these legal and economic rights, the declaration also officially recognizes and sanctions the "distinctive spiritual relationship" of Indigenous peoples and the land, reinforcing the sentiments expressed by Smith and others noted here. Moreover, the UNDRIP reads, "Indigenous peoples have the right to . . . uphold their responsibilities to future generations in this regard."[64]

One of the paradoxes of the legal discourses of sovereignty is that the relationship of a people to the land, particularly the occupation of territory, is both a prerequisite for and the principle benefit of sovereign status. As one legal scholar put it, "Territorial sovereignty is an indispensable attribute of independent nations; the territory is the very basis on which national existence rests." Simply stated, "Sovereignty needs territory on which it is to be exercised."[65] Thus, in the early 1990s, both the need and the right of Indigenous populations to proclaim their relationship to the land were of paramount concern for Native peoples worldwide. This was especially true for the Indigenous peoples of Canada, the United States, Australia, and New Zealand—the four UN member nations that refused to sign the UNDRIP, in part because it contains provisions that call for restitution or compensation made for lands that were unlawfully taken.[66] In the decade after the formal ratification of the UNDRIP, constant pressure by Indigenous groups and their allies has moved all four dissenting nations to publicly endorse the declaration; most recently, Canada formally removed its objector status in a statement made to the United Nations Permanent Forum on Indigenous Issues in May of 2016.[67]

No matter how the articles of the UNDRIP are legally interpreted and enacted in the coming years, it is clear that the language of sovereignty has gradually pervaded every aspect of Indigenous cultural studies.[68] As early as 1994, Osage critical theorist Robert Allen Warrior argued for a broadly inclusive understanding of sovereignty as a communal and individual empowerment: "If our struggle is anything, it is the struggle for sovereignty, and if sovereignty is anything, it is a way of life. That way of life is not a matter of defining a political ideology. . . . It is a decision—a decision we make in our minds, in our hearts, and in our bodies to be sovereign. . . . The struggle for sovereignty is not a struggle to be free from the influence of anything outside ourselves, but a process of asserting the power we possess as communities and individuals to make decisions that affect our lives."[69] Warrior's capacious definition of *intellectual* sovereignty is reflective of a particularly Indigenous epistemology, according to Tuscarora artist and scholar Jolene Rickard. Rickard, whose grandfather Chief Clinton Rickard founded the Indian Defense League in 1925, writes that "This notion of sovereignty as a matter confined to the legal sphere is not the kind of sovereignty that I grew up with among the Haudenosaunee."[70] Rather than accept either the European definition of sovereignty or the U.S. legal interpretation of it, the Haudenosaunee created a unique understanding of the concept "that embodies our philosophical, political, and renewal strategies."[71]

Rickard has long argued for such an approach to Indigenous visual arts, asserting that sovereign thoughts, strategies, and practices cut across the whole spectrum of cultural production. In 1995 she wrote in a special issue of *Aperture* magazine devoted to Native American photography: "As part of an ongoing strategy for survival, the work of Indigenous artists needs to be understood through the clarifying lens of sovereignty and self-determination, not just in terms of assimilation, colonization, and identity politics."[72] In Rickard's view, contemporary works by Native photographers join the discourse of Indigenous sovereignty by asserting presence, as in Zig Jackson's *Indian Man in San Francisco* series (1993). Rickard insists that viewing such works through the "lens of sovereignty" allows us to perceive the shift from "a victimized stance to a strategic one."[73]

Of the many scholars of Native American art and visual culture who took up Rickard's charge, Seneca literary theorist Michelle Raheja deserves recognition for introducing the term "visual sovereignty" to the field in 2007. In an analysis of Zacharias Kunuk's film *Atanarjuat: The Fast Runner*, Raheja defined "visual sovereignty" as an act of artistic resistance and agency: created from an entirely Inuit perspective, Kunuk's film, according to Raheja, effectively supplanted the salvage paradigm bias of the 1922 ethnographic film *Nanook of the North* with a "flow of Indigenous knowledge."[74] The example of *Atanarjuat* suggested to Raheja that works of art might open to a range of sovereign strategies and practices beyond the political. She wrote that "visual sovereignty . . . is not always directly involved in political debates. . . . There is more room for narrative play" than in other forms of sovereignty discourse.[75] In the case of *Atanarjuat*, Raheja argues that the film's construction of imaginative narrative sequences of a spirit/dream world, and its incorporation of humor, parody, and absurdity reveal an Indigenous perspective beyond the strictly legal rhetoric of sovereignty. Nevertheless, Raheja's concept does hinge on a notion of Indigenous agency as construed primarily in opposition to structures imposed upon Indigenous communities from without: she refers to visual sovereignty as a "*corrective* cultural narrative."[76] In this respect, Raheja differs from Rickard, who configures Indigenous sovereignty not as a primarily deconstructionist stance, but rather as an inherently affirmative practice of self-determination.[77]

Rickard concluded her 1995 article on sovereignty as a lens for understanding Indigenous artistic practices with the statement that "[artworks] made by Indigenous makers are the documentation of our sovereignty, both politically and spiritually. Some stick close to the spiritual centers while others break geographic and ideological rank and head West. But the images are all connected circling in ever-sprawling spirals the terms of our experiences as human beings."[78] While Raheja's discernment of the resistant strategies of Indigenous art practices provides useful insight into many of the individual works created in the last quarter century—especially those that clustered around the Columbian quincentennial—Rickard's broader view of visual sovereignty as encompassing *all* works that convey an Indigenous worldview is arguably more useful for understanding contemporary landscape art. Her analysis invites us to see contemporary art produced by Indigenous artists as an exercise of Indigenous visual sovereignty, no matter its subject matter, medium, or even its message. And if contemporary Native American art of the past twenty-five years is best understood as "part of an ongoing strategy of survival," then this is perhaps nowhere more apparent than in representations of land.

CHAPTER TWO

The Emergent Tradition of Native American Landscape Painting

THERE IS NO SUCH THING AS A STATIC LANDSCAPE. EVERY LANDSCAPE IS IN A state of transition, undergoing a neverending process of transformation brought about by forces of wind, water, and plate tectonics. These forces are perhaps nowhere as evident as they are in the Columbia River Gorge in Oregon, at the edge of the Columbia Plateau and the Umatilla Indian Reservation where James Lavadour lives and paints. The gorge, in some places nearly four thousand feet deep, was formed by the force of the Columbia River, which cut into the plateau over the course of millennia, exposing layer upon layer of volcanic sediments that stand as great basalt spires and miles-long saw-toothed palisades. This is a landscape that shaped human history, as the confluence of great rivers flowing a thousand miles from the continent's interior has channeled people into the gorge for more than fifteen thousand years. When Meriwether Lewis and William Clark portaged over the cascades of the Columbia on their march to the Pacific in 1805, they were following in the footsteps of generations of Yakama, Umatilla, and Nez Perce people, into the traditional homelands of the Wishram and Wasco. At Celilo Falls, Lewis and Clark reported that nearly a dozen tribes gathered to fish for salmon and trade at the "Great Mart" of the Columbia.[1]

Lavadour's paintings such as *Salmon Back* (2003) and *Summer Run IV* (2009) capture this landscape in all of its facets, the multiple layers of paint echoing the composition of the cliffs and the glossy yet textured surfaces of the panels refracting light in a manner reminiscent of the way light plays on the surface of a fast-flowing river. For Lavadour the landscape of the Columbia is less subject matter than it is inspiration, however; his work does not strive to picture the river as much as to convey its effects, its energy. Early in his career, when he was still trying to articulate his relationship to paint and to the landscape, Lavadour had an encounter with moving water that he describes as fundamental to his understanding of the forces of nature and his physical body. Hiking along a stream that was swollen with spring runoff, Lavadour came across a "logjam with this single long branch sticking out of it." He recalls that he was "thinking about water, how I couldn't pin it down with my eyes. I grabbed ahold of this stick and all of a sudden I could *feel* the water, the transmission up the stick. And I realized that it was energy. It's that movement. It wasn't something I was looking at, it was something I already knew somehow, I already felt, a way that I already moved. It was like discovering that in myself."[2] As a result of this encounter, Lavadour came to understand his role as an artist as essentially being a conduit for the forces of nature. And he came to fully appreciate the kinetic power of rivers, as both a creative and destructive force.

Lavadour's respect for the irrepressible force of the river is shared and echoed by Kay WalkingStick, who painted a series of diptychs in the late 1980s that featured turbulent rivers cascading through narrow chasms that can barely contain them. *On the Edge*, *The Abyss*, *Grappling with Chaos*, *Loss*, *Uncontrolled Destiny* (all 1989), and *Letting Go from Chaos to Calm* (1990), pair tightly cropped images of churning waters with panels that depict only an abstract symbol such as an arc or wedge bisected by a broad stripe of contrasting color. The color palette of *On the Edge* is the most literal, reproducing the earth tones of the rivers and gorges of upstate New York, where it was painted. For WalkingStick the river paintings are also deeply metaphorical, expressing the grief and anger she felt upon the sudden and unexpected death of her husband, Michael, in 1989. She described these works to an interviewer in 1995: "I saw [the waterfalls] as the unstoppable onrush of our lives. . . . My husband had just passed away and I felt that our lives were like these cascades, which are not dammed but just rush on. There is a tremendous unstoppable power of torrentially racing forward."[3]

Thus, like Lavadour's paintings, WalkingStick's multilayered canvases evoke the momentum of the river, yet as diptychs they also offer some mitigation of that tumultuous force. The abstract panels, which WalkingStick has described as referring to both the past and the future, allowed her to take a longer view, out of the painful circumstances of the present. Taken together, the two sides of the diptychs represent WalkingStick's attempt to restore a semblance of balance to her life. She concluded, "That whole waterfall series was about the onrush of time, combined with the quiet, still, timelessness of abstraction."[4] As previously noted, WalkingStick has been quite blunt in insisting that, no matter how closely her paintings are tied to the landscape, they are not "pictures of a place." Lavadour is a bit less adamant, but he admits some ambivalence toward the subject of landscape when he says that "landscape has always been indelible to my work, it is just what I see in paint. But

I also tried to understand something greater in painting by *denying landscape* and just letting the paint do whatever."[5]

One of the questions taken up in the next two chapters is why both of these artists, whose careers are defined by their engagement with land as subject matter, have consistently "denied landscape." In a 1994 interview with Lawrence Abbott, WalkingStick indicated her rationale for resisting the genre when she stressed that her paintings "are not landscapes in the sense that Thomas Cole or [Frederick] Church painted landscapes."[6] Her reference to the two canonical figures of the nineteenth-century American landscape tradition invokes a whole host of associations with the genre of landscape painting as discussed in chapter 1—including its complicity in colonialist processes. As the interview progressed, WalkingStick made it clear that she was concerned not only with the way that landscape paintings had naturalized the subjugation and displacement of Indigenous peoples but also with the way that the genre had contributed to the destruction of the environment. She said of Cole and Church, "These artists brought in the notion of Manifest Destiny and that the earth is there to be exploited for mankind's use, which is one of the things that has destroyed our United States. Not just the aboriginal inhabitants, but the earth itself."[7]

It is clear then that Lavadour and WalkingStick are not denying land when they deny land*scape*. Focusing on Lavadour and WalkingStick as the preeminent but by no means only contemporary artists to take up this subject in paint, I argue that the desire of Indigenous artists to express and strengthen their connection to the land—without reproducing the tropes or ideologies of the European landscape tradition—has been a motivating factor in the development of Indigenous art in the postmodern period. While the subject of this book is the emerging Indigenous landscape tradition, the European tradition also comes into sharper focus, not only in the course of the analysis, but also in the self-conscious critique of the genre supplied by the works themselves. As Raheja reminds us in the essay on visual sovereignty quoted earlier, Indigenous artists frequently "revisit, contribute to, borrow from, critique, and reconfigure" older artistic conventions in order to establish uniquely creative—and sovereign—forms of self-representation.[8] She writes, "visual sovereignty recognizes the paradox" of critiquing representations of Native American subjects while simultaneously participating in "some of the conventions that produced these representations."[9] In other words, even as we acknowledge the degree to which Indigenous artists engage with and sometimes even reproduce aspects of the European landscape tradition, we must not regard their work as derivative, or their artistic practices as simply or only oppositional. On the contrary, chapters 2 and 3 will demonstrate just how effectively contemporary Indigenous landscape paintings adapt conventions of the genre to convey a uniquely Indigenous worldview.

In choosing to center this discussion on WalkingStick and Lavadour, I am aware that their decades-long careers span the gulf in postmodern art that supposedly witnessed the death and rebirth of painting. Yet, while both WalkingStick and Lavadour have worked in other media, including drawing, printmaking, and to some small extent sculpture, both consider themselves "pure painters," devoting most of their intellectual and artistic energies to the exploration of "this wonderful thing called paint."[10] The similarities in their practices do not end there: both work in series, pursuing particular lines of inquiry over the course of multiple canvases and many years; both work with multipaneled compositions; both affirm the physical objecthood of the canvas or support; and both emphasize nonvisual forms of perception. Despite these affinities in their work and in their artistic practices, WalkingStick and Lavadour have come to abstract landscape imagery from very different experiences. Lavadour, who was born in 1951 in Pendleton, Oregon, is a self-taught artist who lives and works within his tribal community. WalkingStick, who was born in 1935 in Syracuse, New York, earned a master of fine arts degree from Pratt Institute in Brooklyn and has worked in the heart of the mainstream art world in New York City for most of her career.

A SEPARATE INTENTION OF THE EYE

In an important way, neither Lavadour nor WalkingStick is exclusively concerned with the visual properties of the landscape. Lavadour is explicit in his recollection that he was fascinated with the river because he couldn't "pin it down" with his eyes—he couldn't see the river's surface clearly, but he could feel it. While Lavadour's experience was a generative one, ultimately leading him to a fuller understanding of his art, his struggle to fix the river in his vision put him in good company. Henry David Thoreau described a similar difficulty in his account *A Week on the Concord and Merrimack Rivers*, detailing time spent with his brother in 1849. Seeing the surface of a river, he remarked, "required a separate intention of the eye, a more free and abstracted vision . . . than to see the river bottom merely."[11] What Lavadour has developed in his artistic practice is that "separate intention of the eye"—the ability to see the surface of a river and to intuit what is beneath the surface. *River (10)* (2007; figure 2.1) seems almost to illustrate this dual vision. In the top third of the composition a ridge of striated forms stretches into the deep background, terminating in a horizontal line of mist that hovers over the lower two-thirds of the painting. Beneath this placid layer a torrent of brilliant orange is laid down with sharp, angular gestures.

River (10) is a prime example of what Kathleen Ash-Milby called a "compound" image—a single panel that merges the two strains of Lavadour's work, the landscapes and structures discussed at some length in the first chapter of this book. In this context, the image suggests a merging of visual and kinetic forms of sensory perception. In metaphorical terms, *River (10)* may be even more revealing. The year 2007, during which Lavadour produced nearly two dozen paintings in the *River* series, was the fiftieth anniversary of the construction of The Dalles Dam, a hydroelectric project that forever altered the landscape of the Columbia River Gorge.[12] Ten miles upstream from the dam, Celilo Falls and the oldest inhabited community in North America were inundated by the newly formed Lake Celilo. In that anniversary year, however, a sonar survey of the bottom of the lake revealed that the great horseshoe-shaped falls were still intact, flowing beneath the surface. For the tribes of the Columbia Plateau and for Lavadour personally, the sonar images brought enormous relief and a newfound commitment to one day dismantling the aging hydroelectric infrastructure and restoring the ecosystem of the Columbia.[13]

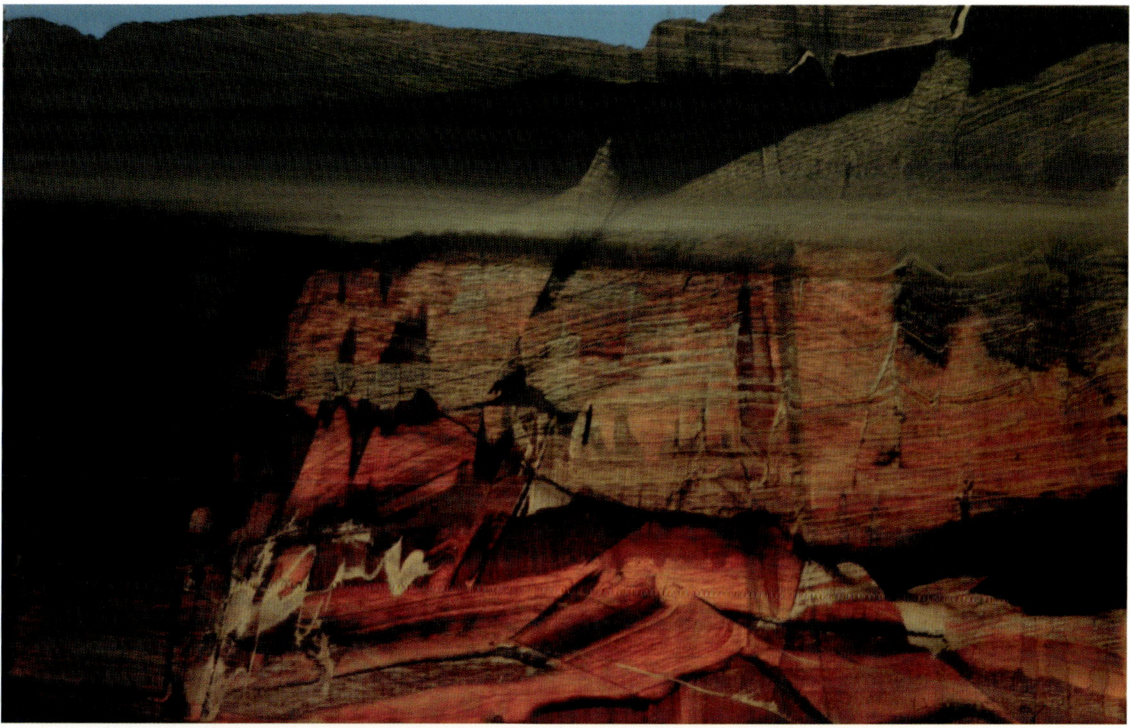

2.1 James Lavadour (Walla Walla, b. 1951)
River (10) (2007)
Oil on panel, 12 × 18 inches
Copyright James Lavadour. Courtesy of the artist.
Private collection

One of the most intriguing of all of Lavadour's works that reference watercourses is *Looking Down on the River* (2010). This panel is oil on wood, like the paintings in the earlier *River* series, but it is monochromatic, and it features the prominent dripping of paint that is characteristic of Lavadour's structures, which tend toward abstraction. And even though Lavadour inverted the panel after the paint dried, causing it to look as if the drips are defying gravity, the association of the river's natural flow and the flow of the paint is not incidental. Since his earliest years as an artist Lavadour has been fascinated with the material properties of paint, particularly its liquid movement. Before he was twenty, Lavadour was actively investigating the way that water-soluble pigments such as food coloring behaved physically. He recalled to interviewer Vicki Halper, "I just did simple things. I would experiment with taking some paint and putting it on a piece of paper and rolling it around; I'd take two or three watercolors and put them in a pot, and pretty soon the different pigments would begin to separate . . . and they would create erosion patterns that were the same as I was seeing on the hillside. Here was a microcosm of that macrocosm. The way this river and this mountain range were formed is the same exact way as this stain was formed here on this paper."[14] Forty years later, *Looking Down on the River* continues that same exploration, except that here the correspondence between the properties of paint and the forces of nature is much more fully articulated. Over and again in interviews and artist statements from the 1990s, Lavadour reiterated his conviction that painting is governed by the same laws as any other geological process—deposition, sedimentation, erosion, scouring, slumping. In 1995 his artistic vocabulary broadened to incorporate terms borrowed from physics, specifically those associated with fluid dynamics, such as "flow," "turbulence," "vortices," and "fingering instability."[15]

Even as Lavadour came to appreciate paint "when it is flowing in mass, and the particles of pigment are like rocks in a flood stream moving and fanning into sedimentary masses," it does not necessarily follow that he would regard his paintings as landscapes.[16] For this to happen, he needed to make the connection between the microcosm and the macrocosm, between the pigment and the land, and he needed to make the perceptual leap to seeing *space* in his paintings. According to Lavadour, space "opens up" between the multiple layers of paint on his panels. Starting with the first mark, which he says is pure "cosmic energy," gestures and pigments accrue, and the two-dimensional surface of the painting becomes literally three-dimensional.[17] Looking into this mass as it is forming, Lavadour recognizes patterns, then familiar structures. Eventually, "it becomes compositional to the point where you create a space that can be inhabited, perceptually inhabited."[18]

WalkingStick had a similar experience, watching the layers of paint and wax build up on her canvases until they conveyed both the illusion and the reality of three dimensions. "The paintings had this feeling of accruing the way the earth has accrued with layers of rock and sediment," she remarked in 1994.[19] But it wasn't until she started varying her colors that she came to regard the works as pictorial landscapes: "As soon as you manipulate color you're manipulating atmosphere; you see space. And so they were taking on . . . a look of real landscape because they were becoming atmospheric."[20] Materializing as they do from the actual canvas, WalkingStick's and Lavadour's landscapes remain intimately tied to the medium of painting. Pigment itself is composed of mineral earth and, when suspended in oil or water, is bound by the physical laws of fluid dynamics; in Lavadour's view the act of painting is akin to the processes of landscape formation—potent with tectonic force. For WalkingStick, paint is an engrossingly tactile material, and the act of painting is both sensual and sacred, an investigation into the spirituality of all things human and nonhuman. The path that WalkingStick took toward the landscape and how she sought to balance the eruptive energies of nature with the profound stillness of abstraction in her diptychs is the subject of the rest of this chapter.

GRIDS

In 1984 WalkingStick was invited to join twenty-five other New York–based artists in paying tribute to the majestic American elm tree. The group exhibition, *Homage to the American Elm*, held in Cooperstown the following year, was not a cause for celebration but a response to a growing environmental crisis: the spread of Dutch elm disease and the near extinction of the stately tree. As the organizers of the exhibition conceived of it, the show offered artists and viewers a chance to reflect on the disappearance of an American icon that Thomas Cole himself had referred to as "that paragon of beauty and shade."[21] WalkingStick's contribution to the show, a diptych painting titled *Death of the Elm* (1985; figure 2.2), pairs two disparate impressions of the tree, one more abstract than the other. The left panel, which contains the more representational image, illustrates what an elm tree looks like, from memory—each branch and leaf is indicated by a thick impastoed stroke of brightly colored acrylic paint, which together fan out across the surface of the paper to suggest the fan shape of the tree.[22] The result is a highly expressionist portrayal that the exhibition's curators could only describe as evocative of "bark-like textures and deteriorating conditions," but for WalkingStick it seemed almost too representational. For more than a decade before she painted *Death of the Elm*, WalkingStick had been working in a purely abstract and severely minimalist style exemplified by paintings such as the *Chief Joseph* series (1974–76), now in the collection of the National Museum of the American Indian; *Genesis/Violent Garden* (1981); and *Cardinal Points* (1983–85).[23] In each of these previous works,

WalkingStick had sought to convey intense emotional, spiritual, and intellectual content in a resolutely modernist idiom, which was to her mind defined as purely abstract. She had not yet arrived at the impressionistic landscape forms that are characteristic of her work from the late 1980s forward. In order to mitigate the nascent realist qualities of the imagery in *Death of the Elm*, her solution was to pair the first panel with one that was more representative of her style at that time, which is to say more abstract.[24]

The painting on the right side of the diptych is a near-reproduction of a somewhat experimental earlier work, *Montauk I* (1983; figure 2.3). Both *Montauk I* and the right side of *Death of the Elm* are painted in layers of acrylic and wax on wood, and both feature only the merest forms—lines scratched into the surface that reveal the colors of the layers beneath. Both are physically impressive works, though at 36 inches square, the panel in *Death of the Elm* is scaled down from the monumental *Montauk I*, which is 56 inches square and, according to WalkingStick, composed of nearly five pounds of acrylic paint and an untold amount of wax layered on a reinforced (doubled) canvas. In its final form, inclusive of its wooden support, *Montauk I* is 4¼ inches deep. The variation in the imagery of the two thickly layered canvases is slight but important to the meaning of the works. *Montauk I* contains a series of lightly etched curving lines distributed loosely through the composition and one

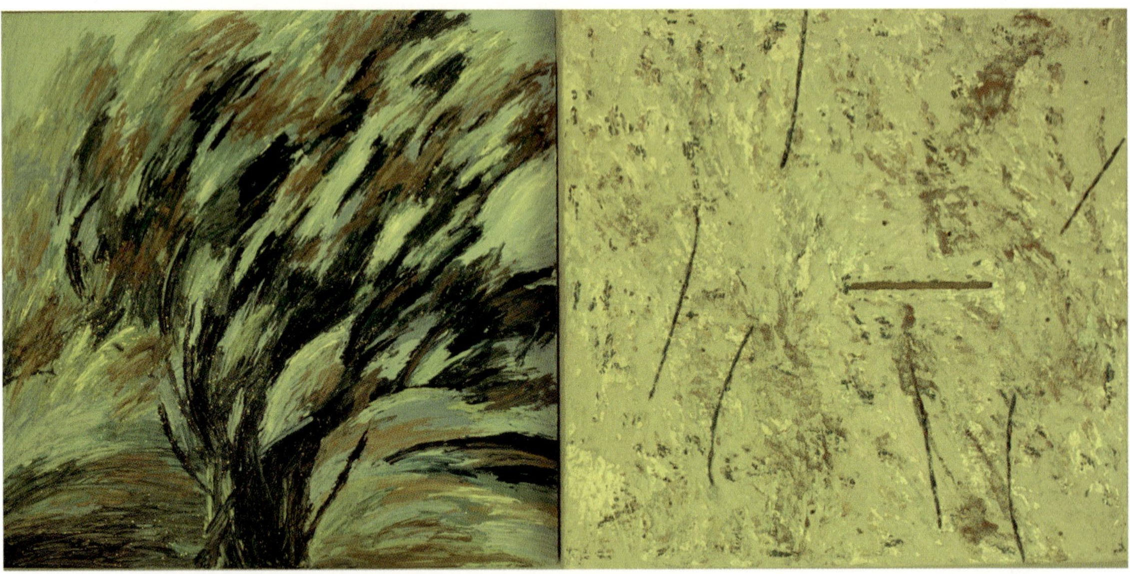

2.2 Kay WalkingStick (Cherokee, b. 1935)
Death of the Elm (1985)
Acrylic, oil, and saponified wax on canvas, 36 × 72 × 3 inches
Copyright Kay WalkingStick. Courtesy of the artist.
No longer extant

deeply gouged, perfectly horizontal line that vibrates with the intensity of its brilliant red color.[25] In *Death of the Elm*, the horizontal line segment is less pronounced due to the lack of contrasting color exposed in the underpaint, but the vertical lines are much more prominent in both color and gestural treatment. In place of the ethereal waving lines of *Montauk I*, these are much more aggressive, slashing across the canvas like wounds to the surface. The most significant difference between the two works, however, is the color palette. The warm light-filled pigments of *Montauk I* are obscured in *Death of the Elm* by a veneer of milky white, and this, finally, conveys much of the meaning of the painting. WalkingStick states that the white represents death in general, and in particular it is reminiscent of the denuded skeleton of a dead tree. Even the horizontal line segment takes on symbolic meaning, the flat line of death or annihilation.[26]

In pairing two forms of imagery in the diptych *Death of the Elm*, WalkingStick found not only that she could mitigate the realist qualities of her initial rendering of the elm but also that the result was actually an increase in affect, or expression. On one side, she presented a fairly literal representation of her subject and on the other a deeply symbolic meditation on loss. WalkingStick recalls that she discovered in this pairing "a kind of symbiosis there that was quite remarkable, that [she] would not have predicted. They spoke to one another. They became more than what they were alone."[27] From this point on, WalkingStick worked almost exclusively in diptych format, a development that I pursue later in this chapter. Considering that *Death of the Elm* is her first diptych painting, it is important to note that while the left panel clearly identifies the subject of the work, it is the abstraction that carries the majority of the expressive content.

The notion that abstraction—even minimalism—was an appropriate and effective vehicle for serious emotional content is something that WalkingStick began to explore in earnest in graduate school. When she enrolled in the master of fine arts program at Pratt Institute in Brooklyn, New York, in 1973, she was thirty-eight years old, already an accomplished painter whose figural work had been exhibited in New York City galleries and garnered positive reviews in the art press. In the two years that she studied at Pratt, however, her work underwent a pronounced change, migrating away from figures into more devout forms of abstraction. By the end of her first year, she was fully committed to the modernist project of abolishing what she regarded as "Renaissance space," or the illusion of three-dimensionality. She began to lay out her compositions with the aid of mathematical formulas and grids and to direct her creative energies toward the exploration of materials and processes, such as pouring paint, staining canvas with ink, and mixing acrylic with wax. Her goal was to paint in a thoroughly modern way, flattening out the canvas and affirming its status as a physical object rather than as an illusionary device.[28]

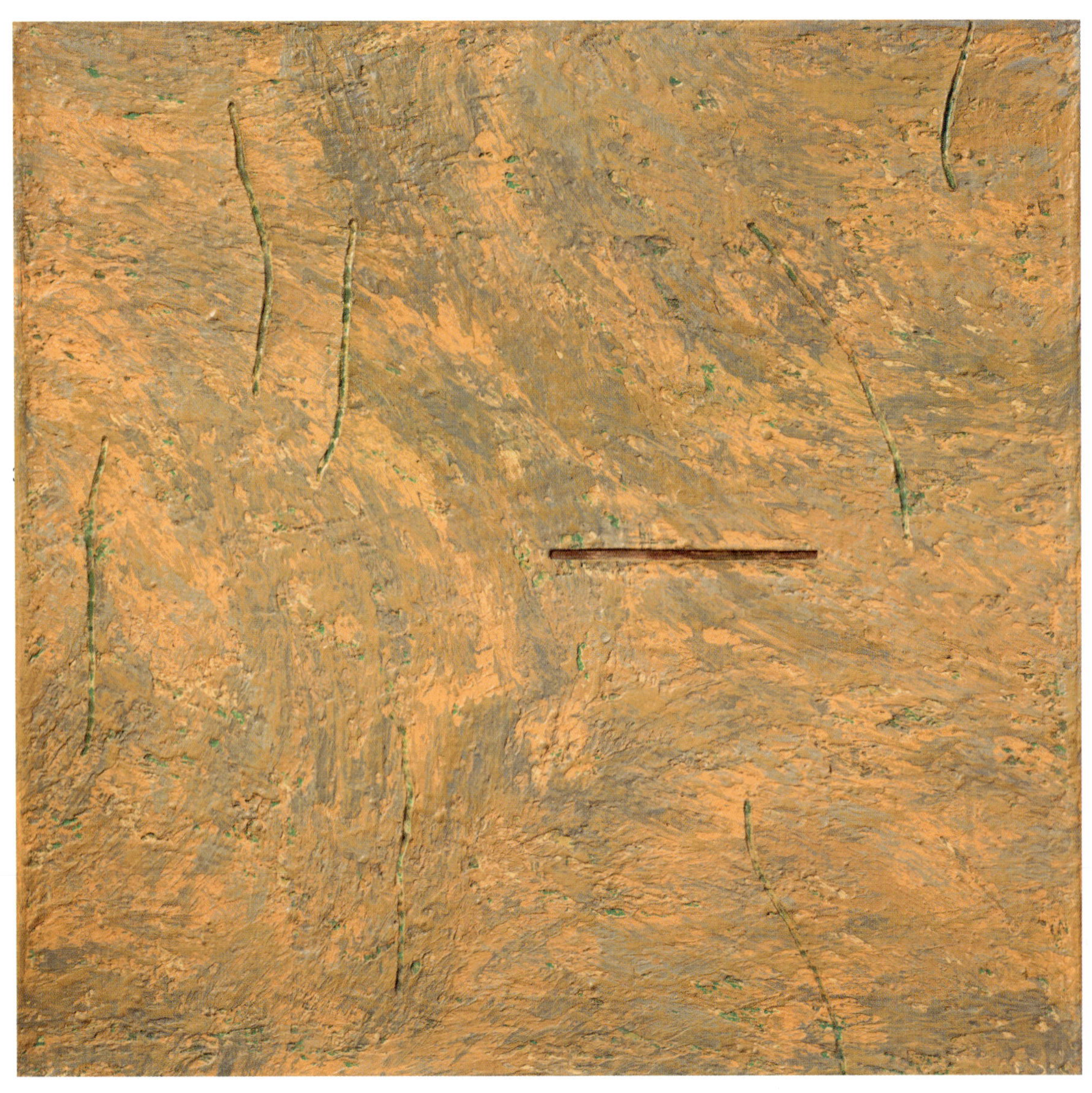

2.3 Kay WalkingStick (Cherokee, b. 1935)
Montauk I (1983)
Acrylic, saponified wax, ink, and pebbles on canvas, 56 × 56 × 4¼ inches
Copyright Kay WalkingStick. Courtesy of the artist.
Collection of the artist

Almost as soon as she began to work in a minimalist idiom, however, WalkingStick became frustrated with the movement's disinterest in or deliberate suppression of content. She noted that "in general they [the minimalists] had tried to avoid expression. They didn't want, not only meaning, but emotion; and they certainly didn't want narrative."[29] This presented a significant problem for WalkingStick, who, like so many other artists in the late 1960s and early 1970s, believed art could be a force for change. Her interest in feminism and the environment had already yielded works with titles such as *Apron Agitato* (1974) and *Pieces of Sky* (1970), and the focus of her attention was shifting toward American Indian history and politics, including her own Cherokee heritage. American Indian activism, such as the American Indian Movement occupation of Alcatraz in 1969–71, the "Trail of Broken Treaties" march on Washington in 1972, and the standoff at Wounded Knee, South Dakota, in 1973 increased WalkingStick's awareness of contemporary politics; closer to home, the publication in 1970 of Dee Brown's *Bury My Heart at Wounded Knee: An Indian History of the American West* also affected her thinking about her identity as a Native woman.[30] As WalkingStick recalls, "I was raised in a time when everybody thought that the only good Indian was a dead Indian. In fact, I did a painting called *For That Only Good Indian*."[31] Reading Brown's account of Chief Joseph, the Nez Perce chief who waged a running fight with the U.S. Army as he tried in vain to lead his people to safety in Canada in 1877, WalkingStick found herself thinking about a comment her father had made to the effect that Chief Joseph was one example of a "good Indian," and she resolved to bring this distinctly Native subject matter into her work.[32] The result, three dozen separate 20-by-15-inch canvases collectively titled the *Chief Joseph* series (1974–76), are some of the most devoutly intellectual and minimalist works of her career, but they are also deeply affecting. WalkingStick's intention in the series was "to make minimalist paintings that had emotion, and an energy, and a kind of narrative."[33] When the series was exhibited at the Bertha Urdang Gallery in New York City in 1978, *Art in America* critic Marjorie Welish praised WalkingStick for "attempting to forge a viable esthetic from American Indian and Minimalist elements together," which was exactly the synthesis that WalkingStick had strived for.[34]

In each of the thirty-six panels of the *Chief Joseph* series, four basic geometric forms are repeated—two small segments of a sphere and two larger ones—arranged vertically inside a rectangular field. WalkingStick created the line segments and arcing forms by scratching through layers of acrylic and wax to reveal the colors of ink-soaked canvases, and in order to ensure that the images were uniform, she traced each element on a grid pattern. The grid governs every aspect of these forms—their placement in the composition, their orientation, their dimension—and, whether or not that grid was entirely obscured or still faintly visible at the end of the process, it was essential to the composition: "I want the grid to be sensed, if you are aware, if you really look at it: this length is a quarter of the whole, this length is a half of the next unit."[35] In this respect, the grid functions as an extension of pure geometry, establishing a mathematical relationship between elements of the composition in a manner that is reminiscent of the search for harmonic proportions in the early history of painting. In modernist painting, however, the primary function of the grid is to affirm the flatness of the picture plane and the material presence of the painting. As Rosalind Krauss argued in her critical essay "Grids" of 1979, the "grid has become the medium for some of the greatest works of modernism." "In the flatness that results from its coordinates, the grid is the means of crowding out the dimensions of the real and replacing them with the lateral spread of a single surface."[36]

"The point was to flatten space," WalkingStick has said, and in the *Chief Joseph* series and the proto-landscape painting *Montauk I*, she achieved this primarily through the use of the grid. Increasingly she also moved to a square format. Even her signature diptychs, which are oriented horizontally, are constructed from the joining of two square panels. WalkingStick explains: "The theory when I was in [graduate] school was that resolving the composition of a square is harder than resolving a rectangle, even if it is only a slight rectangle. It's an easier problem and resolution. But as a matter of fact, that is only when you are talking about Renaissance perspective. If you're dealing with flat space, you're not dealing with a window on the world."[37]

Here at the threshold of WalkingStick's transition from truly nonobjective painting to a decades-long engagement with landscape, it is important to ask what else a painting might be if not a window on the world. Krauss provided at least one answer in "Grids," stressing that the use of the grid resulted in increased attention paid to the painting's material support.[38] She noted that "unlike perspective, the grid does not map the space of a room or a landscape or a group of figures onto the surface of a painting. Indeed, if it maps anything, it maps the surface of the painting itself. . . . Considered in this way, the bottom line of the grid is a naked and determined materialism."[39] This is precisely the kind of materialism that became ever more important to WalkingStick, as she began to mass her materials—acrylic and wax and ground seashells and copper filings—on reinforced canvases. Though the emphasis is always on paint, the medium that WalkingStick was deeply devoted to, the effect of all this massing of material is that the works approach the status of sculpture in their three-dimensionality. WalkingStick regarded them as such, averring, "These *are* objects. The notion of the painting as object was really very big for me when I was doing these. It's like sculpture, and I saw them like sculpture."[40] Critics agreed: writing for *ARTnews* in June of 1981, Deborah Phillips remarked that WalkingStick's new approach to the canvas "rather rigorously defines the work as a physical object" and that this treatment lent "an immediacy and directness to the work."[41] Frederick Castle of *Art in America* noted that the paintings "look somewhat like paintings, which they are, but also somewhat like large, heavy square objects on the wall."[42]

In the summer of 1983, WalkingStick received support from the Edward Albee Foundation to spend a month as an artist in residence in Montauk, Long Island. Almost immediately, paintings such as *Montauk I* and *Montauk II (Dusk)* reflected the change from working indoors in New Jersey and New York City to working near the sea. WalkingStick recalls that she was struck "by the colors that were there, they were so different from the dark colors of [her] attic studio."[43] She continued to build monumental 56-inch-square canvases, layering them by hand with as many as thirty layers of paint and wax and adding in pebbles taken directly from the beach at Montauk. As she scratched through the "twilight tones of muted pink" into the pale green layers below, she was aware that her wavy, vertical lines suggested trees scattered throughout the composition.[44] Enticingly, in both *Montauk* paintings, WalkingStick inscribed a short, thick, straight horizontal line segment in the middle of the composition. Though the placement of each line segment is determined by a mathematical ratio (they are equidistant from the top and bottom edges of the canvas, and each is a quarter of the total width of the canvas in length), it is tempting to interpret them as fragmented horizon lines. After all, there are few places in the natural world that the horizon line is more evident than at the ocean's edge. Nevertheless, despite the presence of trees and this proto-horizon, WalkingStick is reluctant to categorize the *Montauk* paintings as representational landscapes; she is willing to allow only that the paintings had "a little bit more to do with the landscape at Montauk than with just the inside of my head."[45]

Given that she had already overcome "modern art's will to silence, its hostility to literature, to narrative, [and] to discourse," WalkingStick's resistance to the incipient landscape in the *Montauk* paintings seems less a concern with content or even with representation itself, than with the particular subject: the real.[46] Krauss's critique of modernism provided fuel for her unease: "There are two ways in which the grid functions to declare the modernity of modern art. One is spatial; the other is temporal. In the spatial sense, the grid states the autonomy of the realm of art. Flattened, geometricized, ordered, it is antinatural, antimimetic, antireal. It is what art looks like *when it turns its back on nature*."[47] While Krauss was stridently declaring modernism's de facto refusal of nature—due in part to the grid's reflexive emphasis on the material support of the painting as an autonomous object—WalkingStick was experiencing the opposite effect. As noted earlier in this chapter, WalkingStick recalls that the landscapes in her work evolved or emerged of their own accord, as products of a process that emphasized the material surface. She elaborates:

> The paintings became more and more about the earth, the landscape, and they looked, many of them, like seeing the earth in the geological diagrams one sees of the different-layered remains of the various eons of the history of the earth. The paintings had this feeling of accruing the way the earth has accrued with layers of rock and sediment. The surface itself looks very much like limestone. . . . And it has, because of the wax, a very organic quality, so that related to the earth itself, to the ancient earth, to the earth as seen from thousands of miles up.[48]

In this passage, WalkingStick is speaking generally about the encaustic paintings of the early 1980s, but it is clear that all of this was coming to a head in the *Montauk* canvases, which bore the imprint of a particular place and time.

By 1985 WalkingStick's practice was finally overtaken by the landscape, and in *Death of the Elm* we encounter a more literal treatment of natural elements and the artist's first fully realized diptych painting. Though later diptychs such as *On the Edge* (1989; see figure 1.3) pair an "imagistic landscape" with an abstract or symbolic element such as a wedge or arcing form, *Death of the Elm* features landscape elements in both panels.[49] On the left, the limbs and leaves of a tree are depicted in acrylic on paper in colorful expressionistic strokes; on the right, the layering of acrylic and wax shades into landscape. The abstract panel serves its symbolic function (recall that the milky white color is symbolic of death and the short flat line segment signifies annihilation); however, it too can be read in more representational terms. The smooth mottled surface of the canvas is reminiscent of the bark of a dead tree, and the bent vertical lines that in the *Montauk* paintings only hinted at tree forms recur here in a work that is avowedly about trees. Whether one sees the abstraction as an extreme close-up of a single tree or a longer view of a forest replete with a horizon line—or both at once—is a phenomenon relevant to the discussion of contemporary landscape art, as it touches on the artist's ability to represent both a microcosmic and macrocosmic view of nature. As a perceptual phenomenon it features heavily in Krauss's account of the function of the grid in modernist painting.

Rather than speaking of microcosms or macrocosms, close-ups or long views, Krauss parses the difference between *centrifugal* and *centripetal* functions of the grid. The centrifugal reading interprets the space of the canvas as being but a fragment of a scene or space that continues off-canvas. This view is analogous to the characterization of painting as a window that dates back to the Renaissance and was so famously interrogated by Magritte's *The Human Condition* (1933). Yet in Krauss's telling, it is the grid rather than the image that expands beyond the confines of the canvas: "Logically speaking, the grid extends, in all directions, to infinity. Any boundaries imposed upon it by a given painting or sculpture can only be seen—according to this logic—as arbitrary. By virtue of the grid, the given work of art is presented as a mere fragment, a tiny piece arbitrarily cropped from an infinitely larger fabric." The centripetal reading, on the other hand, regards the canvas as a self-contained entity, not contiguous with the world around it. In Krauss's view, the centripetal approach is basically without precedent in the history of art: it is a product of the modernist revolution. It operates "from the outer limits of the aesthetic object inward. The grid is, in relation to *this* reading a *re*-presentation of everything that separates the work of art from the world. . . . The grid is an introjection of the boundaries of the world into the interior of the work; it is a mapping of the space inside the frame onto itself. It is a mode of repetition, the content of which is the conventional nature of art itself."[50]

When Krauss finally asks whether "what we see in a particular painting [is] merely a section of an implied continuity, or . . . the painting structured as an autonomous, organic whole,"[51] our dilemma with regard to WalkingStick's work deepens: it cannot be both, but it is. The right side of *Death of the Elm* alone compounds a microcosmic and macrocosmic view of a tree/forest, and the canvas represents only a fragment of a whole in either regard; the grid functions here as a centrifugal structure. Yet that same canvas is a world unto itself, a tangible and material object that is as self-reflexive as it is representational; the grid acts as a centripetal force. It turns out that WalkingStick's accomplishment would not have been anathema to Krauss, who concluded her investigation into the nature of the grid with the tantalizing admission that a few modern artists had managed to "think about the grid in both ways at once."[52]

SYMBOLIC LANDSCAPES

The inherent contradiction between centrifugal and centripetal perspectives is but one form of duality that WalkingStick managed to accommodate in a single panel before embracing the diptych format.[53] In an interview with the *New York Times* in late 1985, WalkingStick stressed the dichotomies in her paintings: "'First,' she says, 'there is the logical, reductive development of the composition and then the emotive, ritualistic application of paint.'"[54] What WalkingStick discovered in the process of pairing panels in the creation of *Death of the Elm* is that the diptych format allowed her to separate out some of these multiple perspectives: microcosm and macrocosm, centripetal and centrifugal forces, pure geometry and psychological expression. The diptych gave her room to breathe. More importantly, moving to the diptych formula provided WalkingStick a way to preserve her abstractions as such, by relocating the emerging landscape elements to the neighboring panel. In *Late Summer on the Ramapo* (1987), for example, the abstract panel closely resembles those earlier abstractions that had tended toward "becoming landscapes" due to their thick layering effect. It even contains the bent lines that read as trees in

Montauk I and *Death of the Elm*. Nevertheless, the dominant form in this panel is a black scalene triangle that furiously resists interpretation as a landscape element. The landscape has instead migrated to the right panel, where an imagistic scene of a riverbank is depicted in oil paint on an otherwise unmanipulated canvas. WalkingStick's decision to paint in oil instead of acrylic is significant, because the medium allows for a much freer application of paint and results in a much brighter color palette than was available when she worked with acrylic and wax. The difference between the two panels is tangible: the abstract panel stands a full three inches out from the wall, physically overshadowing the much less robust landscape painting. Together, the two square panels make for a monumental presentation that is 48 by 96 inches in dimension.

Despite the dominating physical presence of the abstract panel, the landscape scene on the right of *Late Summer on the Ramapo* commands attention through its vibrant color and sensuous forms. As a view of the landscape, the scene is tightly cropped: the top of the frame bears down heavily on the composition, truncating the trees along the riverbank. Rather than suggesting a continuation of the scene beyond the confines of the canvas, the composition folds back on itself as the reflection of the tree trunks plunge into the middle ground of the painting, and all attention is directed to the undulating surface of the river, where WalkingStick's deft handling of the paint conveys the fluid movement of the water. As the pigment flows across the canvas, the rippling surfaces of the painting and the river become one. As a final touch, the cool green and warm peach tones of the scene lend it temporal specificity: they are the colors of late summer, perfectly appropriate to the subject matter as announced in the work's title.

At this early date WalkingStick's diptych titles often made direct reference to the places that they depict. Along with *Late Summer on the Ramapo*, titles like *Canyon de Chelly* (1984–87) and *Hermosa Ridge* (1988) not only pinpointed locales but also intimated that the scenes were painted "from life," recording distinct temporal, seasonal, and weather conditions. For these very reasons, WalkingStick became disenchanted with her titles, sensing that particularity detracted from her efforts to "describe the earth in general."[55] For the next twenty years, roughly from 1989 to 2009, the artist avoided geographic attributions in her titles and instead insisted that her landscapes were merely *inspired* by particular places. She steadily maintained that her images were nonobjective, filtered through her memory and subjective experience.

In the few years that elapsed between the inception of the diptych format and her husband's death, the works seem to have been primarily about juxtaposing two different forms of representation—abstraction and realism—and it is reasonable to consider their formal aspects, like the cropping of the landscape scenes, in light of WalkingStick's long engagement with modernist aesthetics. In the wake of the tragedy that befell her in 1989, however, WalkingStick's devotion to the diptych format could hardly have been driven by modernist concerns alone. Instead, the diptychs morph almost imperceptibly into vehicles of impassioned expression. Five diptychs, for example, feature a waterfall or cascade in the landscape panel. In each of these—*On the Edge*, *Loss*, *Uncontrolled Destiny*, *The Abyss*, and *Grappling with Chaos*—the cropping of the landscape scene is much more drastic than in previous works, and the effect is dizzying: the viewer is swept up in the maelstrom of WalkingStick's overwhelming grief. The landscape paintings constitute only half of each composition, however; the pathos of the cascades is counterbalanced by the stasis of the enigmatic forms that appear in the encaustic panels. Thus, as discussed earlier, the diptych format came to embody WalkingStick's struggle to regain her own sense of equilibrium during a period of crisis. The artist regarded the images of torrents of churning water as both a metaphor for "uncontrolled destiny" and a "snapshot" of the present; the abstractions represented "both the past and the future," as well as a sense of eternal stillness or calm. Taken together, the two sides of the diptychs express the immediacy of loss while providing solace gained from taking a more existential view.

Looking back on these works years later, WalkingStick remarks that the diptychs of this era were, for her, also an exploration of the corporeal and the incorporeal.[56] This can be interpreted in several different ways. The corporeal aligns with the real time of the present and with the realism of the landscape scenes, while the incorporeal aligns with the timelessness and conceptual nature of the abstractions. In the context of WalkingStick's grief, the corporeal and incorporeal also reference the perceived dichotomies of body and spirit, matter and immateriality.[57] These dichotomies have typically been explored in the history of art through depictions of Christ, whose flesh is said to have become spirit at the moment of transfiguration, resurrection, or ascension. WalkingStick has expressed interest in historical depictions of the subject—such as Renaissance painter Andrea Mantegna's *Lamentation of Christ* (c. 1480), in which WalkingStick says you "can feel the body becoming spirit."[58] What is unique about WalkingStick's approach to the issue of the corporeal and incorporeal in her diptychs of this period is her transference of this investigation from the figural tradition to landscape and abstraction: the corporeal "body" for WalkingStick is not a body at all.

Perhaps fittingly, it is the abstract imagery that bears much of the weight of WalkingStick's expression of the incorporeal, at least at first. A two-panel charcoal drawing from 1989, entitled *Is That You?*, reveals this shift: the right panel again depicts a waterfall, but the fan-shaped element on the left is multiplied and glows with diffuse light. It seems to exist in several dimensions, one beyond the other, each radiating energy. In effect, the abstraction has a ghostly quality that is reinforced by the title of the work: *Is That You?*.[59] Though less ephemeral and spectral than the abstract form in the charcoal drawing, the abstractions of the diptych paintings likewise yield symbolic meaning when read in light of WalkingStick's stated interest in matters of spirit. *Letting Go from Chaos to Calm* (1990) is the last in the series of diptychs that WalkingStick painted in the immediate aftermath of her husband's death. It continues the use of the waterfall as a metaphor for being swept up in life's events, but the title indicates that WalkingStick is emerging from the darkest hour of her grief.[60] The color palette is growing brighter, and the fan shape of the abstract panel is now overlaid with a novel form, a vertical ellipse. Like the fan-shaped segments of a circle and the scalene triangle of the artist's earlier abstractions, the ellipse is an element of fundamental geometry. Here, it forms a strong vertical axis that grounds the abstract panel with its absolute symmetry. Symbolically, the ellipse represents wholeness, completion, or a return—connotations that make sense in the context of WalkingStick's rumination on mortality and her desire to regain her sense of equilibrium.[61]

The ellipse is most significant, however, as a symbol of the *unification* of the corporeal and incorporeal realms. WalkingStick refers to this shape—which she employed in diptychs such as *Night* (1991), the *Spirit Center* series (1991–92), and *Remnant of Cataclysm* (1992)—as a mandorla, an element of medieval religious iconography.[62] "Mandorla," which means "almond" in Italian, is the term given to the vertical ellipse with slightly pointed ends that is formed at the intersection of two overlapping circles. In Christian iconography, the shape represents the union of the realms of spirit and matter or heaven and earth, and it encloses the figure of Christ or the Virgin Mary, rendered at the moment of their transfiguration. For WalkingStick, the vertical ellipse thus represented the promise of transcendence as well as wholeness. By 1992 WalkingStick's journey had come full circle: in a diptych entitled *Spirit Center II*, the vertical ellipse is joined at right angles by one of shimmering substance that seems to exist in another dimension. Together the two inscribe a translucent sphere that enfolds a radiant core. *Spirit Center II* offers further revelation: the rushing rivers and waterfalls of the *Loss* series have given way to an arid landscape scene that is oddly cropped and somewhat difficult to resolve visually. In it, a leafless tree pushes through the crevices in a rocky escarpment and casts its shadow across the dry earth. Where the shadows of the branches fall they seem to penetrate the soil, spreading as roots, perhaps also seeking the center. This imagery both mirrors and is the near antithesis of the abstraction. Whereas the abstraction is becoming ever more ephemeral, incorporeal, and immaterial, the landscape painting remains solidly grounded; its three-dimensionality, deep shading, and recession into space all underscore the mass of its forms.

The relationship of the landscape imagery to the abstraction is vexed in all of WalkingStick's diptychs: sometimes the scenes seem to resonate with a single theme, color palette, or compositional form, and at other times the dichotomy is more pronounced. Even in diptychs that denote spiritual balance, the distinct landscape elements communicate turbulence rather than serenity. WalkingStick is drawn to "rugged" landscapes—to escarpments, mesas, and mountain ranges that "carry a memory of the earth's history[,] . . . that look newly carved and eons old."[63] In effect, WalkingStick's natural features bear the ravages of time, but they are also achronic—in a perpetual state of transformation yet resistant to change. "There's a primalness," she says, "a larger-than-life quality to them. They're not tamed, they're not controlled, they're not farmed, they're not pruned."[64]

One effect of consistently depicting raw and rugged landscape features in these works is the sharp contrast that such scenes offer when juxtaposed with the abstract panels. There is a heightened tension that accrues between the disparate components of the diptychs, which in addition to representing the corporeal and the incorporeal also contrast the "stillness of eternity" with the primal forces of the earth. Both the conflict and the resolution were important to WalkingStick, who understood that her paintings had always been animated by the disparity between the stillness of her minimalist forms and her passionate, expressive handling of paint. A closer look at *Remnant of Cataclysm* (1992) reveals that the contrasting aspects of stasis and dynamism are not exclusively relegated to their respective panels: the craggy, irregular landscape scene on the right contains a relatively stable horizon line, and the static form of the horizontal ellipse on the left vibrates with a corona of agitated marks that pulse like the gaslight of Van Gogh's *The Night Café* (1888).

Nevertheless, each of WalkingStick's diptychs emphasize the unification of distinct forms of perspective and perception. In a special edition of *Art Journal* devoted to Native American art in 1992, for which she served as guest editor, WalkingStick wrote, "To unite two kinds of memory, these two kinds of perception, is important to my psyche. It offers not only a personal wholeness, but also a wholeness in the continuum of humanity. . . . These are not landscapes, but paintings about my view of the earth and its sacred quality."[65] In addition to stressing WalkingStick's holistic approach to her subjects, this passage attests to the degree to which her meditation on the spiritual realm, once expressed primarily through abstraction, came to permeate her landscape imagery. Moreover, WalkingStick's respect for the sacredness of the earth may underscore her appreciation for "primal" landscapes, which in remaining untouched or unaltered by humans represent the earth in its purest or original state. Finally, WalkingStick's affinity for untamed, uncontrolled, unfarmed, unpruned landscapes returns us to the thesis of this chapter. Her penchant for picturing ruggedly inhospitable landscapes and her refusal to temper them imaginatively with roads or clearings or open foregrounds contravene the norms of earlier European paintings. In fact, many aspects of WalkingStick's practice may be considered anti-invitational in the manner that they interrupt the viewer's imaginative access to the landscapes pictured. For example, WalkingStick's retreat from providing place-specific titles and her concomitant assertion that her landscapes do not represent "real" places work against the European landscape's tradition of portraying the colonial peripheries (e.g., the American West, Africa, New Zealand) as *terra nova*—land for the taking.

Perhaps the most devoutly anti-invitational aspect of WalkingStick's diptychs, however, is their assertive materiality. In addition to building up her canvases—notably the abstract panels—with layers of paint and wax and other substances such as sand, canvas, and metal, WalkingStick directs attention to the way that the abstraction literally overshadows the landscape panel. This was the case with the very first diptych, *Death of the Elm*, in which a work on paper was unevenly paired with a heavy encaustic on panel, and it persists in lesser degrees in diptychs like *Uncontrolled Destiny* (1989), where the panels are slightly different sizes and deliberately offset, or where the artist has left a slight gap between panels. WalkingStick explains: "That edge and the center line between the paintings is important. The other day somebody called it a speed bump, which I think is hysterical. It forces you to slow down, to look at one side, then slowly look at the other, then look back."[66] The intent behind these visual effects is to "maintain that sense of [the painting] being an object, of it being concrete: it is real."[67] Once the illusion of space is mitigated by the primacy of the painting as an object, so too is the viewer's progress into that space slowed.

DECOLONIAL LANDSCAPES

It is fitting to note that each of the aspects of WalkingStick's diptychs that effectively block the viewer's imaginative access to the landscape was codified in her practice between 1989 and 1992, precisely the years that heralded the transition in Native American art from modernism to postmodernism. Two of WalkingStick's diptychs, including *Loss* (1989), were featured in *The Decade Show: Frameworks of Identity in the 1980's*, the groundbreaking New York City exhibition of works by ninety-four artists of Hispanic, Asian, African American, Native American, and European heritage in 1990. A collaborative effort between three institutions that were considered somewhat outside of the artistic mainstream—the New Museum, the Museum of Contemporary Hispanic Art, and the Studio Museum in Harlem—*The Decade Show* is now widely regarded as a foundational event in the development of postmodernism.[68] WalkingStick's work was also included in nearly every important Columbian quincentennial exhibition of 1991–92, including *Our Land/Ourselves*, *Submuloc*

Show/Columbus Wohs, and *Land, Spirit, Power: First Nations at the National Gallery of Canada*.

Of the many strains of postmodernist discourse that emerged out of the exhibitions listed above, those that addressed the intersections of Indigenous land, history, and identity stood out strongly. Saulteaux First Nation curator Robert Houle stitched these themes together seamlessly in his description of WalkingStick's work in the *Land, Spirit, Power* exhibition: "Her abstract landscapes, especially the earlier ones, have the strength and inner calm of a warrior combined with passionate execution and an aggressive stance. This emotional intensity directs the viewer to feel the subcutaneous layer of pain of someone who is preoccupied with the land in the way that only a member of a nation that has been dispossessed can be." Though Houle references WalkingStick's personal experience (her biracial identity, the "loss of a life-long partner and friend"), his essay emphasizes the *collective* rather than individual experience of Native peoples on the eve of the quincentennial.[69] Moreover, Houle's perspective as a co-curator of the *Land, Spirit, Power* exhibition is reflective of the larger discourse surrounding the quincentennial, which included difficult but cathartic conversations within Native communities, as well as far more contentious dialogues that challenged the uncritical celebrations of Columbus enacted in the public realm.

WalkingStick herself was galvanized by this discourse, and for a time she channeled her rage at the injustices of history into her work. Two of the diptychs that were featured in the *Land, Spirit, Power* exhibition, *Where Are the Generations* (1991), and *Our Selves/Our Land* (1991), are quite explicit in voicing Native survival. Both feature representational landscape elements—here understood as explicitly Native land—on the right and thick encaustic abstractions on the left. In both works, however, the central motif in the abstract panel is an embedded copper plaque. The plaque in *Our Selves/Our Land* is engraved with a single word written in the Cherokee syllabary. The inscription in *Where Are the Generations* reads in English: "In 1492 we were 20 million. Now we are 2 million. Where are the generations? Where are the children? Neverborn." The inscription ends with WalkingStick's own name, written in Cherokee.[70] WalkingStick's use of writing in these works is astonishing, given the determinacy of language relative to the symbolism of abstraction, which it replaces here. Evidently, she wanted to ensure that the message in the quincentennial works would be clearly heard and understood.[71]

Even as WalkingStick contributed her voice to the charged political dialogue of 1992, she did not abandon her engagement with spirituality or with what art historian Lisa Seppi has termed "metaphysics." In the years just following the quincentennial, WalkingStick returned to the subjects that had occupied her before, creating diptychs with titles like *Eternal Chaos/Eternal Calm* (1993), *Seeking the Silence* (1994), and *Four Directions: Spirit Center* (1994; figure 2.4).

This is no simple return, however; WalkingStick had more reason than ever to seek solace through immersion in the spiritual world. Now she sought to restore balance, not only for herself, but also for humanity. With this turn came the introduction of a new abstract element that is ubiquitous in the diptychs of this period: the equilateral cross of the four directions. The choice reflects her renewed commitment to ever more universal forms of expression. For WalkingStick, the equilateral cross is not only "archetypal imagery" of the kind she had favored in her devoutly minimalist works of the 1970s but also a symbol that has its strongest valence in Native contexts: "I use [the motif] because it can be read in so many ways: as the four directions symbol, as a Christian cross, as a plus sign, which means there's more here—or this adds up. So that symbol, although it has specificity for me, has broad meaning. I also like the fact that it encourages a kind of unity. It's one of the few pan-Indian symbols I know."[72] In her personal papers, WalkingStick stressed the unifying aspects of the symbol, writing that the symbol represented the sacred in most tribes, despite the variations in languages, creation stories, and views of the cosmos held by those peoples.[73]

Four Directions: Spirit Center (1994) pairs the four directions symbol with one of the most representational of all of WalkingStick's contemporaneous landscape paintings.[74] The oil on canvas rendering on the right is a near copy of the rocky escarpment pictured in *Spirit Center II* of two years earlier, but this one is devoid of trees, and the light and color palette are softer. The cropping of the composition is also less severe, allowing a deeper look into the landscape, which recedes to a distant horizon line. The legibility of the landscape scene is significant, for one of the strongest connotations of the four directions symbol is its association with land and the sanctity of the earth. The equilateral arms of the cross represent the four cardinal directions, which extend to encompass all points in space. Moreover, according to Seppi, the motif signifies WalkingStick's "optimistic attitude and inclusive approach towards landscape" because it symbolizes the earth in a state of equilibrium. Further, Seppi writes, "In WalkingStick's view the cruciform motif represents not only the sacred earth, but also 'the balance and harmony therein.'"[75] *The Four Directions: Spirit Center* thus demonstrates the lasting effects of the Columbian quincentennial on WalkingStick's work in that it offers healing from trauma while foregrounding a collective and distinctly Indigenous worldview.[76]

The equilateral cross has not always been so closely associated with Native spirituality in WalkingStick's personal lexicon. Seppi identifies at least three other paintings that featured the motif in the early 1980s, before the advent of the diptych paintings. The single-panel encaustics *Cryptochroma I* (1982), *Positive Field* (1982), and *Cardinal Points* (1983–85) all belong to the period in which WalkingStick was striving to achieve modernist flatness through geometry and use of the grid. The equilateral cross is a fragment of a grid writ large; it

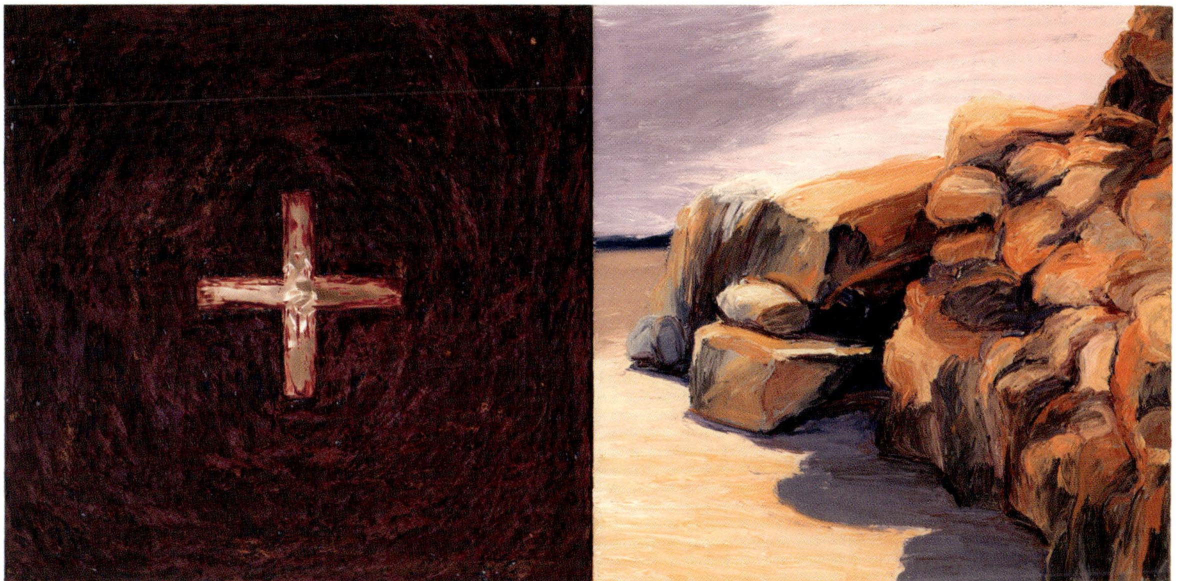

2.4 Kay WalkingStick (Cherokee, b. 1935)
Four Directions: Spirit Center (1994)
Acrylic, saponified wax, and oil on canvas and wood panel, 28 × 56 inches
Copyright Kay WalkingStick. Courtesy of the artist.
Collection of Erica WalkingStick Echols Lowry

is also uniquely oriented to the square format that WalkingStick had adopted in her effort to deny "Renaissance space." Their minimalist attributes notwithstanding, the titles of *Cryptochroma I*, *Positive Field*, and *Cardinal Points* all make punning reference to Christian associations of the cross. Seppi reports that *Cryptochroma* refers to the secret crypts and hidden vaults built under Christian churches, while *Cardinal Points* is a triple pun, referring to the cardinal directions, religious dignitaries of the Catholic church, and the scarlet color of the painting itself. In the latter example, the cruciform motif is rendered in gold metallic paint, another allusion to the interiors of churches.[77]

The original title of *Cardinal Points*, *Resurrection Piece*, marks it as a precursor to WalkingStick's later contemplation of the corporeal and incorporeal, yet in referencing Christian doctrine so explicitly, the title proved to be "too religious" for the artist's comfort.[78] WalkingStick's revision of the title is consistent with her intention to engender multivalent interpretations of her work, but her suppression of the religious content also served to position the work as resolutely modern. A scant few years earlier, Krauss had characterized the prevailing attitude of the mainstream art world toward any and all reference to the sacred as follows: "Given the absolute rift that has opened between the sacred and the secular, the modern artist was obviously faced with the necessity to choose between one mode of expression and the other. . . . Although this condition could be discussed openly in the late nineteenth century, it is something that is inadmissible in the twentieth so that by now we find it indescribably embarrassing to mention *art* and *spirit* in the same sentence."[79]

It would be another decade before postmodernism rehabilitated the sacred, lauding it as a foundational aspect of Indigenous experience.[80] When the equilateral cross motif resurfaced as the four directions symbol in WalkingStick's diptych paintings of 1994–95, it carried with it connotations of both Christian and Indigenous iconography and the syncretism of WalkingStick's own religious background.[81] Moreover, in the diptychs, the motif is invariably partnered with the landscape, which redirects the focus of the spiritual expression toward the earth.[82] The extent to which the symbol came to be associated with land in the diptychs is borne out in the treatment of the abstract form. In place of the gold metallic paint that alluded to sacred architecture in *Cardinal Points*, WalkingStick inserted copper into the cross in *Four Directions: Spirit Center*. Unlike the copper plaques of the quincentennial diptychs *Where Are the Generations?* and *Our Selves/Our Land*, copper is used here as an inlay, lending its substance and symbolism to the abstract form. As an elemental metal, copper is literally what the earth is made of, and for WalkingStick it represents the preciousness of the earth's natural resources.

The inclusion of copper in works like *Four Directions: Spirit Center* may reflect WalkingStick's "optimistic attitude"; however, there is a dark side to her evocation of the earth's bounty as well. In her editorial essay in *Art Journal* in 1992, WalkingStick cited a deep concern for the environment as common to all Indigenous artists; writing of her own practice she noted that the incorporation of copper "represents the economic urges underlying the rape of our land."[83] WalkingStick was likely referring to *Remnant of Cataclysm*, which contains a broad band of copper running vertically through the center of the diptych's abstract panel. Save for the title, little about the diptych signals the catastrophe that WalkingStick references in her written statement: a dark sky hovers over an arid landscape, yet WalkingStick is reluctant to portray "the rape of our land" in graphic terms. Whether her diptychs symbolize trauma or refuge, the landscapes maintain an air of redemptive beauty.

The contradiction of WalkingStick's landscapes as both desecrated and inviolate is especially evident in *Venere Alpina* (1997; figure 2.5). The landscape element, which depicts a mountain ridge that lies perpendicular to the picture plane, is typical of WalkingStick's diptychs in that it is rendered in oil and is much thinner than the abstract panel.[84] The treatment of this landscape is unusual, however, in that it seems deliberately invitational—the gentle, undulating curves of the rolling hills are sensuous and even seductive. Moreover, the mountain ridge recedes into the distance in a manner that beckons the viewer into the space of the landscape. The enticing beauty of the scene is all the more surprising given that it depicts a site in Italy that some five years earlier WalkingStick had told an interviewer that she simply could not paint: "I went to Italy in 1992. I visited a wonderful place, Bellagio, for a month and I found that I just couldn't paint it. I tried; I painted for three weeks and finally realized I was getting absolutely nowhere. . . . It isn't my home, but also the Italian landscape is totally controlled by humans."[85] The abstract panel of the diptych reveals the impetus behind WalkingStick's decision to revisit a landscape that is irrevocably shaped by human activity. The panel is built up of layers of acrylic pigment and wax on wood, but in this instance the entire panel is overlaid with a skin of steel mesh that is scored with faint lines. This metallic grid flattens the composition, except where it is rent by a deep vertical gash that echoes the orientation of the mountain ridge to its left. Within this gash, a subsurface of blue sequins and red and black glitter is revealed. Given the copper-colored patina of the steel, the glistening red that is exposed beneath it, and WalkingStick's own statement about her use of metals as a metaphor for the rape of the environment, it is nearly impossible to regard the abstract panel of *Venere Alpina* as anything other than a violently desecrated body. And a sacred body at that: the title, *Venere Alpina* means "Alpine Goddess." The emergence of the figure in WalkingStick's paintings will be taken up in chapter 5; in this context the anthropomorphic landscape signifies the inherent vulnerability of the earth to the exploitation of its natural resources.

The paradox of *Venere Alpina* is that it juxtaposes sensuousness with violation, sacredness with base economic impulses, beauty with offense. Describing this work, WalkingStick reveals a final enigma: she refers to the shape of the gash as a mandorla—the area of congruence between matter and spirit, corporeal and incorporeal realms. But which is the corporeal side? In previous diptychs, that distinction fell to the landscape, with its strong associations of realism and materiality. In *Venere Alpina*, however, the corporeal is convincingly evoked through abstraction, as a metaphoric body. The incorporeal likewise permeates both panels of the diptych, as a manifestation of the earth's sacredness or spirit. Thus, despite the vast differences in the imagery of the two panels of *Venere Alpina*, the diptych again represents the unity or congruence of physical and metaphysical realms.

Of all the differing forms of perception that WalkingStick's diptychs conveyed over the years, *Venere Alpina* best demonstrates the artist's "separate intention of the eye"—her ability to perceive both surfaces and depth simultaneously. Like *Death of the Elm*, which suggested both a forest and an individual tree, right down to the texture of the bark, *Venere Alpina* captures the landscape from a distance as well as from an intensely proximal vantage point. For the viewer, regarding the diptych as both a microcosmic and macrocosmic view of the earth requires accepting the abstraction *as* a landscape

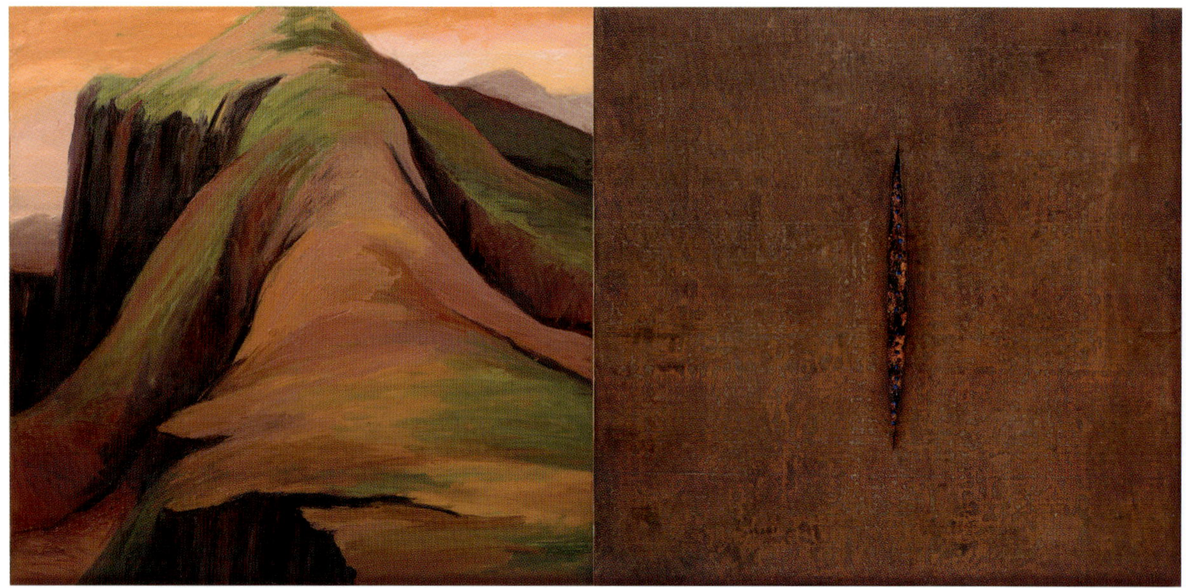

2.5 Kay WalkingStick (Cherokee, b. 1935)
Venere Alpina (1997)
Oil on canvas, rusted steel mesh over acrylic, saponified wax, and plastic stones on wood, 32 × 64 inches

Collection of the artist

or as a form of landscape representation. Over time, the landscape aspect of WalkingStick's paintings spread inevitably into the abstract panel. *Requiem* (2002) returns to the equilateral cross motif of earlier abstractions, but in this instance it is superimposed over the silhouette of a mountain landscape. Further, although the cross in *Requiem* is embossed with gold leaf, the abstract panel is otherwise devoid of mixed media inclusions such as wax that would cause it to overshadow its neighboring landscape scene. The panels appear as basically contiguous landscapes, both painted in oil on wood; the "speed bump" effect of the gap between panels is diminished by the parity in thickness of the panels and by the continuation of the horizon line from one panel to the other.[86]

The superimposition of the symbolic form over the top of a landscape scene continues in WalkingStick's diptychs through to the present day, with one striking difference. In works like *Our Land* (2007), *Rio Grande Gorge* (2011), *The Silence of Glacier* (2013), and many others, the "symbols" are patterns drawn from traditional Native American arts such as parfleche painting, weaving, and beadwork. The bold, colorful, geometric pattern that is draped across the landscape in *Our Land* is of Nez Perce origin: it signifies that the mountains depicted are part of the fabric of the lives of Chief Joseph's people. In 2002 WalkingStick journeyed to these mountains to retrace the path of Chief Joseph's 1,100-mile exodus across Oregon, Idaho, Wyoming, and Montana. A suite of drawings from her pilgrimage was exhibited in 2003 as part of the National Museum of the American Indian's *Continuum 12 Artists* series, where they were shown alongside the three dozen *Chief Joseph* works that WalkingStick painted in 1974–76.[87] One of the drawings, *Bitterroot Mountains I* (2002), served as the preliminary sketch for the diptych painting *Our Land*.[88] Even after the "single image landscapes" made their way into paint in 2006–7, they did not become a prominent feature of WalkingStick's work for several more years. In the intervening period, WalkingStick produced another stunning series of bifurcated diptychs, the *Ramapo River* series of 2009–10.

Ramapo River Early Spring, *Highwater April*, *Blackberry Winter*, *Autumn's End*, *Midsummer* (all 2009), and *Ice Flow* (2010) mark the artist's return to the landscape featured in one of her earliest diptychs, *Late Summer on the Ramapo* (1987). In comparison to the river scene painted more than two decades before—and, for that matter, that of all of her signature diptych paintings—the landscape imagery of the later series is far more representational, offering a greater degree of detail and recession into space and faithfully recording seasonal and atmospheric effects in naturalistic colors. Moreover, the landscape scenes are no longer overshadowed by their abstract counterparts: the thick acrylic and wax accretions are gone, along with the geometric motif itself. In their stead, the diptychs of the *Ramapo River* series each pair an illusionistic oil painting with a companion panel entirely covered in gold or palladium leaf.[89] WalkingStick had used gold leaf before, notably in the equilateral cross in *Requiem* and in figural works discussed in chapter 5; however, in neither of the previous instances did the gold leaf cover as much area as in the *Ramapo River* diptychs. By covering the entire surface and eliminating all intentional marks from the compositions, WalkingStick achieves total flatness in these panels, while preserving the symbolic power of the work.[90] According to WalkingStick, the gold (or other metallic) fields evoke a "separate understanding of space. It is an eternal space rather than a conventional space."[91] Given that her use of gold leaf is directly inspired by devotional paintings from the late Gothic period in Italy, it is clear that WalkingStick's eternal space is a sacred space.

In many respects, WalkingStick's later diptychs continue in the tradition of her earliest ones, though they push ever deeper into both abstraction and realism. Whereas *Late Summer on the Ramapo* (1987) used abstraction to mitigate the illusionist qualities of the imagistic landscape, the later works embrace the particulars of place, space, and time; they also push abstraction nearly to its ontological limits, eliminating form in favor of a purely incorporeal expression. What is less evident in the later diptychs is WalkingStick's physical presence. Gone are the layers of acrylic and wax applied by hand and the agitated scratches and gouges that recorded her bodily gestures. Though the application of the metal foil reveals some trace of the artist's labor as well as her passion, it does not bear the physical immediacy of her expressionist handling of paint. What persists as a record of the artist's presence is her subjective experience of the landscape—the feel of frost in the air, the way light fades on a winter afternoon—these details attest to her existence at a particular place and time. This degree of specificity, which is reinforced in the titles of both the earlier and later *Ramapo* diptychs, was deliberately withheld in the diptychs of the intervening years while WalkingStick was seeking the universal in her work, yet it remains a constant in her paintings after 2009.

New Mexico Desert (figure 2.6), *Rio Grande Gorge*, *New Mexico Arroyos*, *Late Afternoon on the Rio Grande* (all 2011), *St. Mary's Mountain*, *The Pecos*, *Orilla Verde at Rio Grande* (all 2012), and *The Silence of Glacier* (2013) are the most representational landscapes of WalkingStick's oeuvre to date. Each title identifies the site or region that is represented, and each painting features what WalkingStick refers to as a "single image landscape," one that spans both panels of the diptych without a noticeable break between them. These are truly scenic

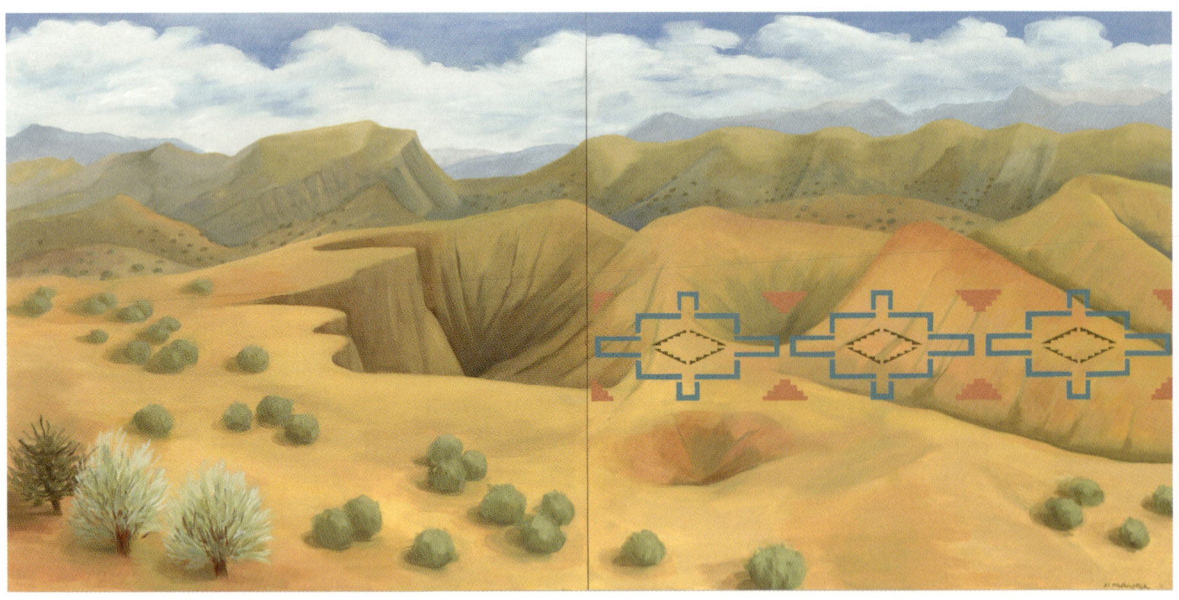

2.6 Kay WalkingStick (Cherokee, b. 1935)
New Mexico Desert (2011)
Oil on wood panels, 40 × 80 inches

National Museum of the American Indian

landscapes, sweeping vistas of sublime beauty that stretch to a far horizon under cloud-filled skies. The only remnant of abstraction in these works is the pattern that is superimposed on the landscape in one of the panels. As described above, the patterns are drawn from the traditional arts of the Indigenous peoples of the region depicted; thus their presence marks the land as Native land.[92] Though the patterns have a flattening effect and call attention to the two-dimensional surface of the painting, these are hardly the minimalist objects of WalkingStick's early career. Neither are they recognizably postmodern, despite the way those same patterns block access to and declare the sovereignty of the Native landscape.

If the recent works are neither modernist nor postmodernist, what are they? According to WalkingStick, they are simply—shockingly—romantic. They are lyrical and sensual and meant to inspire longing as well as reverence and respect. "When I was doing the [older] diptychs," she says, "the landscape was separated from the romanticism, that nineteenth-century romanticism. Now I kind of don't care. Is it nineteenth-century romanticism I'm doing? Fine. That's what I've come to."[93] This, then, is the true spirit of WalkingStick's contemporary landscape paintings: they may be invitational or anti-invitational, visually dominant or haptically charged; they may be landscapes in *exactly* the sense that Cole or Church painted landscapes if the artist chooses them to be. They can be any or all of these things precisely because the hegemony of European landscape representation has been broken, largely due to WalkingStick's own efforts.

CHAPTER THREE

Beyond the Horizon

POSTMODERN PERSPECTIVES ON THE NATIVE LANDSCAPE

All landscape is internal.

Ojibwe artist CARL BEAM

IN THE OPENING PAGES OF THE EXHIBITION CATALOG *OUR LAND/OURSELVES: American Indian Contemporary Artists* (1990), curator Jaune Quick-to-See Smith offered the following caveats about the landscape imagery that the audience would encounter there: "The artists in this exhibit take multiple approaches to describing land/landscape. It is more rare to find a horizon line than not. It is more rare to find political content than not. It is more rare to find realism than not. But however the artists execute their work, whether celebrating human interaction with the land or cautioning the destruction of the land, they weave their distinct conceptions in and through an interior view."[1]

A small contradiction to Smith's observation that "it is more rare to find a horizon line than not," the painting that graced the catalog's cover features a sharply defined, radiant line marking the boundary between water and sky on the surface of a lake. The work, painted in acrylic and pastel on paper and titled *Spirit Path, New Day, Red Rock Variation: Lake Superior Landscape* (1990; figure 3.1), is by George Morrison, one of the most prominent Native American painters of the twentieth century.[2] Morrison, a member of the Grand Portage Band of the Ojibwe, was born in Chippewa City, Minnesota, in 1919, and studied at the Minneapolis School of Art before moving to New York City in 1943. As the first Native American member of the Art Students League, Morrison developed a distinct style of abstraction alongside his friends Franz Kline, Willem de Kooning, and Jackson Pollock. Reflecting on his life in his autobiography, Morrison recalls how he came to absorb the influences of Dada, surrealist automatism, and color-field abstraction in the 1940s: "I was coming around to the idea of making all kinds of scribbles on the canvas. Or putting a bright color here, a big area, then another color beside it. Making arbitrary shapes that didn't relate to anything like clouds or boats or the horizon line, just plain arbitrary shapes that were all over the canvas. . . . Figurative elements in my work were becoming obscure. Finally, I abandoned them and my work became totally abstract."[3]

According to art historian Bill Anthes, the development of Morrison's abstract style during this period stemmed from his affection for his medium. Whereas WalkingStick's and Lavadour's dedication to the physical properties of paint led to the emergence of landscape forms in their work a generation later, Morrison's experimentation with "putting it thick on the brush and then on the canvas with broad strokes, showing the thickness and movement of the pigment," yielded a different result, at least at first: it heightened the nonrepresentational, lyrical, and expressive qualities of his gestures.[4] As his work edged ever closer to pure abstraction, as in *The Red Painting (For Franz Kline)*, circa 1960, Morrison seems to have considered the horizon line as just as much of a detriment to his nonrepresentational expression as figures or three-dimensional objects would have been. Nevertheless, as his career progressed, Morrison came to embrace the horizon as the organizing principle around which compositions like *Spirit Path, New Day, Red Rock Variation: Lake Superior Landscape* are constructed—so much so that he would eventually refer to the horizon line as his "signature."[5] Following Morrison's account in his autobiography, Anthes traces the emergence of this signature element to Morrison's summer residencies in Provincetown, Massachusetts, an artist colony frequented by members of the New York School. In Provincetown, Morrison was struck by the "indelible image" of the ever-present horizon between the ocean and the sky, and the strong associations it evoked of his childhood spent on the shores of Lake Superior.[6] In some respects, the emergence of this motif in Morrison's work is reminiscent of the way that the proto-horizon line appeared in WalkingStick's seaside *Montauk* paintings of the early 1980s, which in turn opened the door to interpreting her minimalist abstractions as landscapes. The same is true in Morrison's case: the presence of the horizon line grounds Morrison's abstractions, establishing an indexical relationship to place, whether or not that place ever comes fully into focus.

The power of the horizon line to read as landscape—albeit as a singular feature—is best demonstrated in Morrison's otherwise-abstract wood collages. Even the simplest of the sculptural compositions that he began crafting in Provincetown in 1965, such as *Art as Illusion* (1967) and *Provincetown, Sky—Seascape* (1970), are arranged and framed in such a way as to cleverly mimic traditional representational landscape paintings. Morrison referred to these works as "paintings in wood."[7] Whether modest in scale or quite large, as in the nearly 10-foot-long *New England Landscape II* (1967) inspired by his friend Louise Nevelson, Morrison oriented his collage compositions around a horizonal line.[8] In his autobiography, he affirmed that the collages were "derived from

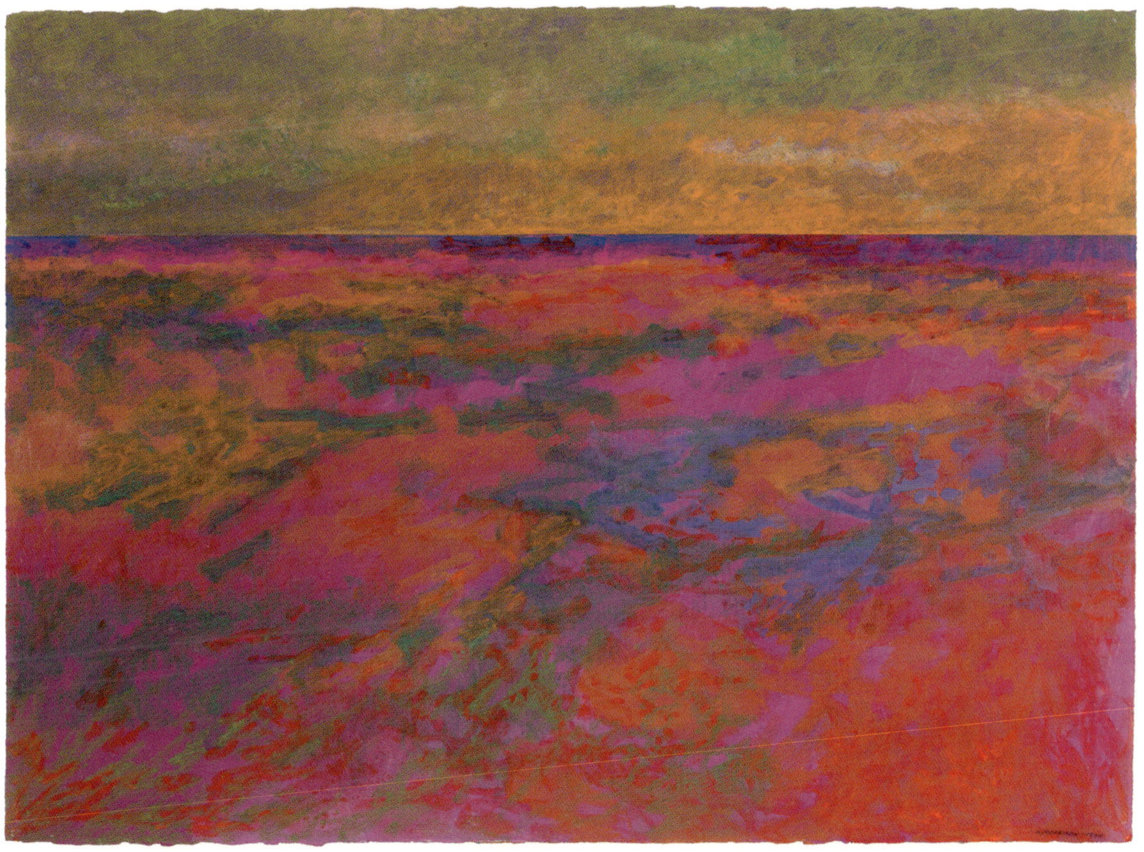

3.1 George Morrison (Ojibwe, 1919–2000)
Spirit Path, New Day, Red Rock Variation: Lake Superior Landscape (1990)
Acrylic and pastel on paper, 22 ½ × 30 ⅛ inches
Collection of the Minnesota Museum of American Art
Purchase, with funds from Mrs. Arthur Savage,
Mr. John R. Savage, Mrs. Harold Searles, Mr. and Mrs. Walter H.
Trenerry, and Mr. and Mrs. Louis N. Zelle, 99.04.02.03

nature, based on landscape. There's a horizon line in each one, about a quarter of the way from the top. That's an absolute straight line, made with a pencil, to help guide the work."[9] The horizontal axis is not as visually pronounced in *New England Landscape II* as it is in *Art as Illusion* or the later *Lake Superior* paintings; nevertheless, the close association of the collage to the landscape is reinforced by the materials used. The driftwood that Morrison incorporated in his large compositions was gathered along the very shores that the works (and many of their titles) reference.[10] As Anthes remarks, Morrison's art, "while abstract, is imbued with the significance of place."[11]

The turn toward the horizon—and, one might add, landscape—came at a time when the artist was seeking to reestablish his connection to place. Between 1943, when he enrolled in the Art Students League in New York City, and 1970, when he resigned his tenured faculty position at the Rhode Island School of Design, Morrison traveled, worked, taught, and exhibited across New England, the upper Midwest, and western Europe.[12] This period of itinerancy coincided with the primacy of abstraction in his work: Anthes suggests that Morrison's abstractions "read as metaphors for the newfound freedoms of his life" beyond the confines of the reservation and the constrictions of the conservative regionalist styles of the Minneapolis art world at midcentury.[13] By the time Morrison was constructing *New England Landscape II*, however, he was longing to move home to Minnesota and his Native community. Anthes writes: "The abstract image of boundless and endless space that embodied Morrison's peripatetic youth as an artist . . . belied his growing desire for emplacement."[14] In 1970 Morrison accepted a teaching position at the University of Minnesota in Minneapolis, where he remained until his retirement in 1983. His joint appointment in studio art and the newly established American Indian Studies Department at the university had a significant impact on his sense of identity, for, as Anthes suggests, Morrison's "new position demanded a process of self-education, as he had not been actively involved in Native American art or Ojibwe culture for three decades."[15] Morrison's own recollection of this time is that he "got involved with the Indian thing again."[16] While this renewed emphasis on his Native identity did not occasion significant changes to the subject matter or formal qualities of his work, it did result in the inclusion of that work in art exhibitions with an Indigenous focus, such as *The Native American Heritage: A Survey of North American Indian Art*, at the Art Institute of Chicago (1977) and *Native American Arts '81* at the Philbrook Art Center in Tulsa, Oklahoma (1981), to name but two.[17]

Upon his retirement in 1983, Morrison returned permanently to the Grand Portage Reservation in Minnesota. From the vantage point of his studio at Red Rock, situated not more than thirty feet from the edge of Lake Superior, Morrison painted scores of expressionist landscapes that he titled the *Lake Superior Landscapes* and, more basically, the *Horizon Paintings* (both series c. 1980–90). Four of the former series were included in the *Our Land/Ourselves: American Indian Contemporary Artists* exhibition in 1990. In addition to *Spirit Path, New Day*, the other *Red Rock Variation: Lake Superior Landscape* paintings featured in the exhibition were titled *Awakening, Time Edge Rising*; *Quiet Light towards Evening*; and *Lavender Wind, the Beyond* (all 1990). As their titles imply, each of these works on paper conveys the sensation of light refracted on the surface of the lake under unique atmospheric conditions. Taken as a group, the paintings are reminiscent of Claude Monet's impressionist masterpieces the *Rouen Cathedral* and *Grainstacks* series of the 1890s;

they may also be usefully compared to WalkingStick's *Ramapo River* paintings that record the passage of light and time on the surface of the river. All four of Morrison's images are structured around a horizon line located in the top quarter of the composition, though the clarity and definition of this line ranges from barely perceptible among the sumptuous lavender hues of *Quiet Light towards Evening* to quite pronounced in the multicolored rendering of *Spirit Path, New Day*.

Despite their particularities, Morrison's *Lake Superior* paintings do not present an objective view of the landscape. Writing on Morrison for the Eiteljorg Fellowship for Native American Fine Art in 1999, David Penney concluded, "These are not pictures of the lake shore, but images derived from an inner state of contemplation, the experience of a 'place' so internalized that it can be reduced to a basic visual language of form, color, and line."[18] The specific tenor of contemplation Penney locates in Morrison's work can be inferred from the abstract concepts that he packed into his painting titles: "spirit path," "awakening," and "the beyond," for example. Like WalkingStick, who penned titles such as *Spirit Center*, *The Abyss*, and *Requiem*, Morrison indicates that his abstractions reach beyond the quotidian into a more existential realm. In Morrison's case, references to the spiritual in his work increased as he faced a sequence of life-threatening health crises in the 1980s.[19] Returning again and again to the familiar landscape of Lake Superior as his inspiration, Morrison created a meditative suite of paintings that express subtle shifts of mood through minute variations in color, perspective, and brushwork. Rushing has described the paintings of the *Horizons* series as representing "a kind of physical and spiritual self-medication" that Morrison practiced over the course of the decade.[20]

Musing on the objective versus subjective content of Morrison's paintings, Rushing offers a further tantalizing observation about the small *Lake Superior* landscapes, such as the 6-by-11-inch acrylic on canvas, *Autumn Dusk, Red Rock Variation: Lake Superior Landscape* (1986). He writes, "like many of the Horizon paintings, this one is conceptual. That is, the transitory patches of color beneath the *waterline* that refer to the rocky *shoreline* would only be observable in 'real life' if you stood with your back to Lake Superior, facing Red Rock, the home and studio that sits high above the shore and lake. In short, two views—one facing the lake and one facing Red Rock—are combined and presented on a single field of gestural color."[21] Rushing's willingness to question the veracity of the horizon line is significant, for as we have seen, the very presence of that line was powerful enough to "transform" Morrison's abstractions into discernable landscapes—in part because it seemed to orient the viewer in space.

That Rushing's analysis of the *Lake Superior* paintings questions where the artist or viewer would have to have been standing in order to see these particular views underscores the degree to which we have traditionally expected landscape paintings to situate the viewer in or above the landscape. This assumption is famously illustrated in Caspar David Friedrich's romantic landscape, *Wanderer above the Sea of Mist* (1818) and neatly encapsulated by landscape theorist Jonathan Smith, who writes, "To the eye that has been properly educated a landscape presents itself as a spectacle, a deportment which in turn creates the position of the spectator. Whether depicted in paint, or rolled out as a tableau vivant below a scenic overlook, a landscape situates its spectator in an Olympian position, and it rewards its spectator with the pleasures of distance and detachment and the personal inconsequence of all that they survey."[22]

While it is nearly impossible to imagine that the postmodern landscape tradition aims to provide the viewer with "the pleasures of distance and detachment," it is intriguing to contemplate just how the position of the spectator is constructed in contemporary Native American landscape paintings. This chapter takes up the questions of literal and metaphorical perspective, asking where the viewer stands in relation to the landscape that is represented and seeking to locate the site from which the image emanates, the "position" of the artist in the land.

GROUNDING

We have already seen, in the case of WalkingStick's work, that a postmodern landscape painting may picture a microcosmic or macrocosmic view, or both at the same time. *Death of the Elm*, for example, suggests three different yet simultaneous perspectives on the elm: the abstract panel can be perceived as either an extreme close-up (the white bark of the dead tree) or a more distant view (of trees in a forest), and the representational painting of the elm's leaves and branches in the companion panel are depicted at a scale somewhere between the other two extremes. Each of these three perspectives posits a different proximity of the viewer to the object or scene pictured, and in a manner reminiscent of the European landscape tradition, all assume a vertically oriented viewer looking ahead to the horizon. We might call this "the view from the ground" or the "ground view." WalkingStick's waterfall paintings of 1989–90, on the other hand, subtly modify a view from *above* the landscape in a way that that enhances their emotional impact. The tightly cropped imagistic landscape of *On the Edge* forces the viewer down into the chasm of turbulent water that represents the sweeping current of events beyond one's control, whereas the slightly altered perspective on an otherwise similar scene in *Letting Go from Chaos to Calm* allows the viewer to hover a bit above the fray, just as WalkingStick herself was surfacing from her grief. By the mid-1990s, diptychs such as *The Four Directions: Spirit Center* paired landscapes deep enough to include a distant horizon line with thick, wax-infused abstractions deployed to slow access into that increasingly recessive space. A retrospective view of WalkingStick's career would suggest that in general the artist's depictions of the landscape progress from intensely tactile, intimately embodied close-ups to a more physically distanced and visually oriented perspective. The monolithic landscape images that make up the majority of her later diptychs are not only more representational and romantic than their predecessors, but they position the spectator (and artist) at some remove from the landscape. As discussed in the previous chapter, this trajectory of WalkingStick's paintings from minimalist objects to imaginative vistas runs against the grain of postmodern painting; however, it is worth noting that the uninhabitable margins (signified by the flattened patterns excerpted from Indigenous art traditions) that intervene between the spectator and the Native landscape function as effective anti-invitational devices.

Clearly there is much at stake in any effort to situate either the artist or the spectator with respect to representations of the Native landscape, not least of which is the question of whether there is a fundamental ideological difference between representations that emanate from *within* rather than from outside of that contested space. Smith implies that Indigenous artists have a unique perspective on the land, one that it is rooted in their very identity as Indigenous people. Reflecting on the words attributed to Chief Seattle—"We are part of the earth and it is part of us"—she writes that despite the differences in their works, all the artists in the *Our Land/Ourselves* exhibition "weave their distinct conceptions in and through an interior view."[23]

Perhaps the best illustration of Smith's perspective on this indexical relationship between the Indigenous artist and the land is her own series of abstract landscapes from the late 1980s, the *Petroglyph Park* series. Painted in response to a cultural and environmental crisis near her home in New Mexico—the proposed development of the west mesa in Albuquerque, an escarpment covered with tens of thousands of ancient and modern petroglyphs sacred to and still used by Pueblo peoples—the images in the series convey an intimate and multifaceted view of a sacred landscape.[24] *Sunset on the Escarpment* (1987; figure 3.2), for example, is a riot of color and form, mixing highly geometricized landscape features with seemingly representational yet entirely symbolic images derived from the petroglyphs themselves. The compositions are agitated, energetic, impassioned, and compelling in their complexity. Like so many of Smith's works, the density of symbols and pictographic elements in these paintings require and reward close looking on the part of a viewer who wishes to decipher their meanings. Carolyn Kastner, author of a monograph on Smith's art, describes one of the *Escarpment* paintings in detail:

The primary colors of Smith's 1987 oil painting *Escarpment* do not describe or map the rugged cliff face formed by volcanic action and erosion of the Rio Grande west of Albuquerque. The flat composition has no horizon line to separate earth from sky. . . . Smith's canvas becomes an expression of human experience from a multitude of views in the landscape, as suggested by the title. The upper third of the canvas offers the prospect of the mesa top, where the drama of the high desert sun is evoked by the arcing gestures of red and yellow against wisps of white pigment over sky blue. At the center of the canvas, jagged lines of white paint set off the vertical field of black, brown, and red, like the sun hitting the surface of the monolithic stones that define the escarpment at midday. The red orb floating between these sectors suggests a coded reference to Sandia Peak (named in Spanish for its brilliant melon color at sunset), also visible from the escarpment.[25]

According to Kastner's reading, the painting depicts at least three different perspectives on the landscape, compressed into a single frame. In this respect, the painting is cubist in its execution, offering these multiple views simultaneously and employing a multitude of short line segments and areas of cross-hatching that flatten the space of the painting and call attention to its surface. Kastner remarks that the flattening effect is reinforced by the geometric forms of the lower canvas, which in their two-dimensionality act as "a firm reminder of the viewer's place in front of the work of art."[26] This effect is far from incidental to the artist's message in the *Petroglyph Park* series: it blocks access to the landscape. While Smith invites the viewer to experience her perspective from within this sacred space, she does not offer them equal access. Kastner concludes that "the canvas refuses to open to the spectator's gaze."[27]

The refusal of Smith's canvases to open into deep space owes much to her elision of the horizon line, which establishes depth of field. In Kastner's estimation, the choice is in keeping not only with the artist's modernist aesthetic but also with her uniquely Indigenous view of the cosmos. She writes that "none of the paintings in the series have a horizon line marking the division of land and sky, because for Smith 'the earth and sky are related in one ecosystem,' a fragile balance that can be easily ruptured by humans, who are unaware of their integral part in the system."[28] The emphasis in this passage is on the inseparability of the environment and its inhabitants, but the absence of the horizon line in Smith's conceptualization also signifies the collapse of physical distance between the artist and the land, for distance is exactly what is required in order to perceive space. In fact, the presence of a horizon line in a landscape painting traditionally signifies two kinds of distance: recession into the perceived space of the painting (relative to the picture plane) and distance between the sights pictured and the site from which the representation emanates—that distance between the landscape and the "Olympian position"

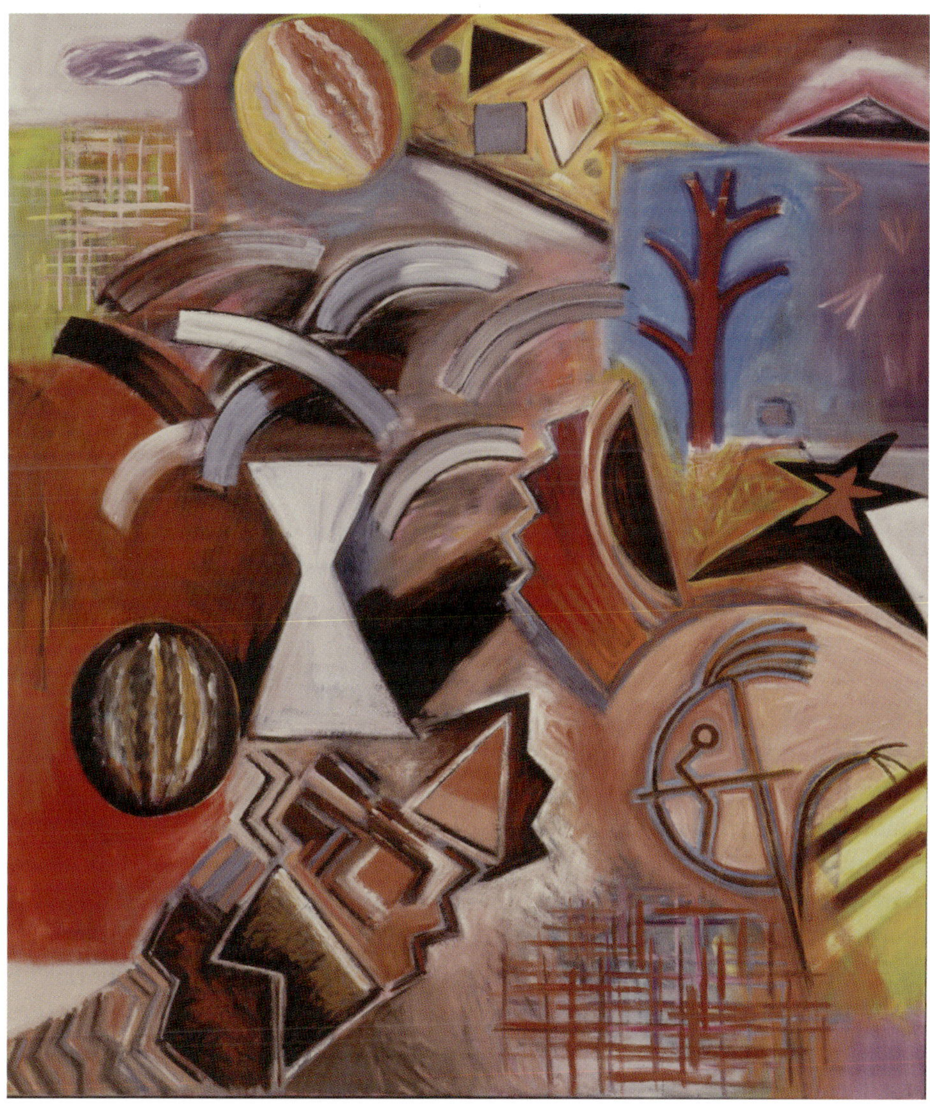

3.2 Jaune Quick-to-See Smith (Salish, b. 1940)
Sunset on the Escarpment (1987)
Oil on canvas, 72 × 60 inches
Copyright Jaune Quick-to-See Smith. Courtesy of the artist.
Peiper-Riegraf Collection, Berlin

occupied by the spectator. Smith's depiction of the Native landscape eschews the "Olympian" view, or what James Duncan has called "the haughty gaze," but the collapse of that space or position comes at some cost.[29] As Kenneth Olwig observes in *Landscape Theory*, the very root of the word "landscape" is the Old English "skipe," indicating that a landscape is intended to describe the "shape" (*not* the "scope" or vision) of a place, which can only be seen from a position of some remove.[30] He writes that the "original" landscape painter, the "nether lands artist, standing on a high elevation (or pretending to do so), gains a wide prospect over the country below, which gives an overall view of the character, or *shape*, of the land that would not be visible closer up."[31]

Thus the postmodern view of the landscape, characterized by the dissolution of distant and framed views in favor of more intimate, haptic forms of expression, offers all the advantages of asserting an Indigenous perspective while avoiding established tropes of power and subjugation. A distanced view, on the other hand, provides a greater "perspective" on the landscape by positioning its representation in the broadest possible context.[32] That the distanced view might serve to concentrate power in the position of the artist or spectator does not necessarily disqualify it from being an effective strategy of Indigenous visual sovereignty because the exercise of that control lies with the artist. These distinctions—between microcosmic and macrocosmic scope, phenomenological and objective approaches, insider and outsider perspectives—are not as great as they once were: rather they constitute a *range* of representational strategies that contemporary Indigenous artists employ in their depictions of the landscape. Lavadour's work provides an excellent case in point.

FLOW

Earlier I singled out Lavadour's multipaneled composition *Deep Moon* (see figure 1.2) as emblematic of the merging of two strains of his imagery, the so-called landscapes and structures. The landscape panels, which are seemingly more representational than the highly gestural and intensely hued structures, dominated Lavadour's work in the 1990s, but by 2000 they were increasingly paired with more abstract counterparts, as in *Deep Moon*. In later compositions such as *Blanket* (2005; figure 3.3), *Cache* (2007), and *Tiicham* (2013; figure 3.4), the landscape and structural elements merge so thoroughly that the distinctions cease to apply; however, it is useful to pause at *Deep Moon* to consider how the work illuminates Lavadour's perspective on distance and proximity.

The central panel of *Deep Moon*, which represents a kind of hybrid form of atmospheric depth and surface effects, capitalizes on the tension that arises with the juxtaposition of several opposing elements, including abstract and (relatively) representational imagery, bright saturated color, and a far more monochrome palette. Each of these variances alters our perception of depth in the painting. The placement of the broad, multicolored band across the middle of the panel, for example, draws attention to the painting's surface, pulling the middle ground into the foreground and thus negating the recession into space that is otherwise conveyed by the hazy atmosphere of the upper half of the composition. Even when mitigated in this way, the central panel nevertheless allows for deeper penetration into the landscape than any of the eight surrounding panels, all of which are basically structures. The placement of the illusionistic landscape in the center of a ring of gestural forms evokes a kind of a peripheral vision: if the viewer opts to focus on the distant horizon of the central panel, the imagery of the outer panels fades into softer focus. The bright colors and sharp, defined lines of the structures do not allow the eye to rest in the distance for long, however: the viewer's attention is drawn back to the resonant surfaces of the outer panels over and again.

As was the case in WalkingStick's paintings, much of the effect of Lavadour's imagery stems from his method of painting. Lavadour builds his paintings in layers, establishing a base layer of oil paint on baltic birch panels prepared with gesso. Before 1987 the underpaint was generally blue, but in that year Lavadour had a transformative experience flying over the Grand Canyon in a small airplane. After viewing the desert Southwest from the air, he recalls that he became nearly obsessed with using red as his base color.[33] The paintings that have elsewhere been characterized as belonging to Lavadour's signature style—those produced between 1987 and 2000, including *Salamander* (see figure 1.1) and *Nest of Suns*—are formed by layering many applications of various earth tones over the red base. Lavadour used his brush to produce a stippling effect in the wet paint, then wiped away areas with a cloth or palette knife before applying the next layer of pigment.[34] Over time, as many as one hundred layers of paint accrued on the surfaces of his panels. The physicality of these layers is crucial to how Lavadour perceives depth in the work. On the one hand, the buildup of paint thickens the surface, affirming the painting's objecthood; on the other hand, Lavadour's scraping and wiping through successive layers exposes the space *between* those layers. In the end, Lavadour insists that "a painting is a three-dimensional thing. There is something behind what I'm looking at. And something behind that, and something behind that. . . . I look at it as a surface that has three-dimensional space *in* it."[35]

The effect of this layering and the paradox of seeing three dimensions on a two-dimensional surface manifests quite strongly in *Salamander*, a nine-panel composition that measures 48 by 60 by 3 inches. All of *Salamander*'s panels can be considered typical of Lavadour's pre-2000 landscapes, yet they vary from one to another in important ways. The central panel of *Salamander* is densely layered and highly textured: the artist's marks and gestures are preserved in the pigment, committing the viewer's attention to the work's surface. By contrast, the panels immediately to the left and right of center plunge us into the deep space of a distant mountain range. In the fully developed foreground of each of these panels, a field of molten red flows across the earth's surface, while in the middle ground billowing smoke drifts through the valley. Lavadour remarks that the imagined vantage point of depictions such as this is deliberately high to promote a sense of recession into space. He explains that "one of the things I wanted more than anything else was this great depth in painting; it's like standing on top of a mountain. I want to see dimension, I want to see the world, I want to see something way back there. Like looking through a telescope, I wanted to know what's way, way, way, way, way back there."[36] The remaining seven panels of *Salamander* exhibit a range of characteristics similar to those already described: in some panels, elements that suggest smoke, lava, and fire mingle with hazy landscape forms, while in others prominent brush strokes and drag marks of a palette knife dominate. In perceptual terms, the variations promote confusion: the viewer perceives both spaces and surfaces—an illusion and a material reality—simultaneously.

On an ideological level, the push/pull, surface/depth alternations of the juxtaposed panels of *Salamander* also block the viewer's imaginative access to the landscape depicted. Even the most representational of Lavadour's landscape images do not provide space for the viewer to "enter" the frame. Where there is a foreground, it is utterly inaccessible—it is either excessively shallow, precipitously sloped, or consumed by fire. Moreover, scenes that depict depth are often joined by panels in which the scale is so radically altered that the illusionism of the landscape in question is shattered. Lavadour acknowledges that his landscapes are perceptually uninhabitable, especially when combined in multipaneled compositions.[37] In *Salamander*, for example, the five panels that constitute the center and four corners exhibit a similarly subdued tonal range, evident brush marks, and low degree of recession into space compared to the remaining four panels that are more illusionistic and of higher contrast. The landscape of these latter four is engulfed in flames. The checkerboard pattern created by contrasting two sets of images is even more pronounced in Lavadour's later compositions of landscapes and structures, such as *Deep Moon*; in both cases, the arrangement of panels has a marked effect on the viewer. First, the eye is forced into constant motion, unable to rest anywhere in the landscape. Second, the composition itself seems to be set in motion in *Salamander*, with the two sets of images rotating around the center panel at different velocities. Lavadour likens this optical effect to a vortex, one that both captivates and expels the viewer: "These are vortices with fulcrum points," he says. "You want to go around them and then go out. You don't want to get stuck. So there's a geometry to the painting—the fulcrum pulls you in and then spits you out."[38]

Leaving aside for the moment the anti-invitational aspects of this compositional layout, the recurrence of the vortex is fundamental to how Lavadour perceives the landscape and his own work. Lavadour recalled for interviewer Anastasia Mejia in 2011 that the motif surfaced in many early single-panel paintings, as well as in multipaneled compositions such as *Nest of Suns* (1998) and *Sunflower* (1999), both of which are composed of five panels arranged in the shape of a horizontal cross: "I discovered that I wasn't making landscapes, I was making a vortex. Every single painting was a vortex, sometimes it's stretched out or compressed or elongated or broken into smaller vortices, but it's all that type of action and it's what flow is all about."[39]

In short, just as the horizon line became George Morrison's leitmotif, so has the vortex become Lavadour's. While the presence of the vortex affects how both the artist and the viewer perceive the landscape, it is not a purely optical phenomenon. For Lavadour the fascination of the vortex is its association with theoretical physics, which ultimately impacts our understanding of geological processes. During a printmaking residency at Rutgers University in 1995, Lavadour met and befriended the physicist Norman Zabusky, who introduced him to key concepts in the theory of fluid dynamics, also known as "flow."[40] Lavadour came to understand that vortices, surface tension, turbulence, and viscosity are all terms of fluid dynamics that describe the way that fluids move across surfaces. For a man who had been experimenting since the age of twenty with how water-soluble pigments and oil paint behaved on paper, the physics of flow provided a new language for processes that he had long observed or intuited.[41] Moreover, the theoretical discourse bolstered Lavadour's conviction that the physical processes that govern painting and geology are one and the same.[42]

As early as 1991, Lavadour was drawing explicit connections between the way layers of paint accrued on his canvases and the way the landscapes of the Columbia Gorge had been formed. *ARTNews* reviewer Lyn Smallwood intuited this aspect, noting that "gradually, through a process that itself seems to replicate the natural course of mountain building—deposition, erosion, accretion, and finally demolition—legible forms begin to coalesce" in Lavadour's paintings.[43] In Lavadour's own words, painting "is an event of Nature—not a depiction of nature—with hydrology, erosion, mineral sedimentation occurring. All the things that happen out there on the land happen on the canvas."[44]

Some of the ramifications of this unifying theory of flow, especially the artist's increasing sense of himself as a conduit for the forces of nature, have been touched upon in chapters 1 and 2 of this book. Here it seems prudent to consider how the forces of geometry and physics converge in the phenomenon of the vortex and how these bear upon Lavadour's depiction of the landscape. The vortices that are formed in the multipaneled compositions, for example, are visible *as* geometry: the careful arrangement of individual panels creates a sensation of motion swirling or rotating around a stationary core. No matter how gestural or illusionistic the image in the central panel may be, the panel becomes fixed—it acts as what Lavadour calls the "fulcrum" (the point on which everything turns). In fact, vortices are three-dimensional, they rotate around axes rather than points. Thus, the axis that orients a multipaneled composition such as *Salamander* is perpendicular to the picture plane, which explains why a viewer, drawn into the vortex, is drawn deep into the imagined space of the image.

As for the vortices that occur in individual panels—the ones that Lavadour describes as occurring in "every single painting," whether they are "stretched out or compressed or elongated or broken into smaller vortices"—they are more illustrative of fluid dynamics than geometry. In order to perceive them, we must be attuned to the energy and flow of pigments and to the movement of Lavadour's body. In this context, the vortices invoke the processes of creation on both microcosmic and macrocosmic levels, even as they attest to the basic material reality of the art of painting. While all of these complexities of fluid dynamics are evident in Lavadour's landscape paintings from the 1990s, they became even more apparent after he began merging landscapes with structures in 2000. The convergence of strains of imagery was accompanied by changes in the artist's method as well. Eschewing the "scalloped textures" of his earlier paintings, Lavadour increasingly favors birch panels with a high gloss finish.[45] According to the artist, these panels have "surfaces as smooth as glass. . . . They are the most explicit surfaces I've ever worked on because every nuance, every little mark or touch, or brush mark or drip or scrape . . . shows up."[46] To complement the smoother surfaces, Lavadour has also thinned his paint to the extent that it can be manipulated with a brush, a cloth, or even a squeegee.

In transitional works such as *Scaffold* the radical impact of the introduction of structures is not yet as apparent as it is in later compositions such as *Deep Moon* or *Blanket*. *Scaffold* incorporates five landscape panels that are quite similar to those that appear in *Salamander*: each depicts a smoky, atmospheric mountain scene sketched in subdued earth tones. As in *Salamander* and *Deep Moon*, the central panel of *Scaffold* is perhaps the most static and illusionistic. It suggests a distant and elevated view of a mountain lake nestled into an alpine bowl under the light of a full moon. Interspersed with the five landscape panels, however, are four new structures—panels in which paint drips and courses across the wooden surface in total defiance of gravity. The juxtaposition of the two strains of imagery in *Scaffold* is so reminiscent of *Salamander* that the effect on the viewer is virtually the same: she is pulled into and expelled by the vortex inherent in the work's geometry.

On the level of the individual panels, Lavadour's new structures provide ample evidence of fluid dynamics. Scrims of opaque paint spill across the

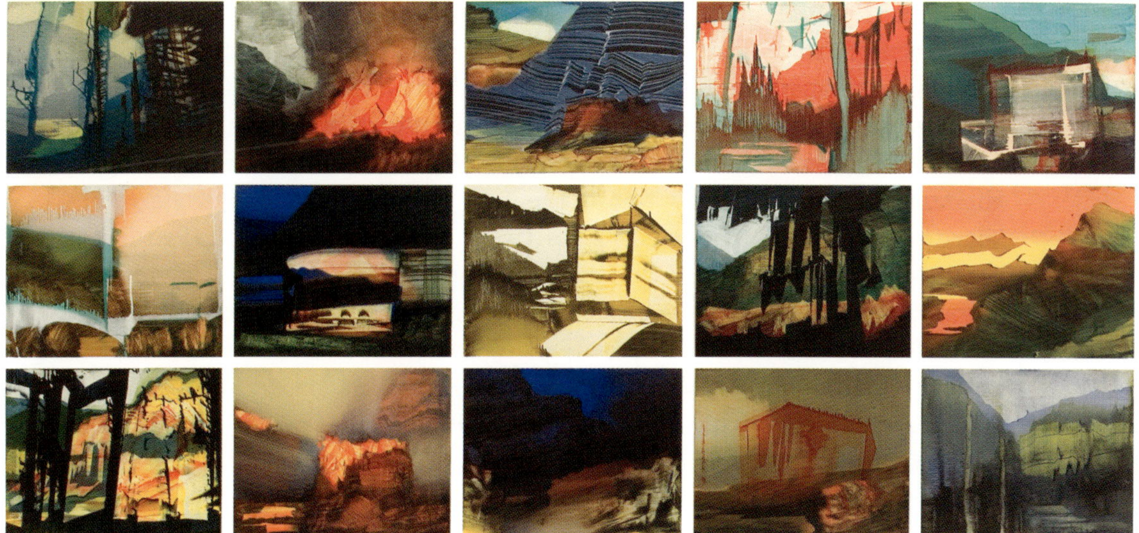

3.3 James Lavadour (Walla Walla, b. 1951)
Blanket (2005)
Oil on panel, 72 × 150 inches
Copyright James Lavadour. Courtesy of the artist.
National Museum of the American Indian

surfaces, piling up and folding back on themselves, obscuring the landscape images that lie beneath them. The forces of flow on display here are spectacular and dynamic: raw color erupts in volcanic gestures, and the eons-long processes of sedimentation and erosion are eclipsed by the explosive energy of plate tectonics. Even the glacial flow evoked by *Ice* (2007) seems less a slow, ponderous occurrence than a massive, unstoppable force. Like the paintings in Lavadour's contemporaneous *River* series, *Ice* is attuned to surfaces and what lies submerged beneath them. In this case, a stratum of molten red roils in the painting's lower register, emanating inverted drips that rise like fissures of steam. According to Rebecca Dobkins, *Ice* represents "the maturation of [an] extraordinarily productive period" in which Lavadour's experimentation with paint led him to devise "a technical means to make both the layers and the process of perception visible."[47]

Oddly enough, despite the preponderance of drips and flows of paint in these works (ample evidence of their creation out of a fluid medium), and in contradiction to the implicit subject matter of panels like *Ice*, in Lavadour's telling the concept of flow does not strictly apply to his structures. Detailing the organizing principles of his post-2000 works, Lavadour remarks, "I use two elemental structures, a landscape and an architectural abstraction (a vortex and a grid). There's the flow of landscape and then the intersection of the architectural structure."[48] In other words, though Lavadour considers all of his paintings to be determined by and illustrative of natural processes, he views the structures as abstractions that are shaped in part by another important force: the human mind. He elaborates, "There's two things going on. There's the human structural perception of the world, which is [architectural]. Then there's the universal cosmic flow of particles and sedimentation and vortices and all the elements of nature and the properties of paint. I needed some way to examine that instead of it just being this big flood of indistinguishable currents. To put a grid over that is to create a little room for myself to be able to contemplate the universe."[49] Thus, Lavadour locates in the structures a kind of organizing principle for his work. That he would refer to this structure as a grid rather than a vortex is important.

The structural elements of paintings like *Tremor III* (2012) and *Spring* (2012) are visually enhanced by a radical shift in Lavadour's color palette after 2000. There is no uniform color of the base layer in the paintings of this period, though Lavadour admits to going through phases of being nearly obsessed with "pure" orange and a "gelatinous" hot pink.[50] What matters most to Lavadour is the *contrast* between adjacent layers of color: if he begins painting with deep orange he will then proceed with an application of violet, "and then there has to be another layer and another layer."[51] Or if he begins with red, he will proceed to green, then, "I squeegee and I start to look for patterns. If I see something there, I put something contrasting over the top and scrape through that and see what happens."[52] Because it is necessary to let layers of paint dry between applications, Lavadour typically has as many as fifty panels in active rotation at any one time. In a single day he may work on five to ten paintings, adding a single layer of color to each. Fortunately, Lavadour's studio space is large enough to accommodate dozens of paintings arranged on drying racks, allowing him easy access to works in progress. As the layers of paint accrue, space becomes visible between them, as it did in the landscapes before 2000; however, the effect is more pronounced in the structures due to Lavadour's use of contrasting colors and his tendency to move his squeegee or brush at right angles to the layer of color beneath. In *Blanket*, for example, the length and direction of Lavadour's gestures produce a variety of optical effects. In the richly hued panel that is second from left in the middle row of *Blanket*, the squeegee marks limn a series of nested rectangles, each suggesting a different degree of recession into space. The orange fields are particularly, if unintentionally, illusionistic: the central scene is oddly reminiscent of a postcard view of a lake at sunset, superimposed over a similar but more proximate vista. The precise latticework of lines to the right of center creates a jarring contrast to the spatial illusion, however, and reorients the image in two-dimensional terms. In the monochrome panel to the right, the abrupt changes in direction of the squeegee strokes produce a more overtly architectural effect, in that the intersecting planes seem to obey traditional rules of perspective.

While these forms pose internal contradictions, they are nevertheless in concert with the wider aesthetic of Lavadour's paintings after 2000, which are maelstroms of chaotic energy. All of these panels are characterized by eruptions of color, exuberant movement, and sweeping gestures, and they employ a vast arsenal of techniques and materials, from the application of paint with palette knives, brushes, and squeegees to the addition of mica and clay to the use of thinning agents and washes. It is no wonder that Lavadour felt the work needed structure in order to avoid being overcome by this "big flood of indistinguishable currents." Lavadour's solution was to employ the organizing principle of a grid system. On the level of the individual paintings, grids are created by cascading parallel lines of dripping paint, by the right angles of Lavadour's gestures, and by the contrasting colors of separate strata built up on the surface of the panel. According to the artist, the grid needs only to be implied for its effects to be felt: a single space held open in the deepest recesses of the painting can serve as an anchor for the turbulent abstractions.[53] On the macro level of the multipaneled compositions, the grid is far more explicit. The fifteen separate panels of *Blanket* are precisely ordered into three rows of five panels each. The imposition of the matrix format not only stabilizes the overall composition but imparts to the panels a kind of serial regularity, despite the complexity and variation of the imagery.

In both its form and its function, then, the grid is the structural opposite of the vortex. Whereas the vortex conveys the swirling energy and movement of elemental forces in Lavadour's landscapes before 2000, the grid manifests as a stable, regularizing structure. The spatial constitutions of the two phenomena are also radically different: the orientation of the vortical axis perpendicular to the picture plane implies three dimensions, whereas the grid is an emphatically two-dimensional construct. Lavadour's interjection of elements of a vortex into the nine-panel compositions *Scaffold* (2000) and *Deep Moon* (2004), as well as in *Flag No. 1* (2002), *Feral* (2003), and *Wash* (2007), allowed him to transcend the two-dimensional limitations of the grid. The vortex form cedes entirely to the matrix, however, in the fifteen-panel compositions such as *Blanket*, *Straight Ahead* (2010), and *Tiicham* (2013) that visually reinforce the grid with distinct margins between rows and columns of panels. Yet even in the latter works, the grid imposes order without annihilating space.

Unlike the "modernist grid," which Krauss characterized as "flattened, geometricized, ordered[,] . . . antinatural, antimimetic [and] antireal," Lavadour's structures are organic, dynamic forms alive with dimensionality.[54] Indeed, because he employs the grid strategically, rather than accepting its conditions wholesale, his practice represents a postmodernist approach to the grid. He

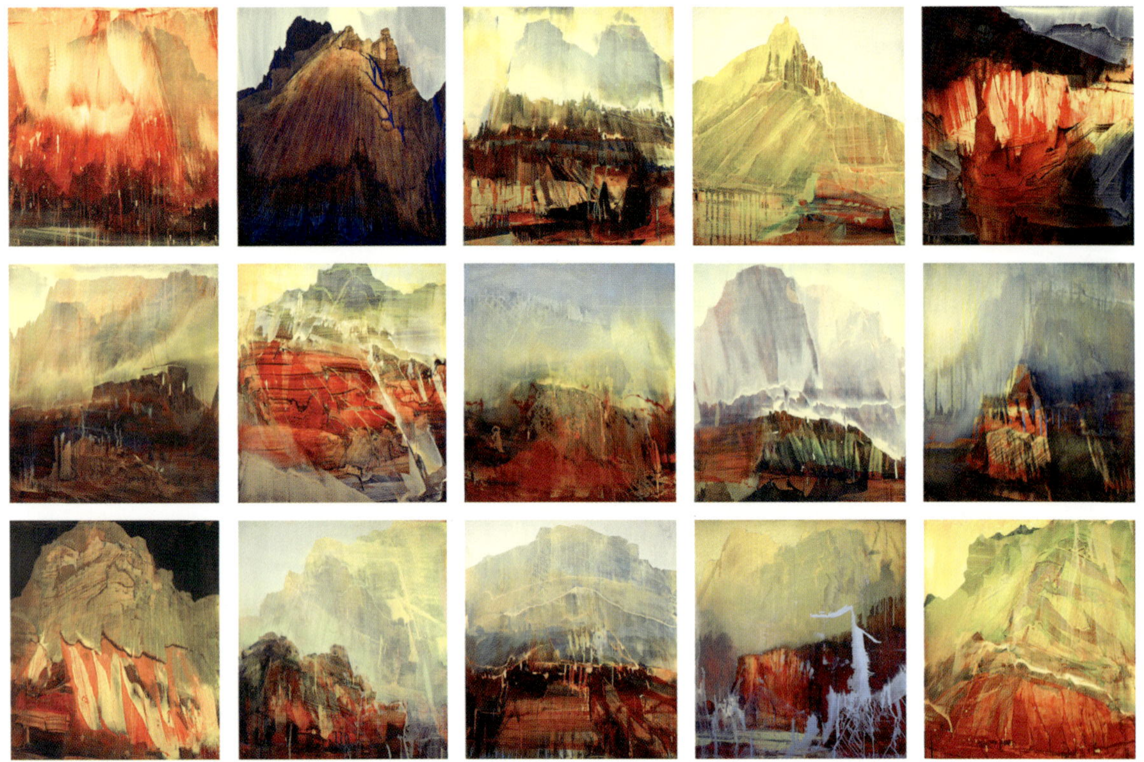

3.4 James Lavadour (Walla Walla, b. 1951)
Tiicham (2013)
Oil on panel, 102 × 152 inches

Private collection

embraces its serial form and lateral spread, but he refuses to "turn [his] back on nature."[55] On the contrary, Lavadour's paintings attest to just how evocative art can be when it opens itself fully to nature.

FRAMING THE LANDSCAPE

In Lavadour's work, the grid is used to create enough space from which to "contemplate the universe," but it stops short of trying to impose order upon the land itself. This is no small distinction, and Lavadour is aware that the format carries with it a legacy of subjugation of the Native landscape, both on the canvas and off. Vernacular landscape theorist John Brinkerhoff Jackson, for example, described the partitioning of land into regular units as a basic component of the American psyche. He writes that the wide open spaces of the Great Plains in particular are an "excellent place to observe how overpowering the national grid system can be. It is easy to suppose that when the first settlers confronted this monotonous sea of waving grass they must have longed to divide it into squares and rectangles in order to give it something like a human scale."[56] That the open space in question was already occupied by Native peoples does not figure into Jackson's telling. His point is that the grid system has long been considered the "most practical and speediest way to deal with lots of space" when settlement, ownership, or administration of land is at issue.

This legacy is so strong that Lavadour's use of the grid, especially in the arrangement of his multipaneled compositions, has been misconstrued by some critics as an expression of desire to assert control over the landscape. Writing for *Art in America* in 1990, Ron Glowen argued that the artist's experience as a land-use planner for the Confederated Tribes of the Umatilla Reservation is discernible in his work: "Lavadour's panels are a metaphor for the division of land into parcels subject to ownership and exchange. The fragmentation of each ensemble represents the ruptured harmony of nature. The segmented panoramas and desolate landscapes might reflect Lavadour's particular relationships to the land—as Native American, as witness, as modern-day bureaucrat and sovereign."[57] Glowen's use of the term "sovereign" here should not be conflated with the concept of Indigenous visual sovereignty as we have come to understand it in the past decade. Whether the assumed partitioning of the landscape is cast as a positive aspect (a "practical way to deal with space") or a negative one ("representing the ruptured harmony of nature"), the implication stems from what is in essence a non-Native perception of the landscape. Lavadour rejects the premise altogether, choosing to focus instead on the generative and untamable forces of nature, a perspective that he considers distinctly Native.

Ironically, Lavadour's appreciation for nature as an irrepressible force aligns his use of the grid more closely with Krauss's critique of modernist painting than with critical reflections on the vernacular landscape. As noted in chapter 2, Krauss concluded her examination of the centripetal and centrifugal characteristics of modernist painting with the observation that "logically speaking, the grid extends, in all directions, to infinity." Lavadour's multipaneled compositions affirm this reading of the grid, his paintings, *and* the land: there is no limit to their expansiveness. Yet even in this respect, Lavadour's paintings refuse to conform entirely to a structure that extends, theoretically, in all directions equally. In Krauss's analysis, the equilateral spread of the grid accounts for the square format favored by many modernist painters, from Mondrian to Agnes Martin and, we might add, Kay WalkingStick. As we have seen, WalkingStick embraced the square format in a deliberate repudiation of what she calls "Renaissance space."[58] In the place of spatial illusion or representation, WalkingStick pursued abstraction and resolute flatness, which she ultimately achieved through her use of the grid and pure geometry. In this sense WalkingStick indeed "turned her back on nature" for a period in the 1970s; however, this did not last. WalkingStick continued to construct square panels, but once she began pairing them in the diptychs, the resulting compositions were consistently rectangular and horizontally oriented. This fundamental change in her format occurred at precisely the moment that her subject matter was shifting toward the natural world.

What we encounter in Lavadour's painting is neither the modernist square nor the vertical rectangle of traditional easel painting. Lavadour works exclusively in a rectangular format, both in individual panels and multipaneled compositions. Moreover, the orientation of his rectangles is generally horizontal: they conform to the classic landscape format.[59] There are exceptions to this rule in Lavadour's practice, especially at the level of the individual panels, but also occasionally in the multipaneled compositions, such as *Totem* (1999), which is stacked vertically. *Tiicham*, the work that Lavadour exhibited at the Venice Biennale in 2013, is the most vertical of all his compositions. Though the three-by-five-panel grid stretches horizontally (the overall dimensions are 102 by 152 inches), each individual panel is taller than it is wide, and the imagery emphasizes that vertical thrust at every opportunity. Nearly every drip, scrape, and gesture runs vertically, coalescing into majestic, jagged mountain peaks that crowd and sometimes penetrate the upper boundaries of the composition.

By and large, however, Lavadour favors the horizontal: even the square grids (the three-by-three-panel compositions *Deep Moon* and *Scaffold*, for example) become horizontal rectangles in their overall dimensions. In other instances, Lavadour accentuates the horizontal by arranging multiple panels in a single row. *North Bank* (2012) exhibits the narrowest proportions of Lavadour's recent work: the three-panel row is more than 6 feet long but only 18 inches tall. A subtle yet important feature of *North Bank* is the degree to which the horizon lines within the individual panels align across the full composition. Lavadour brackets the central panel, with its horizon line situated in the top third of the painting, with flanking panels in which the horizon starts high but plunges into the middle of the scene. The result is somewhat disorienting, the implication being that either the height of the landscape features or our proximity to them is shifting from panel to panel. On the other hand, the relatively close correspondence of the horizon line from the first to third panels unifies the composition.

Whether they are continuous or discontinuous, prominent or somewhat obscured, Lavadour's horizon lines are crucial to our perception of his paintings—even the structures—as landscapes. The power of the horizon line to transform even the most abstract work into a landscape was evident to the artist early on: he recalls that he discovered through his experiments with pouring and swirling paint on paper that he could "just cut the top off and there was a perfect landscape."[60] Lavadour draws upon that lesson to this day, using torn strips of paper as templates to form the silhouettes of mountain peaks and ranges at the top edge of many of his panels.

The works discussed in this chapter demonstrate how effortlessly the presence of a horizon line transforms an abstract image into a landscape because it orients the viewer in space. This was especially true in George Morrison's *Lake Superior* paintings, though the space in question cannot be construed as "real" in the objective sense. As Rushing reminds us, Morrison's landscapes, like Lavadour's, are entirely subjective expressions. Nevertheless, the horizon line grounds the viewer in the space of the paintings, establishing a vantage point located on or near the ground plane. This perspective might be likened to a "boots on the ground" point of view, in the sense that the viewer is both imaginatively emplaced *and* embodied, standing in the landscape looking out toward the horizon. This is in sharp contrast to the aerial view that posits a disembodied spectator looking down on the earth from above. Images created from the latter perspective are by definition devoid of a horizon line.

This is no small distinction, in part because the two different perspectives are strongly associated with different technologies and bases of experience, ranging from an unmediated view of walking in the land to being elevated above it to encountering it only through mediated technologies such as aerial photography. Jackson, for example, suggested that a shift in orientation from the ground plane to aerial view was ushered in with the transition in American culture from the age of the automobile (and one might add the train) to the airplane.[61] More recently, visual culture theorists have extended Jackson's argument to include the age of the smart bomb and predator drones.[62] As drone technology continues to expand beyond its military applications to private use—as evinced in the filming of *Mirror Shield Project: Water Serpent Action* at the Oceti Sakowin Dakota Access Pipeline protest camp—the implications of the aerial view will continue to affect our reading of contemporary landscape representation.[63]

It may be that the horizontal or ground view has been more prevalent in contemporary Native landscape representation than the aerial view to date because the artists wish to establish their perspective from *within* the landscape—thus also establishing their own position as insiders—as discussed in the beginning of this chapter. There are instances, however, of the more distant and disembodied perspective of the aerial view occurring in the Native landscape tradition. WalkingStick's account of the emergence of landscape imagery in her abstract paintings, for example, not only likens the layers of paint and wax on her canvases to layers of earth sediments, but she recalls that the paintings came to look to her like "the earth as seen from thousands of miles up." In Lavadour's case, the massing of paint and other organic materials create strata that he too regards as analogous to the geological processes of deposition and erosion; however, the strata in his paintings are not as easily located with respect to spatial perspective. One of the paradoxes of Lavadour's work is that the materials accrue on his canvases in layers that are parallel to the picture plane, yet the imagery suggests strata that are perpendicular to that plane. In other words, the geological features that are implied in Lavadour's gestural abstractions appear in cross-section view, exactly as they would in the Columbia River Gorge or the Grand Canyon, where the cutting action of rivers and erosion have exposed eons of geologic history.[64]

The facility of Lavadour's work to combine aerial and ground views as well as microcosmic and macrocosmic perspectives was brilliantly—and unexpectedly—illuminated through a collaborative process that he undertook with the Walla Walla Foundry in 2012. The commercial foundry, which has provided opportunity for many contemporary artists to stretch beyond their usual media into bronze, steel, and other metals, invited Lavadour to cast one of his paintings in a sculptural medium.[65] Lavadour brought to the project a monochrome painting that he describes as "a watery kind of abstract," which the designers at the foundry photographed, scanned, and imported into an architectural modeling program.[66] Watching the process, Lavadour recalls that "all of a sudden the stains and the watermarks had dimension to them. . . . It went from a painting to a mountain."[67] Remarkably, the models that were generated and eventually cast in brightly colored urethane resin in two editions entitled *Ruby Lift (I, II, and III)* and *Red River* closely resemble topographic relief maps of the Columbia Plateau.[68] For Lavadour the astonishing naturalism of the models affirmed what he had been saying for years about the correlation between his artistic practices and geological processes: "I realized that the whole thing about how there are rivers and mountains in a brush stroke was true. It was absolutely true."[69]

In the course of creating *Ruby Lift I, II, III* and *Red River*, of literally extrapolating two dimensions into three, Lavadour and his collaborators could not fully divest the work from the issues that attach to the medium of paint or the genre of landscape painting. But they did radically alter the playing field, so to speak: with the transition from painting to sculpture, the question of whether the viewer is permitted to enter the landscape is rendered moot. As a sculptural form, the landscape now enters the space of the viewer.

CHAPTER FOUR

Centering

SITE-SPECIFIC AND LAND-BASED ART PRACTICES

WHEN ROSALIND KRAUSS STARED DOWN INTO A PIT IN A FIELD IN LONG ISLAND in 1978 and asked rhetorically what sculpture is, she could hardly have been more prescient. In the years since her writing, the sculptural field has expanded to encompass a vast array of objects, installations, and artistic gestures that occupy space and evoke place. One such installation confronted visitors to the Art Gallery of New South Wales during the Sydney Biennale of 2012: *Do You Remember When?* (2012; figure 4.1), by the artist collective Postcommodity, comprised a 2-by-2-foot concrete slab excised from the gallery floor and displayed on a plinth, leaving a dirt-filled hole in the middle of the room. *Do You Remember When?* is in part a riff on minimalist sculpture of the 1960s, which often featured square objects cast from industrial materials displayed in stark arrangements in otherwise empty galleries.[1] In the broadest terms, minimalist installations (including *Do You Remember When?*) demonstrated the unique ability of sculpture to occupy, shape, or share literal space in a way that other art forms cannot. As Donald Judd put it in his treatise on modern sculpture in 1965, "Three dimensions are real space. . . . Actual space is intrinsically more powerful and specific than paint on a flat surface."[2]

This chapter is not concerned with sculpture per se but with exploring the ways that Indigenous artists have employed site-specific works to literally ground themselves and their viewers in the particulars of place. In the case of *Do You Remember When?*, for example, Postcommodity's exposure of the earth beneath the building challenged viewers to question the authority of the museum and to acknowledge the aboriginal lands beneath their feet.[3] In this respect, *Do You Remember When?* diverges from its minimalist genealogy and aligns itself with a distinctly Indigenous tradition of installation art, one that can be traced back to the early 1990s and especially to the quincentennial

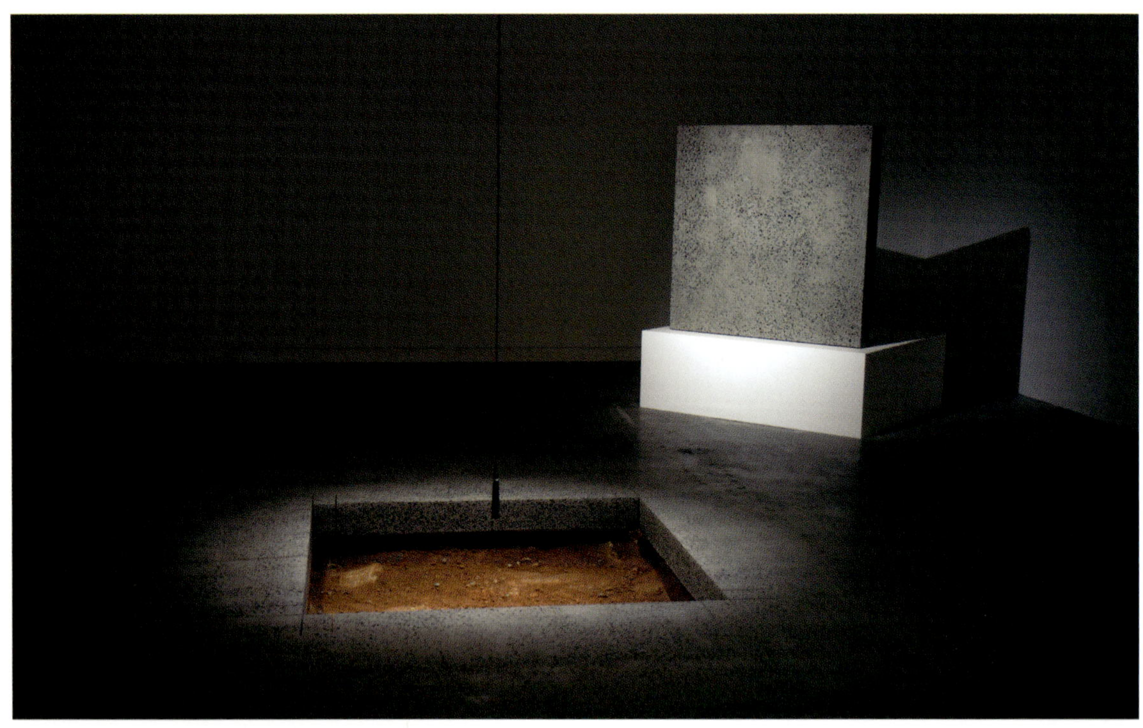

4.1 Postcommodity (artist collective)
Do You Remember When? (2012)
Cut concrete, exposed earth, light, sound. Mixed media installation; cut concrete, 24 × 24 inches
Installation view, Art Gallery of New South Wales, Sydney
Copyright Postcommodity. Courtesy of Postcommodity.

exhibitions.[4] Ho-chunk artist Truman Lowe's monumental sculpture *Ottawa* (1992; figure 4.2), for example, which was constructed for and installed in the *Land, Spirit, Power* exhibition, gestured to the natural environs of the National Gallery of Canada, albeit in a less invasive fashion than *Do You Remember When?*. Lowe's sculpture honored the life-sustaining waters of the Ottawa, Gatineau, and Rideau Rivers that converge near the site of the museum. The work, which is more than 31 feet long, 8 feet wide, and 5 feet high, is constructed of unfinished strips of pine that cascade down onto the gallery floor, "as if the river were spilling into the viewer's space."[5] The shape of Lowe's sculpture suggests the flow of water along the river's course while also evoking the geological features that underlie such flowing bodies: willow sticks that hang below the undulating laths refer to the "wellsprings that feed the river" and to "moisture seeping down into the earth."[6]

A similar sentiment informs Anishinaabe artist Michael Belmore's *Flux* (2010; figure 4.3), a sinuous chain of stones that seeps and spreads across a gallery floor, transforming the exhibition space into an abstracted streambed. While Postcommodity's and Lowe's works conjure the local geography, however, Belmore's *Flux* evokes a sense of place at some remove. Installed in the National Museum of the American Indian's George Gustav Heye Center in New York City, it indirectly referenced a site seventy miles north of Toronto, where the sculpture's ideological double, *Upland* (2005), is permanently integrated into the landscape. *Upland* is arranged in an actual streambed, where Belmore has subtly carved each river rock to nest with its neighbor, suggesting a current or foam of bubbles on a surface.[7] The stones in *Flux* are similarly altered, and in the gallery version the junctures between the stones are lined with gold leaf. While the glittering metal hidden within *Flux* escapes the notice of many viewers, others are rewarded for their deeper investigation. One writer has observed that "the viewer has to get down on his or her hands and knees to view and verify; this is not conventional gallery behavior."[8] Conventional or not, this posture brings viewers closer to the earth. In 2017 an invitation to participate in an immense group exhibition in Canada's national parks provided Belmore with an opportunity to revisit these materials and to expand on the idea that a series of related installations could move us to feel connected to places close at hand and across vast distances. *Coalescence* (2017), Belmore's contribution to *LandMarks* 2017,[9] is a four-part series of site-specific installations reaching across thousands of miles of Manitoba and Saskatchewan. In each location—beginning at the mouth of the Churchill River at Hudson Bay and extending to Grasslands National Park north of Montana—Belmore set copper-lined stones as markers along the path of the great glacier that once covered much of North America.[10]

Ojibwa artist Bonnie Devine's *Letters from Home* (2008) likewise references a landscape that is temporally and spatially remote: four glass sculptures elevated on birch plinths bear the imprint of the earth's surface, cast from granite slabs that line the Serpent River where Devine grew up. The immense stones are part of the Laurentian Shield, the geological bedrock of Ontario that was formed in the Precambrian period. According to Robert Houle, *Letters from Home*, which addresses natural features as sentient beings, conveys the "imprints of the grandfather, the glacier stone," as a form of recollection and reclamation of the Native landscape.[11] For Devine, employing sculpture to stake one's claim to space and place is both a personal ritual and a sovereign act. Whatever their form—representational or abstract, discrete sculptures or complex installations—all of the works discussed in this chapter gesture toward the earth as they seek to establish a connection to place. Or, as the title of Postcommodity's installation in Sydney graphically reminds us, site-specific works often seek to *re*-establish a connection that has been severed by time and the historical legacy of the dispossession and dislocation of Native peoples.

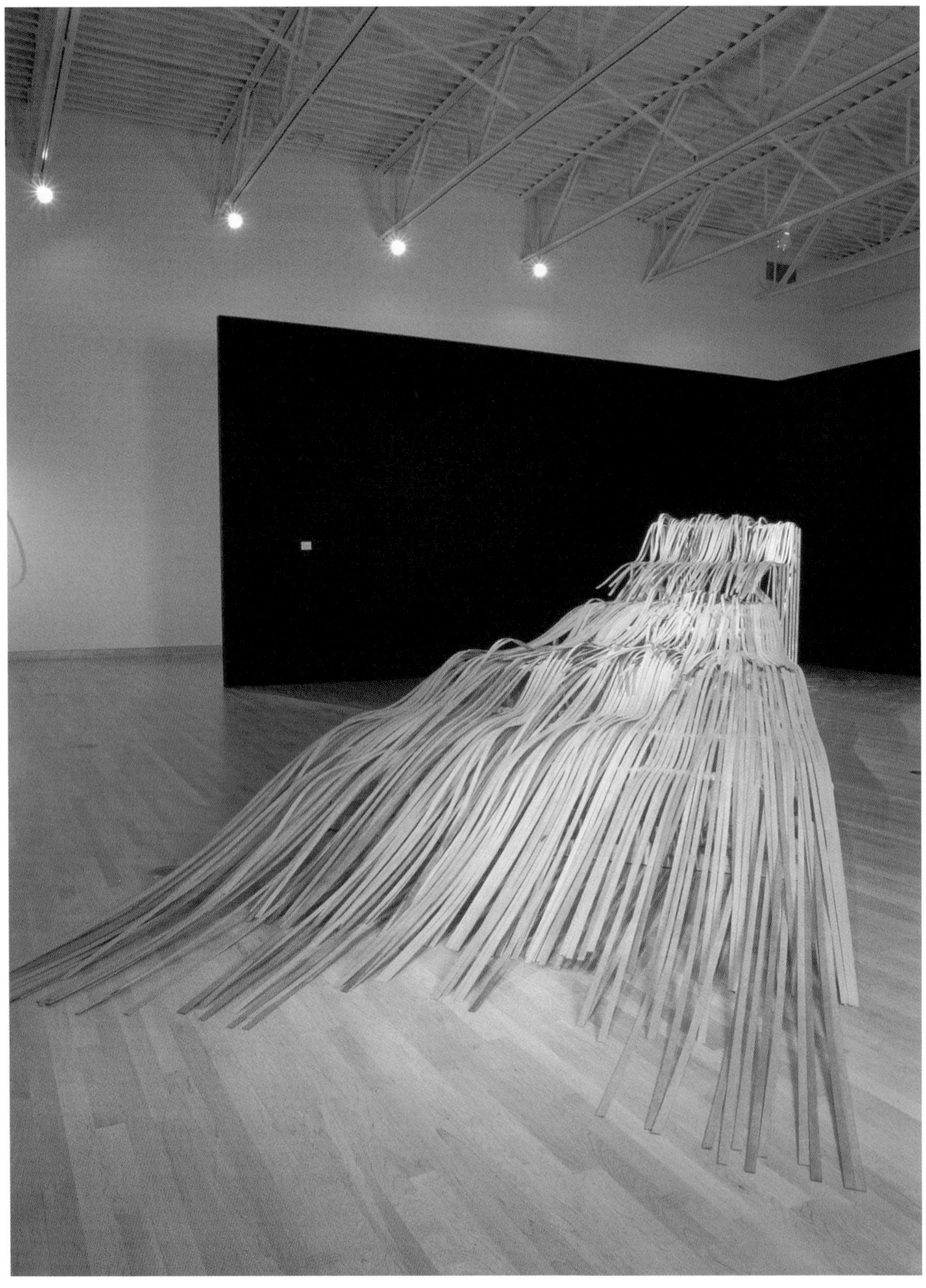

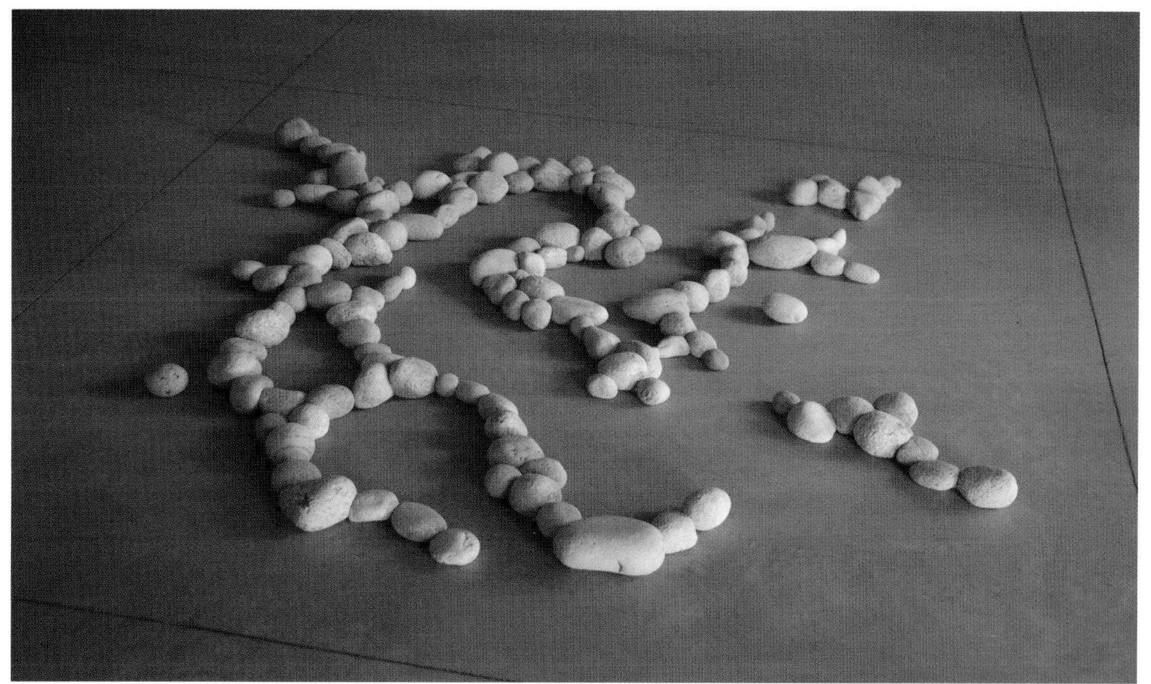

4.2 (*facing page*) Truman Lowe (Ho-chunk, b. 1944)
Ottawa (1992)
Wood, 60 × 36 × 3½ inches
Installation view, National Gallery of Canada, Ottawa
Courtesy of the artist. Photograph courtesy of the National Gallery of Canada.
Collection of the artist

4.3 (*above*) Michael Belmore (Anishinaabe, b. 1971)
Flux (2010)
River stones, gold leaf. Floor installation, 96 × 108 inches
Installation view, National Museum of the American Indian, New York
Courtesy of the artist. Photograph courtesy of the artist.
Collection of the artist

SITES AND NON-SITES

In 1993 New Yorkers walking through Washington Square Park would have seen dozens of limp muslin forms hanging in sheets in the windows of New York University's Grey Art Gallery, illuminated at night by soft orange light. What they made of this installation by Mohawk sculptor and videographer Alan Michelson depends on whether they were aware of the place that Washington Square played in Manhattan's history: the forms evoke the burial shrouds of thousands of victims of yellow fever, most of them poor, who lie buried in unmarked graves beneath the park. Michelson, who earned his master of fine arts in painting from the School of the Museum of Fine Arts in Boston, is a voracious researcher, and when he moved to New York City in the mid-1980s, he submerged himself in studies of the city's past. The discovery of (and subsequent public controversy over) an African American burial ground in Lower Manhattan in 1991 inspired Michelson to create a series of installations to mark the sites of urban cemeteries that had been obscured by development. In addition to *Cult of Memory*, Michelson also fashioned *Permanent Title* (1993), a series of muslin "shroud" bags coated in wax, each one bearing a charcoal rubbing or impression of the stone surfaces of buildings and sidewalks constructed over lost burial grounds. The bags of *Permanent Title* were displayed on-site at various locations, directing attention to what lies beneath the surface of the city's streets.[12]

Though these works engage only indirectly with the Indigenous history of New York City, Michelson, like many other Native artists, has long been interested in the impact of urbanization on the cultural and natural landscape. Two more of his New York City–based works—*Earth's Eye* (1990; figure 4.4) and *Mespat* (2001; figure 4.5)—address the devastation of the environment directly. *Earth's Eye* employed cast concrete markers to trace the contours of the now-extinct ecosystem of Collect Pond, the freshwater source that sustained Manhattan residents until it became so hopelessly polluted by tanneries in the eighteenth century that it had to be backfilled. Today only a remnant of the water source still flows, powering the cooling system of the Manhattan Criminal Courts building. In a method akin to Devine's, Michelson cast each marker with the impression of a plant or animal that was native to the vanished habitat to bring this subterranean history to light and to symbolically arrest the destruction of the pond's fragile ecosystem. The environmentalist ethic that underscores the work is made all the more evident in the title, which is taken from the writings of America's first conservationist, Henry David Thoreau. In *Walden* Thoreau wrote, "A lake is the landscape's most beautiful and expressive feature. It is earth's eye; looking into which the beholder measures the depth of his own nature."[13]

Noting that many of Michelson's works in the 1990s "became focused on intersections of the temporal and the spatial—and of ways of bringing

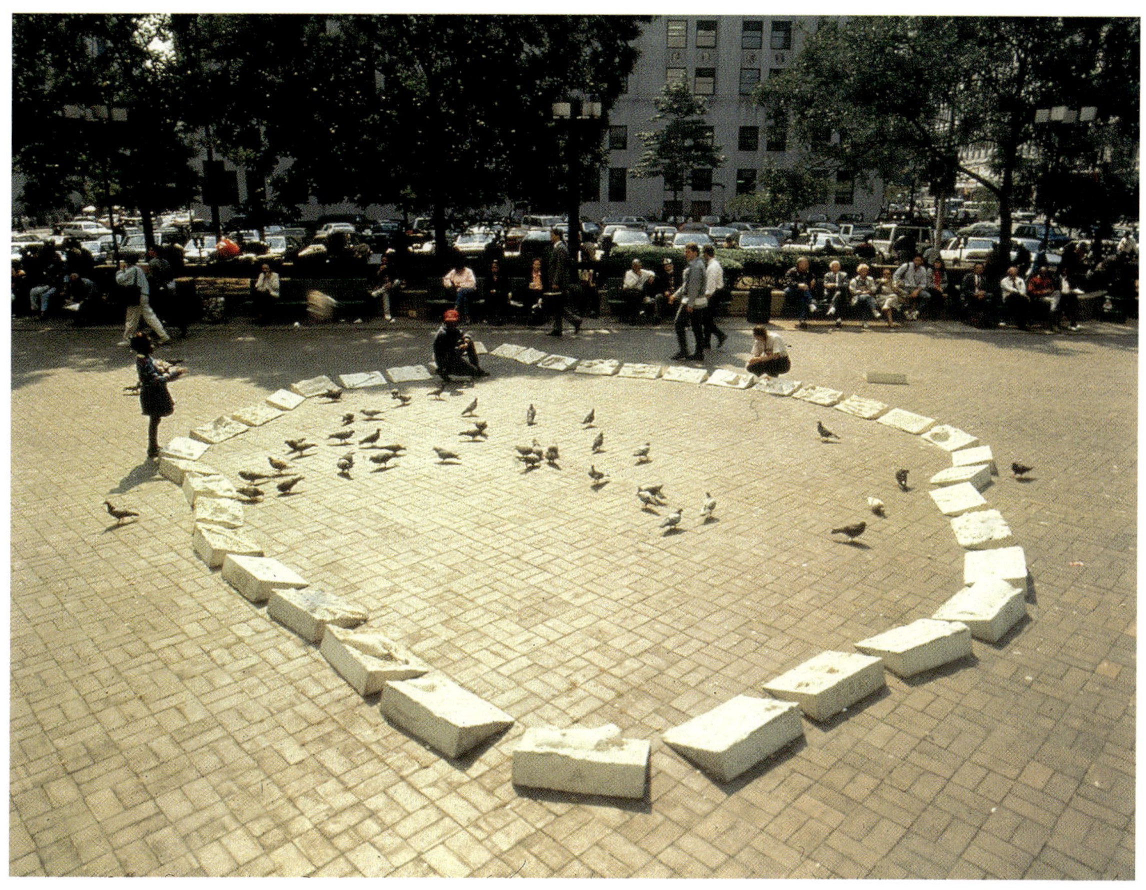

4.4 Alan Michelson (Mohawk, b. 1953)
Earth's Eye (1990)
Cast concrete, forty markers, each 22 × 14 × 6 inches
Installation view, Centre Street, New York
Courtesy of the artist. Photo by Peter Loppacher.

previous states of a locale into the here and now," *Sculpture* magazine critic Deborah Everett referred to *Earth's Eye*, *Cult of Memory*, and *Permanent Title* as "non-sites," cleverly evoking Robert Smithson's hugely influential New York City art gallery installations of the late 1960s.[14] Smithson defined his non-sites—installations of dirt and rocks brought into Manhattan from the pine barrens of New Jersey—as referents to remote places. He explained that "the site, in a sense, is the physical, raw reality—the earth or the ground," whereas the non-site, in the gallery, is but an "abstraction" of that place.[15] His purpose was to employ physical material to evoke a place but also to affirm its absence, to attest to its existence somewhere else. By transporting materials from the outliers (the site) into the urban core of New York City (the non-site), Smithson seems to have strengthened the dialectic of center and periphery, yet his actions also suggest that the center cannot hold: as critic Craig Owens wrote in 1979, the non-sites are relegated to being "a vacant reflection of the site."[16]

Everett's evocation of Smithson's work enables us to view other contemporary landscape installations in similar terms. Belmore's *Flux* is perhaps the most analogous, as it is constructed from rocks brought into a New York City gallery from far afield, and Devine's *Letters from Home* also gestures to a landscape that is both metaphorically and physically distant. Michelson's Manhattan-based works function differently, however, because they lack any reference to the periphery. Installed on the aptly named Centre Street in Manhattan, *Earth's Eye* hinges on the relationship between presence and absence, yet the installation materializes in the exact location of the site to which it refers, the destroyed ecosystem of Collect Pond. The same can be said for *Permanent Title* and *Cult of Memory*, which underscore temporal rather than spatial dislocations. In Michelson's urban installations it is time rather than space that intervenes between the fact and the referent: both *Earth's Eye* and *Cult of Memory* figure the present as only the uppermost stratum of the historical landscape. Lowe's *Ottawa* and Postcommodity's *Do You Remember When?* address similar instances of cultural amnesia, and in all of these cases, the in situ placement of the artwork, the symbolic representation of a previous state of being, draws that distant memory back to the surface.[17] *Do You Remember When?* goes a step further in establishing that what has been forgotten is specifically *Indigenous* knowledge; Postcommodity delivers this message through the addition of a sound element in the piece.

When *Do You Remember When?* was first conceived and exhibited at the Arizona State University Art Museum in Tempe in 2009, the room was filled with the sounds of Native voices singing a social dance song taught to the members of the artist collective by the local Pee Posh (formerly Maricopa) community. When the work was reprised for the Sydney Biennale in 2012, Postcommodity commissioned local Australian Aboriginal musicians to record a variety of Aboriginal instruments, songs, and calls to the animals of the region.[18] Considering that the composition of *Do You Remember When?*—extending as it does into the earth—would classify the work as site-specific no matter where it is installed, the customization of the piece through the inclusion of local Indigenous voices carries much of the work's meaning. As the members of Postcommodity see it, *Do You Remember When?* "becomes a spiritual, cultural and physical portal . . . from which emerges an Indigenous worldview."[19] The inclusion of the calls to the animals of the environment in particular reveals that the Indigenous worldview is *place-based*.[20] *Do You Remember When?* asserts that the only way that we might restore our contemporary relationship with the land and the environment is by peeling back the membrane (institutional or other) that separates us from Indigenous knowledge. Finally, it can be argued that in filling the void in the center of the gallery with the sound of

Indigenous voices, Postcommodity deftly overcomes the intrinsic problem of Smithson's sites and non-sites: rather than vacating the center, *Do You Remember When?* permeates it with Indigenous knowledge, reclaiming the space as Indigenous space.

RISING INTO RUIN

If the intention of all of these installations, especially Michelson's New York–based works of the early 1990s, was to literally unearth place-based knowledge, this is not as evident in *Mespat*, the other devoutly environmentalist work mentioned alongside *Earth's Eye*. *Mespat* is a departure in medium for Michelson, from site-specific sculptural installation to digital video, in this instance shot from aboard a boat traveling up a New York City waterway in 2001.[21] The work became an installation only when finally exhibited, first at the State University of New York at Stony Brook and then at the National Museum of the American Indian in 2006. In both of those venues, Michelson chose to project the twenty-minute video onto an 11-by-14-foot screen of white turkey feathers, in honor of the Indigenous inhabitants of the now-blighted landscape of Newtown Creek, a three-and-a-half-mile estuary that snakes between the boroughs of Queens and Brooklyn. It was along this estuary, which the Lenape Indians knew as Mespat—"bad water place"—that Indigenous peoples and European settlers first cohabitated and from which Native peoples were subsequently displaced. In the video, which has ambient sound but no narration, an endless succession of rusting barges, metal scrap yards, and chemical storage tanks glide past the camera lens, a nonverbal testament to a long history of environmental and cultural devastation.

When Michelson began his journey up the East River by boat in 2001, his intent, surprisingly, was to produce a "contemporary version of a nineteenth-century moving panorama," a visual format that has its roots in the romantic landscape tradition.[22] Rather than reproducing a picturesque scene, however, Michelson had a more somber vision in mind. He intended to capture a sequence of images of Rikers Island prison complex, an overt symbol of institutional power. Michelson recalls that when his party arrived at Rikers he found the view disappointing: "The island was smaller than we imagined, and from our distance the jail complex was clinical and benign-looking, more like a college campus than a notorious penal colony."[23] Michelson abandoned this subject in favor of the industrialized wasteland of Newtown Creek, which was a change in direction but hardly in dystopic character. Michelson knew that the estuary was severely polluted (so much so that it is now a Superfund site), and he was aware of the area's long history as a site of cultural contact and conflict. For Michelson, then, Newtown Creek was a landscape somewhat

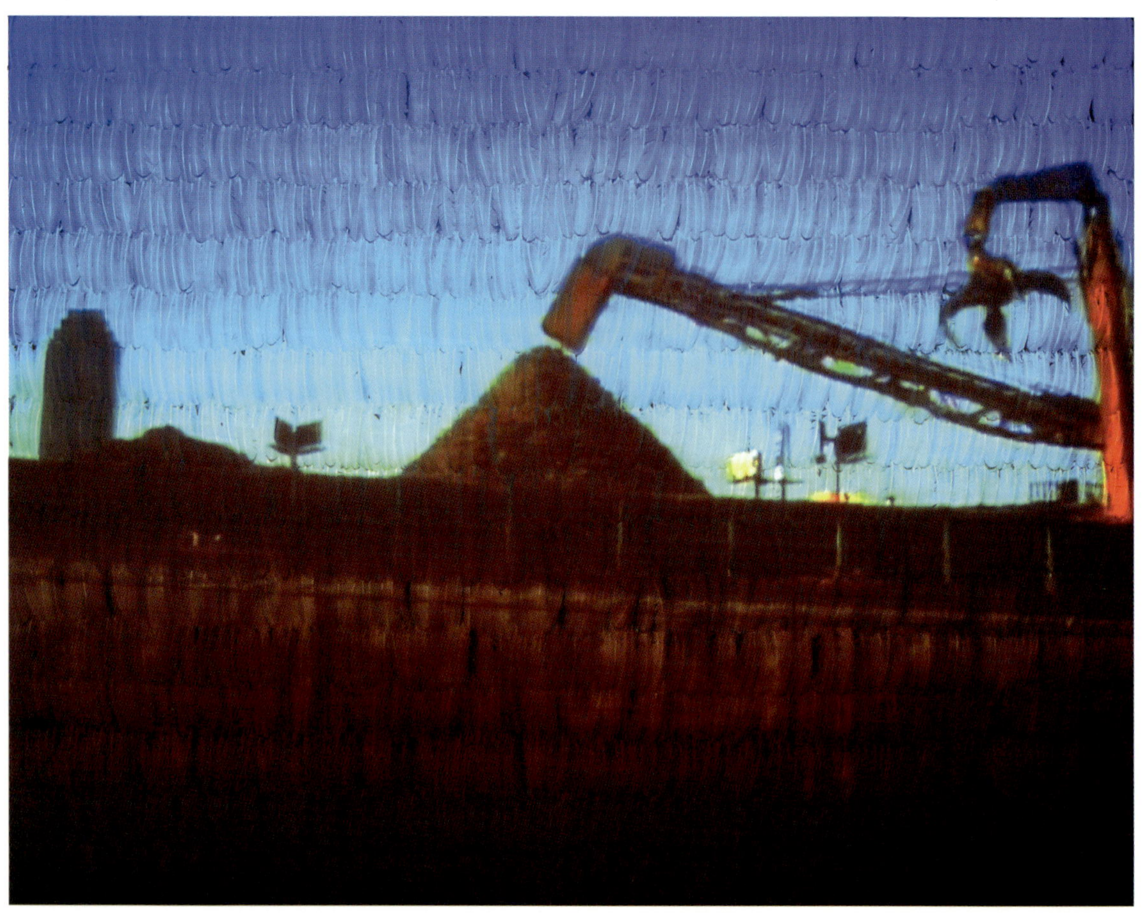

4.5 Alan Michelson (Mohawk, b. 1953)
Mespat (2001)
Video (19:24 min.) with original soundtrack by Michael J. Schumacher, turkey feathers, Monofilament, 69 × 489 inches
Courtesy of the artist. Photograph by Katherine Fogden.
National Museum of the American Indian

like Rikers Island in that it symbolized the darker side of civil society, albeit in a subtler form. *Mespat* is an unrelenting visual recital of industrial ruin: for twenty minutes, piles of broken concrete and scrap metal, sewage pipes, derelict cars, and deteriorating highway supports pass across the screen. The pace is mesmerizing, steady, and without punctuation, an effect underscored by the composed soundtrack of low gurgling and thrumming noises that segue into eerie electronic tones. Everett described *Mespat* as "seductively calm," having "a drifting, somnambulant quality" and the "uneasy familiarity of a recurring bad dream."[24] Michelson himself has likened the work to "a contemporary *Heart of Darkness*," referring to that work's nightmarish qualities as well as to its metaphoric use of the journey upriver as a search for origins.[25] Less evident in *Mespat* is the Native history that drew Michelson to Newtown Creek in the first place; the video can do little more than register the absence of Lenape people and culture in their traditional homeland. In preparing to exhibit *Mespat* in 2006, however, Michelson contrived an ingenious way to reinscribe the Native presence: he crafted his projection surface out of the material of traditional Lenape garments.

The characteristic of *Mespat* that most clearly distinguishes it from Michelson's earlier work and the other site-specific sculptures described above is that it is not particularly symbolic or metaphorical: the video is an unmediated record of a contemporary place. In this respect, *Mespat* is reminiscent of another canonical work by Smithson, a photographic essay entitled "The Monuments of Passaic," published in the December 1967 issue of *Artforum* magazine.[26] Like *Mespat*, "The Monuments of Passaic" chronicles an artist's journey up a severely polluted urban waterway: Smithson spent hours wandering along the banks of the Passaic River in New Jersey, photographing various structures with a Kodak Instamatic camera. When he returned, he published a series of his snapshots of rusting bridges, pumping derricks, and empty parking lots alongside a narrative of his activities and thoughts. This mock travelogue is important to us today—not only because it contains the amusing anecdote that the author was disappointed to find that his new paperback, *Earthworks*, was about soil shortages rather than sculpture—but also because the article documents Smithson's growing interest in both site-specific monuments and the concept of time. Smithson's walk among the derelict structures of Passaic brought him a "new consciousness of the post-industrial terrain" and a renewed respect for the inevitability of such processes of historical decay.[27] In his eyes even future structures such as the new highway he watched being built were doomed to obsolescence. He deemed these "ruins in reverse," asserting that "buildings don't *fall* into ruin *after* they are built but rather *rise* into ruin before they are built."[28]

It seems an understatement to call Smithson's vision dystopic, yet Owens discerned a glimmer of optimism in it. Writing on Smithson just after the artist's untimely death in 1973, Owens described his output as "entropy made visible," an affirmation of a universal law that prescribes the reduction of all systems to their least complex state.[29] Owens's interpretation was grounded in his analysis of Smithson's writings, especially "The Monuments of Passaic," but also in consideration of his site/non-site installations and sculptural projects such as *Asphalt Rundown* (1969), *Partially Buried Woodshed* (1970), and *Spiral Jetty* (1970). Each of these seemed to Owens a demonstration of Smithson's preoccupation with structures in decline. If, in effect, Michelson's video *Mespat* can be considered an animated corollary to "The Monuments of Passaic," the two works taken together would appear to attest to the centrality of dystopic vision in both modern and postmodern American art. *Mespat* may, on the other hand, represent something of a transitional moment for Michelson in which he was coming to terms with the decimation of Indigenous landscapes and cultures yet still actively seeking visual strategies to counter that erasure. In the works that followed *Mespat*, Michelson redoubled his efforts to assert Indigenous presence. One of those works took him out of New York City to the farthest reaches of the state, to another river that forms the very border of the nation.

Third Bank of the River (figure 4.6), a 6-by-40-foot sculptural construction that was permanently installed within the United States Port of Entry at Massena, New York, in the summer of 2009, is a stunning affirmation of Indigenous presence in every sense. Funded by the U.S. government's General Services Administration and prominently displayed within a U.S. border control station, *Third Bank of the River* is resonantly site-specific: it is a graphic representation of a particular place and of the geopolitical relationships between the United States, Canada, and the Mohawk Nation that are enacted there.[30] *Third Bank of the River* is composed of hundreds of photographs of the Saint Lawrence River that Michelson digitally joined in a series of luminous purple and white horizontal bands.[31] Once again, Michelson took his photographs from aboard a boat to map the territory from a variety of perspectives and to adequately convey the complexity of the cultural and geographic landscape of the border zone. On the northern shore of the Saint Lawrence River at this location is the Canadian city of Cornwall, Ontario, and on the southern shore, Massena, New York. In the center of the main channel of the river, anchoring the two long spans of the Seaway International Bridge, is Cornwall Island or Kawehno:ke, the northernmost territory of the Akwesasne Mohawk Nation.[32] Thus *four* shorelines are visible in *Third Bank of the River*: at the top is the bank of the river at Massena; below this is the south channel of the river bounded in mirror fashion by the (upside-down) southern shore of Cornwall Island. The lower purple stripe can be considered the northern channel of the river, with the north shore of Cornwall Island above and the Ontario mainland opposite, below.[33] At the far left of the composition all four anchorages of the Seaway International Bridge are shown, and as the panorama pans to the right, other local landmarks appear, such as a now-demolished brick-making factory near Cornwall and the Alcoa plant at Massena. The seamless blending of Michelson's digital photographs creates a middle territory comprised of an ephemeral cloudscape; nevertheless, the placement of Kawehno:ke at the literal center of the composition reinscribes the vital placement of the Akwesasne Mohawk Nation at the heart of the Three Nations International Crossing. As a statement of Indigenous presence (and a concomitant claim to territory), *Third Bank of the River* is a bold proclamation of Indigenous sovereignty, a point that is further underscored by the format of the work: the overall design is that of a 40-foot-long Haudenosaunee treaty belt.[34]

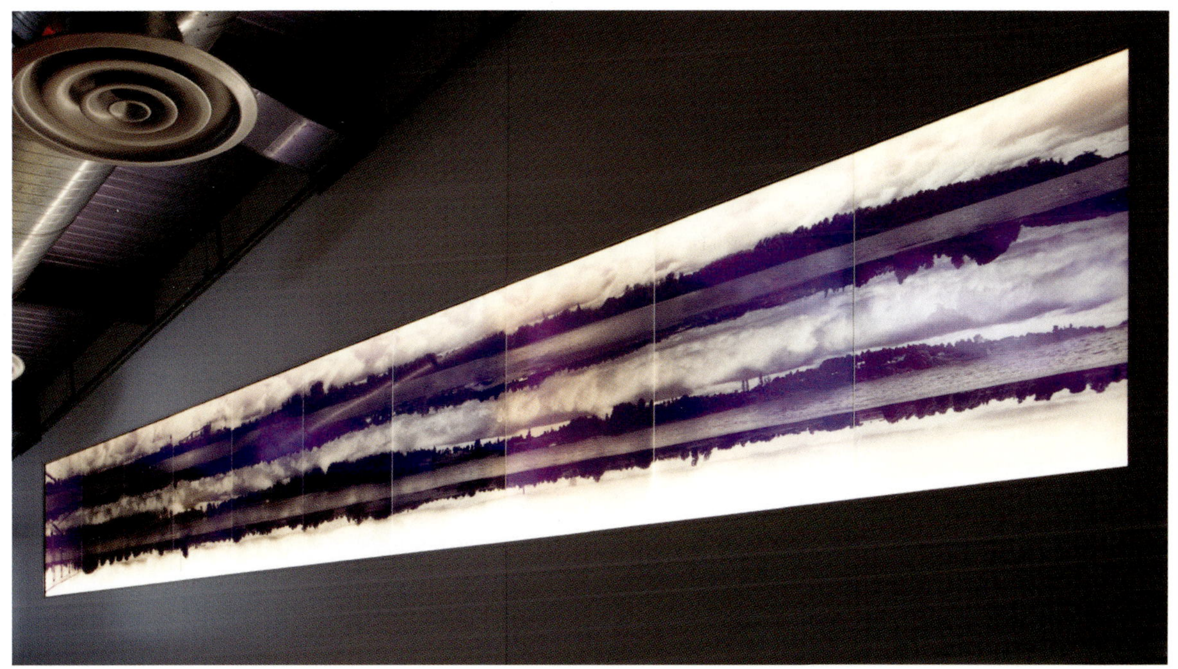

4.6 Alan Michelson (Mohawk, b. 1953)
Third Bank of the River (2009)
Etched glass, 69 × 489 inches
Courtesy of the artist. Photograph by André Costantini.
United States Port of Entry, Massena, New York

The particular treaty that Michelson references in *Third Bank of the River* dates to 1613, when the Iroquois entered into a reciprocal pact of non-interference with the Dutch. In the symbolic language of the Guswenta Treaty, the two cultures—Native and European—were described as two vessels traveling down a river on a parallel course. These vessels, a birchbark canoe and a European ship, represented the laws and customs of each people; the agreement stated that neither would impede the other's progress. The historic Two Row Wampum, a woven beaded belt that formally ratified the agreement and also embodied it in graphic form, represented the two vessels as parallel purple stripes against a background river of white. The importance of the treaty coupled with its compelling graphic representation and metaphoric narrative have made it a recurring subject in contemporary First Nations art. Algonquin artist Nadia Myre's monumental digital photograph *For Those Who Cannot Speak: The Land, the Water, the Animals and the Future Generations* (7½ by 188 feet; figure 4.7) invokes both the treaty and the contemporary political protest movement Idle No More, also known as the Broken Treaty Movement.[35] Myre explains that the work was "inspired by a declaration read by Algonquin kokoms (grandmothers) on

Parliament Hill on 11 January 2013. Like the movement Idle No More, the kokoms demanded greater respect for Aboriginal peoples. At the end of the text, they said they were making these demands on behalf of those who cannot speak, namely the earth, water, animals and future generations."[36]

The first time Michelson invoked the symbolism of the wampum belt and the river as a metaphor for contact and coexistence was in a video work aptly titled *TwoRow II* (2005). Exhibited at the National Museum of the American Indian in 2005 and subsequently acquired by the National Gallery of Canada, *TwoRow II* is a four-channel video installation that projects images of the banks of a different river—the Grand River—as it flows through the Six Nations Reserve in Ontario. The Grand River holds great significance for Michelson, as it defines both his ancestral homeland—his grandparents were born and raised on the reserve, and many of his relatives still live there—and the collective territory of the Six Nations. By the terms of Great Britain's Haldimand Proclamation of 1784, the Haudenosaunee were deeded a six-mile tract of

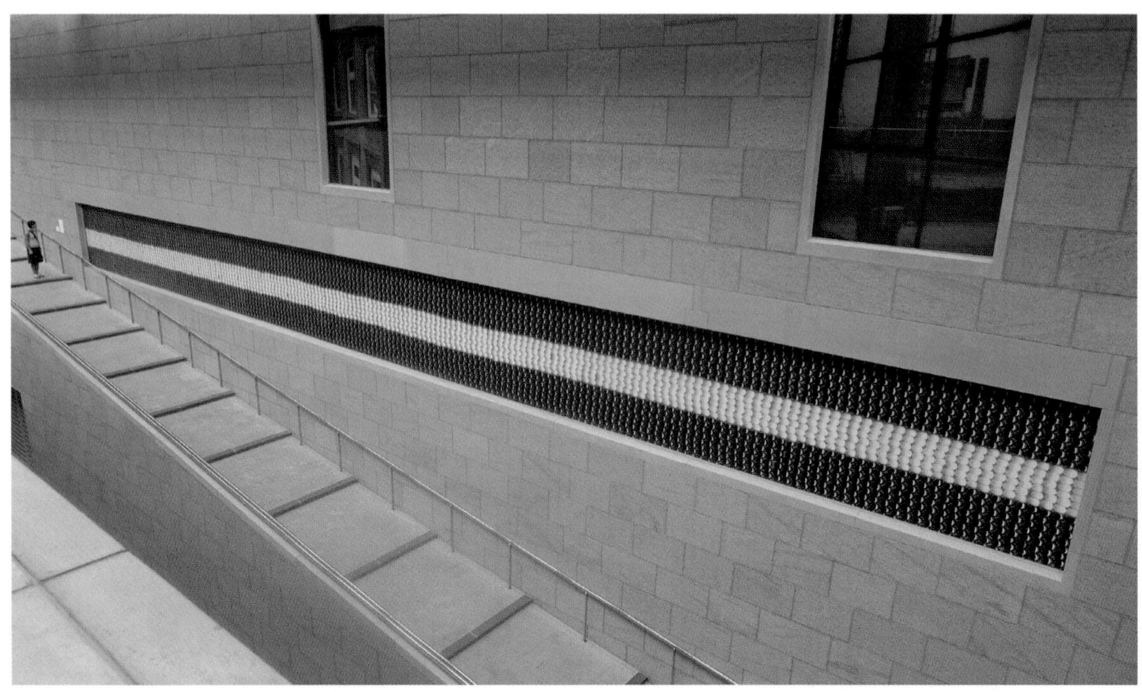

4.7 Nadia Myre (Algonquin, b. 1974)
For Those Who Cannot Speak: The Land, the Water, the Animals and the Future Generations (2013)
Digital print 7 ½ × 188 feet
Installation view, National Gallery of Canada, Ottawa
Courtesy of Art Mûr Gallery, Montreal. Photograph by Guy L'Heureux.

land on either side of the Grand River from mouth to source; today the river forms a boundary between the reserve and non-Native townships.[37] To create *TwoRow II* Michelson again took to the water, videotaping each bank as a separate entity from the vantage point of a tour boat as it navigated the river on a summer dinner cruise. Along with the video of the banks, Michelson captured the audio narrative of the non-Native tour director describing the history of the river and its people to his passengers.

After the cruise, Michelson returned to Six Nations to produce a second soundtrack, recording stories of the river as told by Six Nations residents.[38] In the gallery, the two soundtracks run simultaneously, competing and conflicting as narratives but never quite canceling one another out. As if to further underscore the degree to which the two cultures—the two sides of the river—are alienated, Michelson set the two video tracks moving in opposite directions; the Native and the non-Native worlds literally run at cross purposes. As a multisensorial depiction of discord, *TwoRow II* deftly conveys the complexities of life in a border zone, with the river and its banks serving as an apt metaphor for cultural interaction and exchange. Further, the work reminds us in literally graphic terms that the treaties and agreements made between Native and European Nations have not been honored: part of the soundtrack recorded at Six Nations details the loss of nearly 90 percent of the reserve's land base promised by the Haldimand Proclamation. Six Nations resident Amos Keye Jr. states in the *TwoRow II* voiceover, "Of an estimated 675,000 acres of land promised in the Haldimand deed only approximately 69,000 acres remains Six Nations land. And this has been another 'Grand Moment.'"[39] Michelson himself has lamented, "the brother-to-brother relationship [of the Guswenta Treaty] has not been respected; it needs to be shored up. The whole power thing has to shift."[40]

A significant difference between *TwoRow II* and the later *Third Bank of the River*—in addition to the increased number of sovereign entities in the mix—is a changing perspective on borders as immutable geographic features of the landscape. Ironically, though it is a literally moving image, *TwoRow II* figures the river as a kinetic yet insurmountable barrier between cultures. *Third Bank of the River*, on the other hand, finds Michelson willingly transgressing boundaries, moving through the waters of the Saint Lawrence in such a way that his actions demonstrate not only the fluidity but also the permeability of the border. I would argue that the shift in Michelson's perception of the border from a contoured boundary to a porous membrane is due to his encounter with the complex cultural geography of Massena. This is, after all, a landscape that has inspired other works of art, such as the Academy Award–nominated film *Frozen River* (2008), that feature the border crossing experiences of the Akwesasne.[41]

BORDER CROSSINGS

Border crossing—as both a noun and a verb—has been an important recurring subject in Native American landscape representation. Throughout the 1990s, for example, Mandan/Hidatsa/Arikara photographer Zig Jackson employed still photography to record his passage through various reservation landscapes. *Entering Laguna Indian Reservation* (1990) and *Entering Fort Berthold Indian Reservation* (1997) are shot in black and white, lending a documentary feel to the images, yet Jackson's subtle hand with the compositions lend them a particular inflection: the landscapes are majestic and expansive, and the boundary markers are ineffectual at best. In the absence of either borders or controls, the Indigenous landscapes in Jackson's photographs are readily penetrated by highways that pass into and through them. Perhaps for this reason Jackson began a new series of works invoking reservation boundaries in 1997. In the later series, *Entering Zig's Indian Reservation* (figure 4.8) the artist appears in various urban settings, wearing a feathered war bonnet and standing beside a sign that reads in part, "Entering Zig's Indian Reservation / No Picture Taking / No Hunting / No Air Traffic / New Agers Prohibited." In this new series Jackson establishes himself as a sovereign entity: he reclaims Indian territories, dictates his own boundaries, and writes, rather than is subjected to, the rule of law. With the prohibition against "Air Traffic," he even institutes his own no-fly zone. Still, it is important to note that Jackson has not surrendered his mobility. Instead, the series affirms the artist's modern nomadism; he, his sign, and his territory are itinerant but not ungrounded.

Less than a year before Jackson began his series of interventions into public spaces, the installation of a more permanent sign in Albuquerque, New Mexico, sparked considerable public debate with its stark imagery of a borderland. *Cultural Crossroads of the Americas* (1996; figure 4.9) by Chiricahua Apache sculptor Bob Haozous was commissioned by the University of New Mexico and installed at the edge of campus on Albuquerque's Central Avenue—historic Route 66. Taking its place among the neon signs and kitschy monuments that line Route 66, the 29-by-20-foot Cor-Ten steel billboard cites this local history of tourist travel with its images of cars and camping trailers driving past iconic monuments and McDonald's golden arches. The billboard also features a trio of figures moving across the Mexican desert toward the United States. In stark contrast to the corporate, urban environment of the United States, Mexico is represented as a preindustrialized state: the human figures are drawn in the style of Mixtec codices, and the migrants make their long journey on foot.[42] The cultural crossroads of America (Route 66) become the cultural crossroads of the *Americas* in Haozous's vision, which centers on the border, represented here by a pyramid-shaped factory belching pollution that drifts both north and south. Haozous recalls that he was thinking

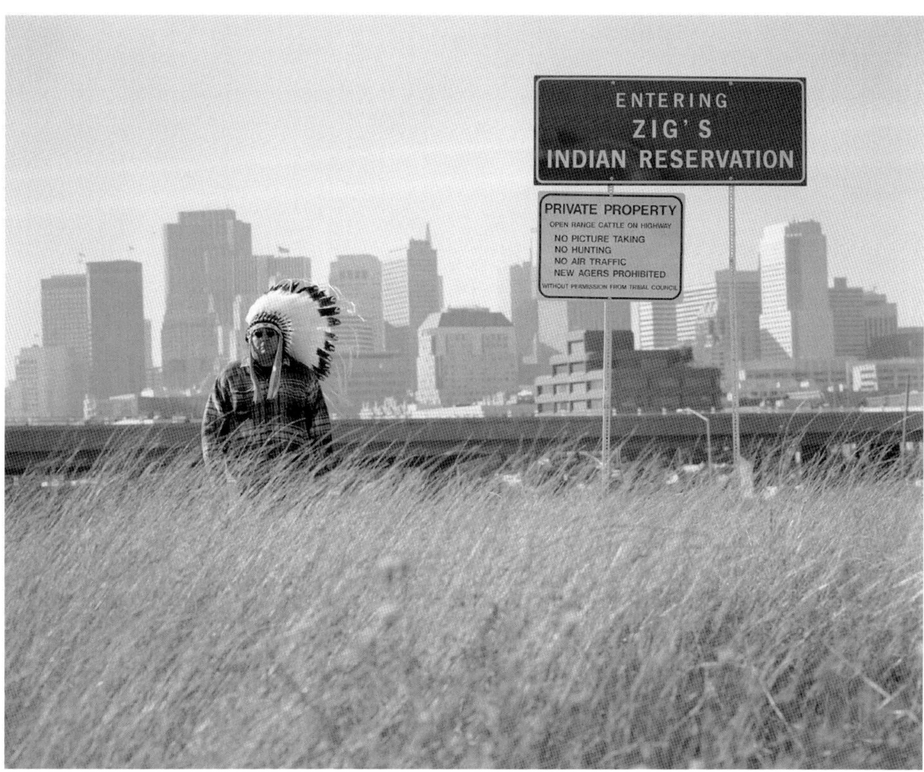

4.8 Zig Jackson (Mandan/Hidatsa/Arikara, b. 1957)
Entering Zig's Indian Reservation (1997)
Black and white photograph, dimensions variable
Courtesy of the artist
Collection of the artist

in particular about the experience of migrants passing through that zone: "They're all coming to America to gain what we have to offer, and what do we have to offer? The McDonald's, the cross, the dollar sign, the Statue of Liberty, the pollution, the war machine, all these things that America has to offer the world and is well-known for."[43] Despite its bleak humor (especially noteworthy is the exhausted figure slouching on his equally exhausted horse; Haozous has wryly substituted a cowboy in place of the Indian in the *End of the Trail* monument), *Cultural Crossroads of the Americas* is a scathing indictment of America's military industrial complex.[44] The United States is depicted as a cultural landscape dominated by banking corporations, fast food, Christianity in its most corporate form, and even by a corrupted ideology of patriotism, freedom, and opportunity (symbolized by the Statue of Liberty perched atop an office building). This side of the landscape is devoid of actual humans; only machines and structures are visible in this militarized zone.[45]

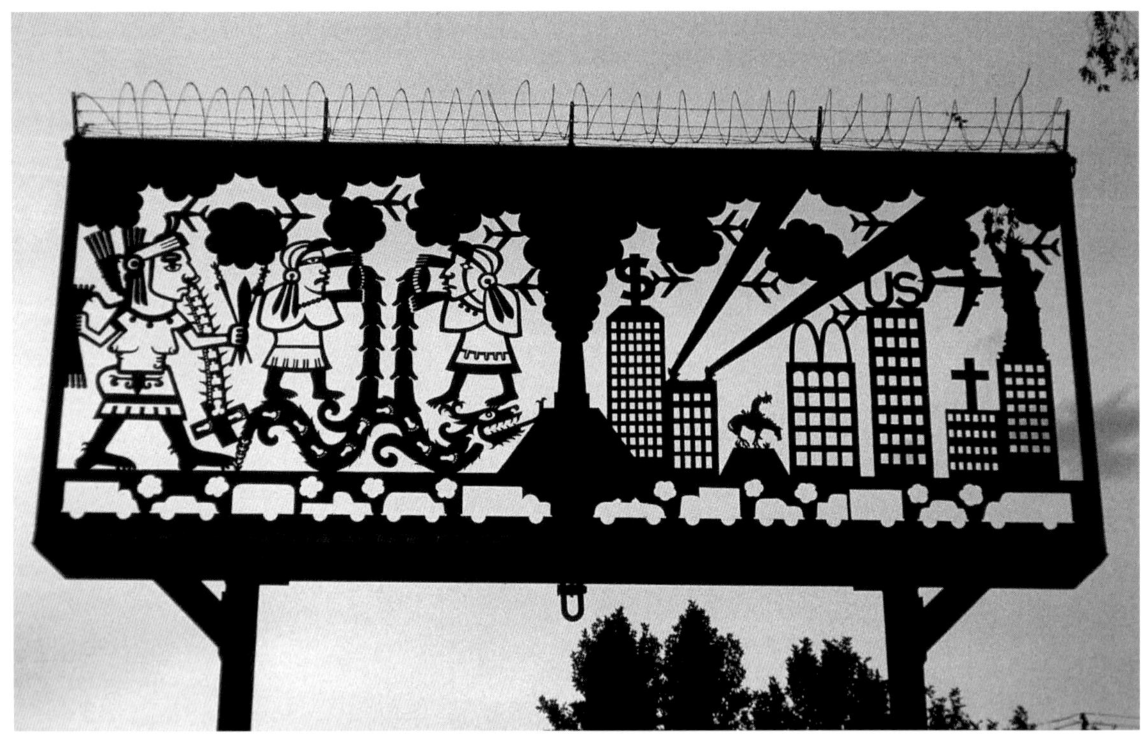

4.9 Bob Haozous (Chiricahua Apache, b. 1943)
Cultural Crossroads of the Americas (1996)
Cor-Ten steel, 348 × 300 inches
Courtesy of the Albuquerque Public Art Program
Yale Park, Central Avenue, Albuquerque, New Mexico

Many of the images featured in *Cultural Crossroads*—the silhouettes of planes soaring through a crowded airspace; the lines of cars, trucks, and trailers progressing bumper to bumper across the bottom margin; the framing device of clouds of pollution billowing from the center of the composition—are reminiscent of a curiously little-known earlier work by Haozous entitled *Spirit of the Earth* (1994; figure 4.10).[46] Commissioned by the federal Art in Architecture Program in 1992, *Spirit of the Earth* was installed at the United States Port of Entry at Otay Mesa, just southeast of San Diego on the U.S.-Mexico border. Given its location on the actual border, the cut steel sculpture can be considered an indirect precursor to Michelson's *Third Bank of the River*. In *Spirit of the Earth*, the cultures of Mexico and the United States are once again represented as separate entities relegated to the corners of the composition: Mexico is symbolized by a codex-style figure, and the United States by a squawking, distressed eagle. The two cultures are united in the shared responsibility for creating an environment impacted by cars, commerce, and pollution.[47]

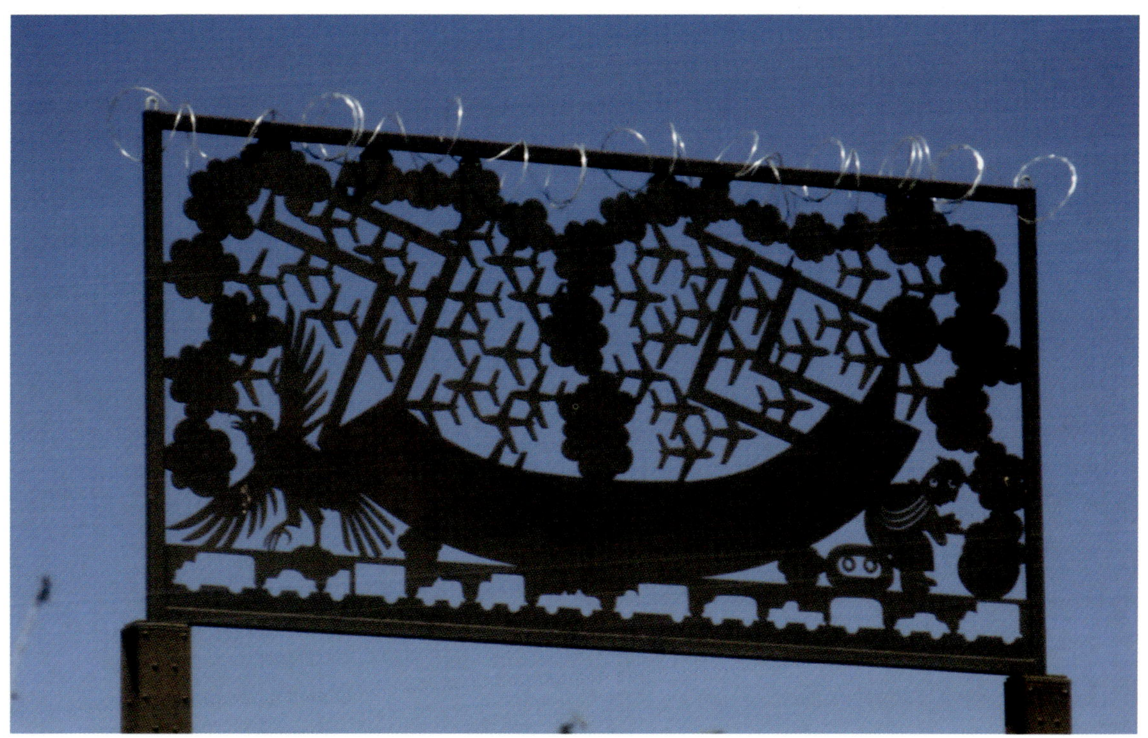

4.10 Bob Haozous (Chiricahua Apache, b. 1943)
Spirit of the Earth (1994)
Cor-Ten steel, dimensions unknown
Courtesy of the General Services Administration
United States Port of Entry, Otay Mesa, California

According to federal Art in Architecture Program historian Ivy Schroeder, the final composition of *Spirit of the Earth* was something of a compromise on the part of the artist and the work's sponsor. Haozous's original design for the piece divided the work into discrete halves, with the United States portrayed as a wholly commercial culture dominated by advertising logos and dollar signs and Mexico portrayed as frozen in the past of a nostalgic, pre-Columbian era. Federal program administrators were not as concerned with the generally critical tenor of the imagery as they were with the perceived dichotomy between the two nations. They asked Haozous to tone down this aspect of the design, and he complied by diminishing though not removing the dividing line in the composition.[48] The government clients had a final, more startling request: they asked the artist to string coils of barbed wire across the base of the sculpture. Haozous recalls: "After I put [the billboard] up, they said, 'We're worried about graffiti. Can you put some razor wire on it?' I said, 'Yeah, I will.' They wanted me to put razor wire on the columns, [to] ensnarl these little kids with their spray cans. But instead I put it on top. It was such a powerful symbol of the border, of the separation, and this entitlement concept."[49] In its final form, then, *Spirit of the Earth* astutely reveals the paradox of the border crossing experience, picturing an unimpeded flow of commerce in the figures of vehicles moving along the lower edge, juxtaposed with an emblem of entanglement and obstruction along the top.[50]

When Haozous revived and adapted the original design of *Spirit of the Earth* for *Cultural Crossroads of the Americas* two years later, the controversy it provoked had little to do with the aspects that troubled the General Services Administration. In fact, what sparked fierce public debate in Albuquerque was the coil of concertina (barbed) wire that Haozous strung along the top edge of *this* structure. The University of New Mexico objected to this element of the composition, and because the artist had not included the wire in the designs approved by either the university or the City of Albuquerque, the university peremptorily removed it. After a series of public hearings on the matter, Haozous sued to have the wire restored, but his suit was unsuccessful.[51]

Haozous's intention (realized or not) to install barbed wire along his billboard sculptures allies the work with others that pictured the border in the 1990s. Haozous himself created an eight-thousand-pound, 9-by-12-foot painted steel sculpture entitled *Border Crossing* (1991) that features on one side images that are by now familiar to us in his work: bomber aircraft, a Christian cross, an armed border guard, a thick tangle of barbed wire, and a locked door that represents the entrance into the United States. On the reverse, however, the steel is painted with a serene yet stereotyped New Mexico landscape, replete with Georgia O'Keeffe–style puffy white clouds. This side of the monument is worlds removed from the bleak symbolism of the militarized zone, and for Haozous that is the point: "It exposes racism and environmental racism issues very clearly. . . . I drew a piece that shows the American viewpoint. It's kind of like rose-colored glasses. And the other side is the reality of this country—of this world. The gate's locked and there's no way to get over here because we're defending our entitlement."[52] Other artists mining similar thematic veins in the early 1990s chose to focus on borders closer to home. Luiseño artist James Luna, for example, stretched barbed wire across the length of a museum gallery during his performance, *Creation and Destruction of an Indian Reservation: An American Dilemma* (1990). Over the course of four acts, Luna dramatized the various stages in the development of the reservation system (one of which entailed the subdivision and fencing off of reservation land in the early twentieth century). The final product of Luna's performance is an installation in which barbed wire bisects a gallery that is lined with rural mailboxes and littered with beer cans. In this last iteration, Luna's wire functions as an ironic substitution for the velvet ropes more typically found in art institutions. It also ideologically bars audiences from entering Indian territory, much like the anti-invitational aspects of WalkingStick's and Lavadour's paintings discussed in the previous chapters did. The presence of the fencing in Luna's installation contradicts the official language of the highway sign behind it that reads "Entering La Jolla Reservation."

A similar two-dimensional work, Pit River/Paiute artist Jean LaMarr's print *Some Kind of Buckaroo* (1992), also depicts a strand of barbed wire separating the viewer from Indian territory and from an Indian man in cowboy hat and chaps standing on the curve of an abstracted earth. A Victorian carpet pattern beneath the man's feet attests to the transformation of the Native landscape in a manner reminiscent of Haozous's sculpture, and LaMarr's vision also includes airplanes streaking across the sky. The airplanes in this instance are fighter jets, though it is unclear whether they menace or safeguard the figure in the foreground: critic Lucy Lippard described the space of LaMarr's *Buckaroo* as "simultaneously comforting and dangerous." The citizen, Lippard wrote, is "fenced off on a reservation as though imprisoned, or, perhaps, protected."[53] In any case, the depiction of the border (whether a reservation or international boundary or both at once) as a fence or impermeable barrier is troubling because the very nature of borders is that they must be at least selectively traversed. The issue, especially as configured in contemporary Native American landscape representation, is not whether boundaries exist but who exercises the right of passage into these spaces and who has the authority to control that access?

Jolene Rickard, who has stated that her intention is to use her art to reinforce the "borders of sovereignty," explicitly claims the right of free passage across borders as a tenet of Indigenous sovereignty.[54] Rickard echoes the lifelong efforts of her grandfather, Tuscarora Chief Clinton Rickard, whose role in founding the Indian Defense League of America (IDLA) in 1924 was mentioned in the first chapter. Since 1928 the IDLA has enacted an annual border crossing celebration to affirm this basic right of Indigenous people, and photographs of the annual event appear in Rickard's work *Corn Blue Room* (1998), installed at the Canadian Museum of Civilization as part of the exhibition *Reservation X: The Power of Place in Contemporary Indigenous Art*.[55] The photographs show Iroquois people displaying an IDLA banner as they walk, without passports, across the U.S.-Canada border at Niagara Falls.[56] The action is a demonstration of rights guaranteed to Indigenous peoples in Great Britain's Jay Treaty of 1794,[57] rights that are also quietly affirmed by Michelson's installation some three hundred miles away at the United States Port of Entry at Massena.[58] As we have seen, Michelson's *Third Bank of the River* references the Guswenta Treaty and is thus a stark reminder of the nation-to-nation relationships that must be honored in any diplomatic negotiation regarding territorial boundaries. The multiplication of the river and its banks, however, and especially the way that those banks mirror one another across the river channels in

Third Bank of the River, exhibits a complexity beyond the compositional tenets of the Two Row Wampum belt. The spatial ambiguities of the composition and the depiction of the island of Kawehno:ke in particular as an ephemeral cloudscape impart a sense of fluidity and mixing that belies the more orderly metaphor of cultures set on parallel courses. In addition to satisfying the aspirations of the commissioning agency to "convey a sense of openness and welcome" at the United States border, *Third Bank of the River* asserts the distinctly Native prerogative to move without hindrance across the arbitrary boundaries drawn by settler nations.[59]

Despite the fact that the modern international boundaries bisect countless Native communities, the right to traverse those borders is not guaranteed by treaty for most Native Americans. In the Southwest along the U.S.-Mexico border south of Tucson, Arizona, members of the Apache, Tohono O'odham, and many other smaller tribes have experienced a gradual choking off of their ability to move through their traditional homelands. From the Tohono O'odham Reservation to Douglas, Arizona, Native communities on both sides of this 140-mile stretch of border have been increasingly impacted by the escalating rhetoric—and the reality—of contemporary border politics. This contested landscape, where tens of thousands of people pass legally through border-crossing stations every day and tens of thousands more endeavor to effect illegal passage through a border zone saturated with an estimated 3,800 U.S. Border Patrol agents, is the setting for two Postcommodity works, the most recent being *A Very Long Line* (2016), exhibited in the 2017 Whitney Biennial.

A Very Long Line is a four-channel video that runs on a continuous loop, showing footage of video shot along the twenty-six-mile stretch of border fence that separates Douglas, Arizona, from Agua Prieta, Sonora. The perspective of the piece is from a car traveling along a dirt road on the U.S. side of the border, allowing viewers to glimpse the landscape of Agua Prieta only through punctuated gaps in the border fence. The experience that the piece captures is something of a novelty, not only for viewers who have never been to the edge of the Sonoran desert, but also in the sense that few people move in parallel to the border. Perhaps the perspective mimics that of U.S. Border Patrol agents, whose experiences have informed other Postcommodity works.[60] Nevertheless, as was aptly demonstrated in Michelson's *Third Bank of the River*, the more common experience of movement in the borderlands is *across* the border, and that is exactly the experience that is metaphorically evoked in Postcommodity's *Repellent Fence* (2015; figure 4.11). This temporary installation of 26 tethered helium balloons, each 10 feet in diameter, floating 100 feet in the air, stretched for more than 2 miles along a line that would connect rather than separate Douglas and Agua Prieta.[61] In other words, the line created by *Repellent Fence* would not function as a fence at all; it transects the border between the United States and Mexico. For Postcommodity, both *A Very Long*

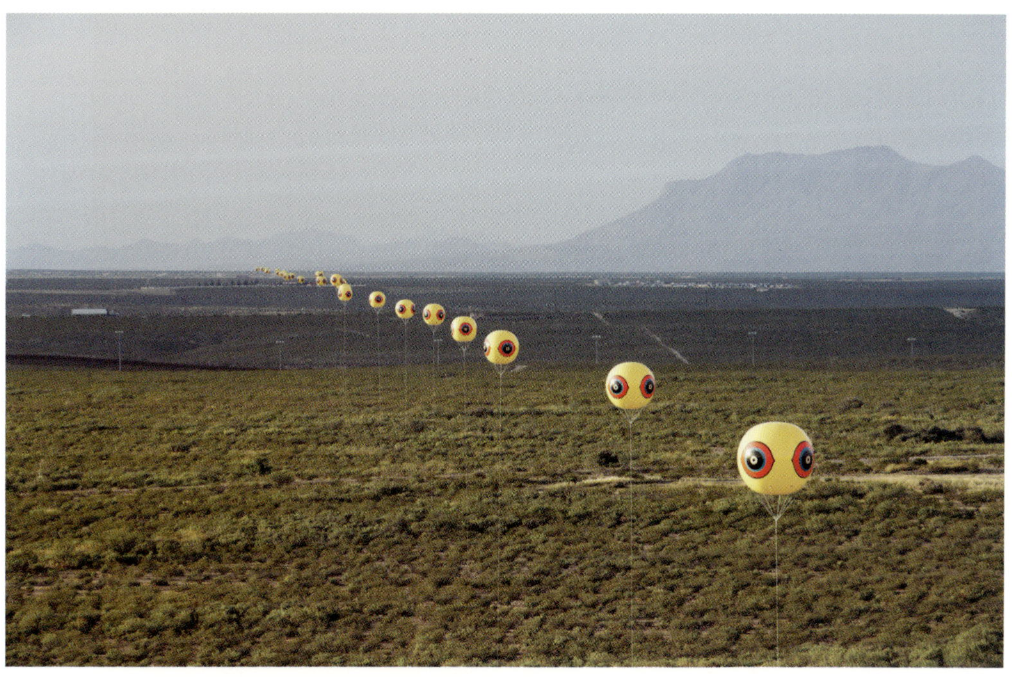

4.11 Postcommodity (artist collective)
Repellent Fence (2015)
Earth, cinder block, paracord, PVC spheres, helium; 26 units,
each 144 inches in diameter; installation length 2 miles
Installation view, U.S.–Mexico border, Douglas, Arizona–Agua Prieta, Sonora
Courtesy of Postcommodity

Line and *Repellent Fence* are intended to recognize the Indigenous peoples "that are intermeshed in the theater of the contemporary immigration crisis of the Americas," including those "who are following the ancient indigenous trade routes in search of economic opportunity" and those who "are coping with the militarization of their ancestral homelands."[62]

While the orientation of the line created by *Repellent Fence* carries much of the work's meaning, a final point is made in the choice of graphics for the balloons themselves. Each balloon is imprinted with four "scare eyes," a design utilized in bird repellent products intended for use in backyards and gardens. The repellent balloons are meant to warn off unwanted birds by mimicking the shape of a predator's eye—an apt metaphor for the militarized border zone. Nevertheless, as Postcommodity notes on its website, the commercial product tends to be ineffective after a few days, and this is an important part of the message of *Repellent Fence*. Like Michelson's *Third Bank of the River*, Postcommodity's installation acknowledges the border while also attesting to its permeability: the settler state may attempt to control the movements of its citizens and noncitizens, but it cannot fully abridge their individual sovereignty.

DECOLONIAL MONUMENTS

The spatial ambiguities of *Third Bank of the River*'s composition that do so much to hold open the possibility of movement through the border zone are derived not from the legislative sphere but from a quite unexpected source: early American tourism. Michelson modeled his complex format—in which the banks of the river are shown in opposing views, one right side up and the other upside down—on pamphlet maps that were provided to passengers on turn-of-the-century Hudson River boat tours. These souvenir guides printed photographs of each bank of the river in multipage panoramas, with prominent landmarks clearly identified. Pamphlet users would follow one stream of images along the top of each page, proceeding to the end of the pamphlet—the turnaround point of the cruise. When the boat began its return tour, passengers would flip the book over and follow along with the images of the opposite bank, progressing again from left to right back to the tour's origin point.[63] Whether printed in multiple-page folios or accordion-style pamphlets, the beauty of this obsolete, mirrored-panoramic form is its ability to convey the experience of moving continuously forward. Though the terms of the commission for *Third Bank of the River* at Massena dictated that the work be permanently fixed, Michelson's resurrection of a century-old representational tradition enabled him to convey something of the actual experience of travel—of transience, of moving through space—in the work.[64]

Michelson's recurring treatment of the themes and mechanisms of riverboat tourism, from the actual cruise that provided the raw audio and visual material for *TwoRow II* to the printed matter that inspired *Third Bank of the River*, returns us to a subject that was raised in the first pages of this book, namely the relationship between sculpture and monuments or, more specifically, what Krauss referred to as "the logic of the monument."[65] Monuments may seem at best a latent motif of *TwoRow II* and *Third Bank of the River*, in part because the works themselves are more readily regarded as visual representations than as three-dimensional objects; nevertheless, in engaging with the history of tourism they directly engage with the history of the erection and consumption of monuments. In Michelson's hands, that history is specifically configured as an exploration of institutional power, cultural memory, and the processes through which the passage of time produces "history." These ideas are best exemplified by a video-based work that Michelson created even as *Third Bank of the River* was being installed at Massena: *Shattemuc* (2009; figure 4.12), commissioned for inclusion in Skidmore College's Tang Art Museum exhibition *Lives of the Hudson*.[66] Like *TwoRow II*, *Shattemuc* is a digital video shot from the perspective of a boat cruising along a river, but in this instance the river in question is the Hudson River, and the video was shot at night, with the aid of a marine searchlight. In this footage, scenes of a serene woodland environment drift slowly by the lens for long stretches of time, interrupted intermittently by channel markers that loom into view in the foreground and then are left behind as the boat continues upriver. Eventually, the landscape changes, segueing into scenes of an urban and industrialized shoreline marred by factories, quarries, and loading docks, all eerily quiet in the middle of the night.

For modern viewers, Michelson's move to filming at night with the aid of a marine searchlight conjures visions of military surveillance, an association reinforced by the fact that the video was filmed from the deck of a decommissioned police launch. Nevertheless, the introduction of the spotlight here is also a direct reference to earlier traditions of viewing along the Hudson, many of which were documented in the *Lives of the Hudson* exhibition. Between the turn of the century and World War II, night tours complemented the type of tourist experiences mentioned above in reference to the pamphlet maps that inspired the format of *Third Bank of the River*. During the day passengers lounged on the decks, enjoying views of Bear Mountain and the Palisades, and at night searchlights mounted on the bridge of the ship directed their attention to monuments along the shore. What shifted with the transition from day to night tours was the focus on what might be considered scenic. Night tours gravitated away from the picturesque landscape scenery of the Hudson River School and focused instead on the monuments of civilization: the Statue of Liberty, Grant's Tomb, and palatial houses such as the Vanderbilt Mansion at Hyde Park. These are the kinds of constructions that seem worthy of the term "monuments"—thus they are the antithesis of what Robert Smithson deemed the monuments of Passaic. For Smithson the derelict structures of Passaic were "anti-monuments . . . the opposite of the romantic ruin."[67] Smithson's tour had no highlights to offer; it repudiated the anticipatory tone of romantic travelogues in favor of a litany of the commonplace.[68] Michelson's monuments of the industrial infrastructure—piers and loading docks, channel markers, rusted barges, factories, and power plants—are also remarkably quotidian structures. Their power lies in repetition: the panoramas of ruin that we confront in both *Mespat* and *Shattemuc* are devastating precisely because of their ubiquity.

Shattemuc compresses the two viewing experiences of the Hudson River cruises—those that focused on the natural, scenic landscape and those that focused on manmade monuments—into a single nighttime sequence, but the progression from the first type to the next is maintained. In his exhibition notes, Michelson elaborates on the significance of this sequencing, writing that the earlier segment is "nature-dominated" and focuses on the densely wooded shoreline along Hook Mountain State Park, while the second segment "depicts the largely industrial shoreline of Haverstraw, the site of major mining and brick plants in the eighteenth and nineteenth centuries,

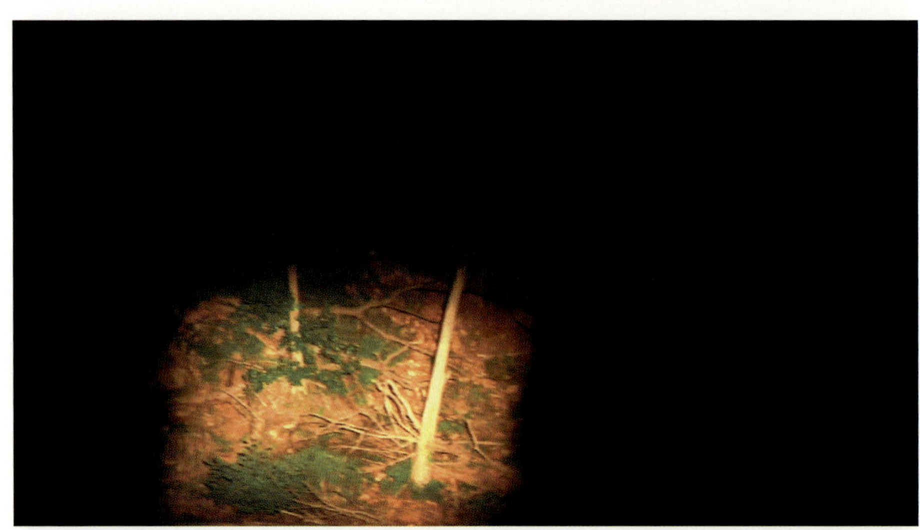

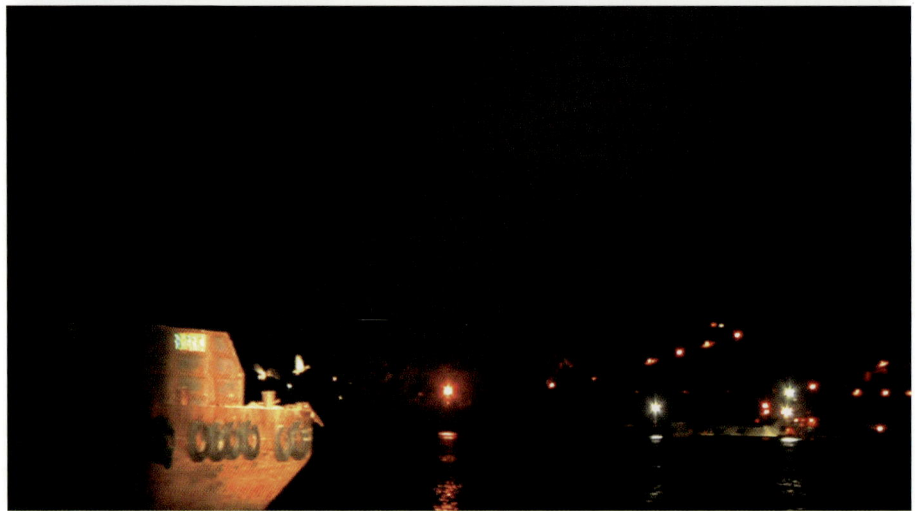

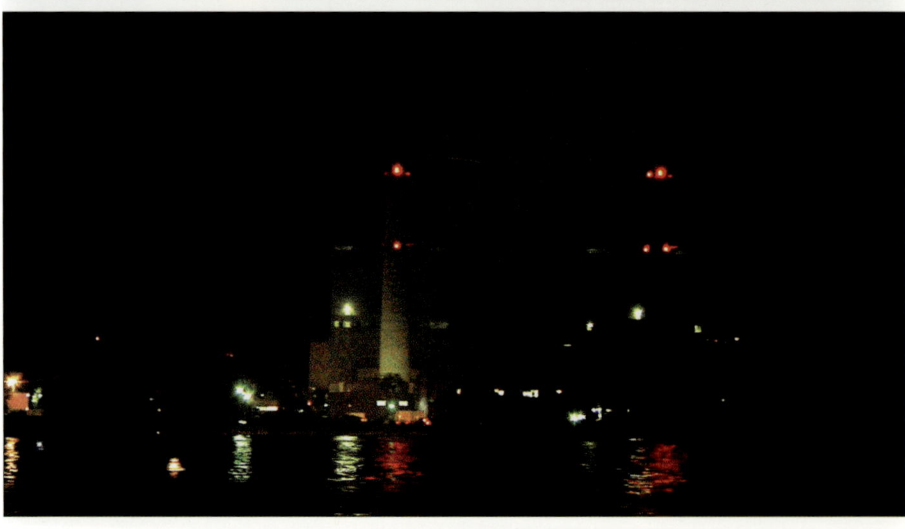

and the present site of rock quarries, a gypsum plant, and a coal-burning power plant."[69] Both shorelines are documented in the present, but they become symbolic of different eras, with Hook Mountain standing in for both the precolonial and colonial periods. Michelson describes the landscape of Hook Mountain as a place "which for eons sheltered Indian tribes and in 1609 was the site of a bloody battle between Henry Hudson's crew and the local Indians over a pillow and shirts."[70] Read in this way, the landscape segments of *Shattemuc* seem to roll out in succession from the precolonial to the colonial period and from there into the present, the decolonial era. Or to put it another way, the landscape transitions from a preindustrial to an industrial state and, given the derelict structures shown at Haverstraw, quite possibly a postindustrial state as well. This sequencing imparts to *Shattemuc* a narrative structure that neither *Mespat* nor Smithson's "The Monuments of Passaic" nor even Michelson's *TwoRow II* demonstrate, despite the contributions of literal narrators in the latter two works.

The implied temporal narrative of *Shattemuc* allies the piece with a series of three video canvases that Michelson produced for the Royal Ontario Museum in Toronto, titled *Of Light after Darkness* (2007). Each thirty-one-minute digital video in this installation shows the sun going down in real time at a site that is integral to the history of colonialism or industrialization in Ontario. The first work in the series pictures Fort York, a military garrison erected by the British in 1793 that is now a national historic site, the second video captures images of the Stelco Steel Mill belching smoke into the skies over Hamilton Bay, and the third is of wind turbines located at Port Burwell on Lake Erie. In a rather sardonic gesture toward the sublime landscape tradition, Michelson displayed the videos on monitors framed in gilded wood, in the guise of nineteenth-century landscape paintings.[71] In fact, *Of Light after Darkness* is explicitly modeled after the work of Cole, one of the founding members of the Hudson River School of painting. Cole was known for his scenic views of the Catskills, the Connecticut River Valley, and the Hudson River, as well as for allegorical series such as *The Course of Empire* (1832–36) and *The Voyage of Life* (1842). As a graduate of the School of the Museum of Fine Arts in Boston, Michelson is well-versed in the romantic traditions promulgated by the Hudson River School painters, and it was Cole's *The Course of Empire* that provided inspiration for *Of Light after Darkness* and, I suggest, for *Shattemuc*.[72]

4.12 Alan Michelson (Mohawk, b. 1953)
Shattemuc (2009)
Video (30:59 min.), soundtrack with original music by Laura Ortman
Courtesy of the artist. Photograph by André Costantini. Collection of the artist

Cole's series consisted of five separate majestic landscape compositions, each intended to portray a stage in the cycle of human civilization. The empire is fictitious; it progresses from a vaguely American *Savage State* (peopled by tiny American Indian hunters "attired in skins," pursuing their prey through the wilderness) to an *Arcadian State*, then through more explicitly Romanized versions of *Consummation of Empire* and *Destruction of Empire*. The series ends in a final state of *Desolation*.[73] According to the authors of *American Encounters: Art, History, and Cultural Identity*, Cole's series reflected his growing concern with Jacksonian-era notions of progress, unfettered growth, and westward expansion: "He believed that no society, however powerful, could endure forever. Civilizations, like individuals, begin in youth and glory but conclude in disillusionment and death. For Cole's American viewers, the issue was not whether his vision was correct, but whether it applied to *them*. Was the doom foretold in *The Course of Empire*—the passage from greatness to destruction—a record of past civilizations or a prophecy about the future of the United States itself?"[74]

Time passes in the course of Cole's series, the sun rises and sets, and the seasons change; however, all the events take place in a single location, and the environment is irrevocably scarred in the process. The three panels of Michelson's *Of Light after Darkness* compress this cycle into fewer "moments" and distribute the impact of empire building over three separate landscapes, but they also progress sequentially. According to Michelson, "Each site represents a different environmental era—past, present, future—in the colonization and development of the area."[75] Like Cole, Michelson assigned each panel a different title—*Gloom of Approaching Night*, *Dying Day*, and *Glorious Light of the Setting Sun*—all aptly chosen for scenes filmed at sunset, and all culled from the writings of photographer Edward S. Curtis (1868–1952), master perpetrator of the trope of the "vanishing Indian."[76]

Adopting *The Course of Empire* as his model for *Of Light after Darkness*, Michelson expanded the investigation of ruin that commenced with *Mespat* to consider the *inevitability* of the decline of systems, infrastructures, and even civilizations. With this turn, Michelson also deepened his engagement with Smithson, whose intention (as cited earlier in this chapter) was to "make entropy visible." Entropy is sometimes defined as the degree of disorder or randomness in a system, but in Smithson's view, the most compelling aspect of the second law of thermodynamics is the assurance that all systems *progress* toward a state of randomness. Entropy tells us that nothing can stay in suspension forever; dissolution is inevitable. In part, Smithson's dedication to showing structures in decline is what led Owens to conclude as early as 1979 that Smithson's work was a fundamentally postmodern project. Owens recognized Smithson's output as a poststructuralist attack on language and narrative, a deconstruction of hierarchy, and an emptying out of the center (in this case New York City) through engagement with the peripheries.[77] A postmodern condition that Owens failed to locate in Smithson's work is an attack on the idea of progress itself, though it seems clear in retrospect that Smithson's careful documentation of the decline of industrial infrastructures was exactly that. Moreover, it is this latter aspect of Smithson's practice that resonates strongly in Michelson's work, particularly in *Shattemuc*, where the notion of progress is conflated with settler colonialism, and thus its dissolution can be regarded as not only a postmodern but a distinctly decolonial condition.

It may seem paradoxical to think of decline in positive, even optimistic terms, but this makes particular sense for Indigenous peoples whose populations, cultures, and natural resources have been relentlessly assaulted in the name of progress. In her article "Settler Monuments, Indigenous Memory: Dis-membering and Re-membering Canadian Art History," Ruth Phillips argues that the efforts of Indigenous artists to interrogate, undermine, and ultimately "dis-member" settler monuments—such as Onondaga Iroquois photographer Jeffrey Thomas's portraits of Native people posing on the plinths of the Champlain monument in Ottawa—are best understood in the wider context of decolonial political movements. Thomas's photographs, such as *Seize the Space, Buffalo Boy* (2012; figure 4.13) wrest control over public discursive space, and in so doing, they seriously disrupt the master narrative of Canada's settler society.[78] According to Phillips, this is especially important for signaling the decline of the colonial era in North America: "In contrast to former external colonies, for internally colonized peoples there have been no definitive acts of political liberation, and no formal closure to the colonial era. . . . The lack of formal closure on a political level has given special prominence to activist projects within the sphere of the visual arts."[79]

The strategies of these "activist" art projects vary considerably, even within the oeuvre of a single artist. In Michelson's case it can be argued that *Mespat* and *Shattemuc* hasten recognition of the closure of the industrial era by documenting it in ruins; Michelson's adoption of Smithson's stance on "anti-monuments" further undermines the mythologies of settler colonialism. *Shattemuc* and *Third Bank of the River*, like many of the other works discussed in this chapter, also extend the sites of Indigenous intervention into the colonial narrative from the centers of power (emphasized in Phillips's essay) to multiple sites on the peripheries. In Phillips's estimation, however, the most effective strategy for reclaiming ideological territory—for intervening in the "commemorative landscapes of settler nations"—is the simple but profound declaration of contemporary Indigenous presence. She writes that a "key strategy of [Thomas's] interrogation of the Champlain monument is the juxtaposition of images that contrast the specificity and immediacy of living people and popular culture with the generality and romanticization of historic monuments."[80]

Writing in 2002, Phillips concluded that the sustained efforts of activist artists to that date had made significant inroads into destabilizing the rhetoric of settler monuments but that they had not yet affected a total sea change in this regard. She wrote, "Interventions similar to those discussed in this essay have steadily increased in major Canadian institutions of art and culture for almost two decades, but they have not yet destabilized the fundamental narratives in which settler monuments are embedded. [Robert] Houle and Thomas, like their contemporaries, do not resolve the problem of

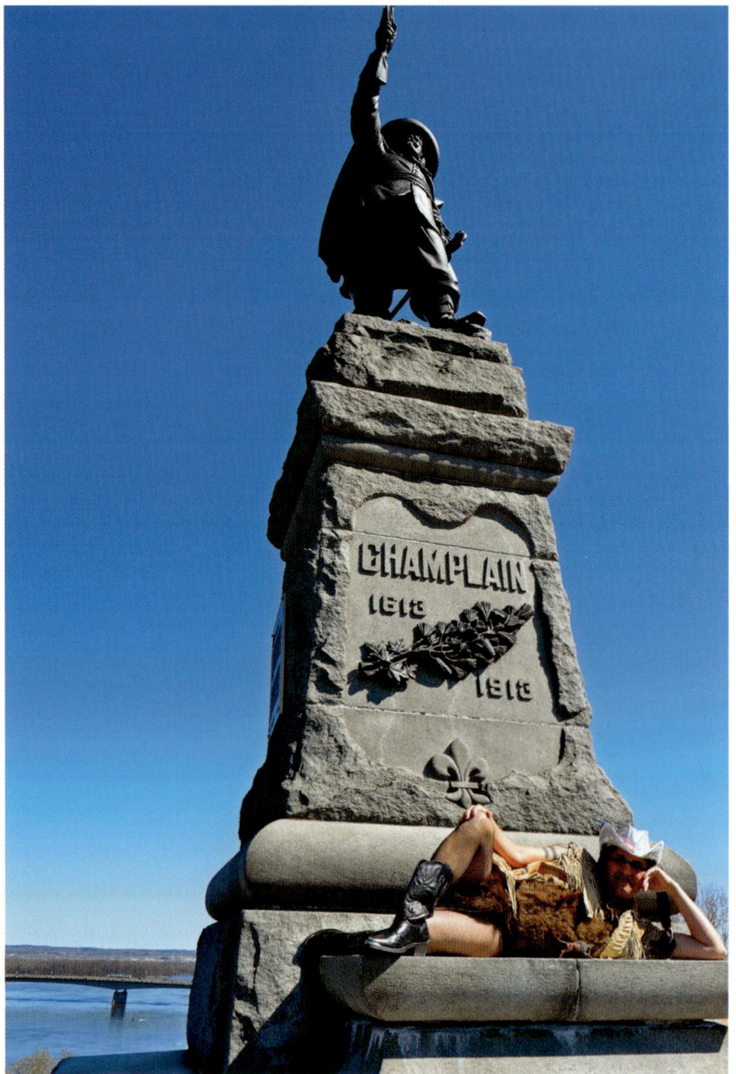

4.13 Jeffrey Thomas (Onondaga Iroquois, b. 1956)
Seize the Space, Buffalo Boy (2012)
Pigment print on archival paper, 20 × 30 inches
Courtesy of the artist
Collection of the artist

postcolonial memory, but, rather, place quotation marks around the monuments of settler historical memory."[81] It is fair to say that in the years since the publication of Phillips's article, there has been a shift in artistic energies away from the interrogation of settler monuments toward the construction of entirely Indigenous ones. Expanding on Phillips's argument, I have posited in this chapter that virtually all of the site-specific, land-based installations discussed herein—from Postcommodity's *Do You Remember When?* to Michelson's *Third Bank of the River*—assume the function of monuments by simultaneously marking space and claiming place. Once again, however, their temporal ethos is different from that of settler monuments, which are oriented toward the past. Indigenous monuments look to both the past and the future while rooting us firmly in the present.

Consider Michelson's video trilogy *Of Light after Darkness*, for example: even as Michelson seems to embrace the inevitability of decline, he does not leave us in desolation as Cole did. While the titles of the individual works in the trilogy (e.g., *Dying Day*) reinforce Edward Curtis's notion of the sun setting on the Indian race, the title of the series itself contradicts it, suggesting instead that there is hope—or light—on the horizon. Indeed, Michelson explicitly designates the final frame of the series, which depicts an Ontario wind farm, as a vision of the future. *Of Light after Darkness* leaves open the possibility that with the fall of empire comes the possibility of renewal, of a more sustainable future. In *Shattemuc* too there is room for reinterpretation of the final scene: in the closing moments of the film, the camera pans away from the shoreline of the Hudson River and out onto the surface of the water in the center of the river channel. In the final seconds, as the image fades and the end title appears, there is a fleeting moment of regression, as if the boat is turning or *re*-turning to its point of origin.[82]

Michelson's work conceives of time on a vast scale, then, but one that unfurls as a boundless spiral rather than on a linear course.[83] This perspective, which situates moments of closure within a larger cycle of processes of renewal, is made explicit in the plans for the artist's most recent land-based installation, *Mantle* (2018; figure 4.14). Commissioned by the State of Virginia for installation in Richmond's Capitol Square Park, *Mantle* is a true monument in every sense of the word: it is a large-scale public installation intended to commemorate the events of human history, in this case to acknowledge and honor the original inhabitants of the Chesapeake region.[84] Michelson's design pays homage to the revered seventeenth-century Chief Powhatan (d. 1618) and the confederacy of thirty-four Algonquian tribes that were united under his leadership. *Mantle* refers in its title and its design to a ceremonial deerskin garment known as Powhatan's Mantle that is embellished with shell embroidery in the shape of spiral motifs that are said to represent the tribes of the confederacy.[85]

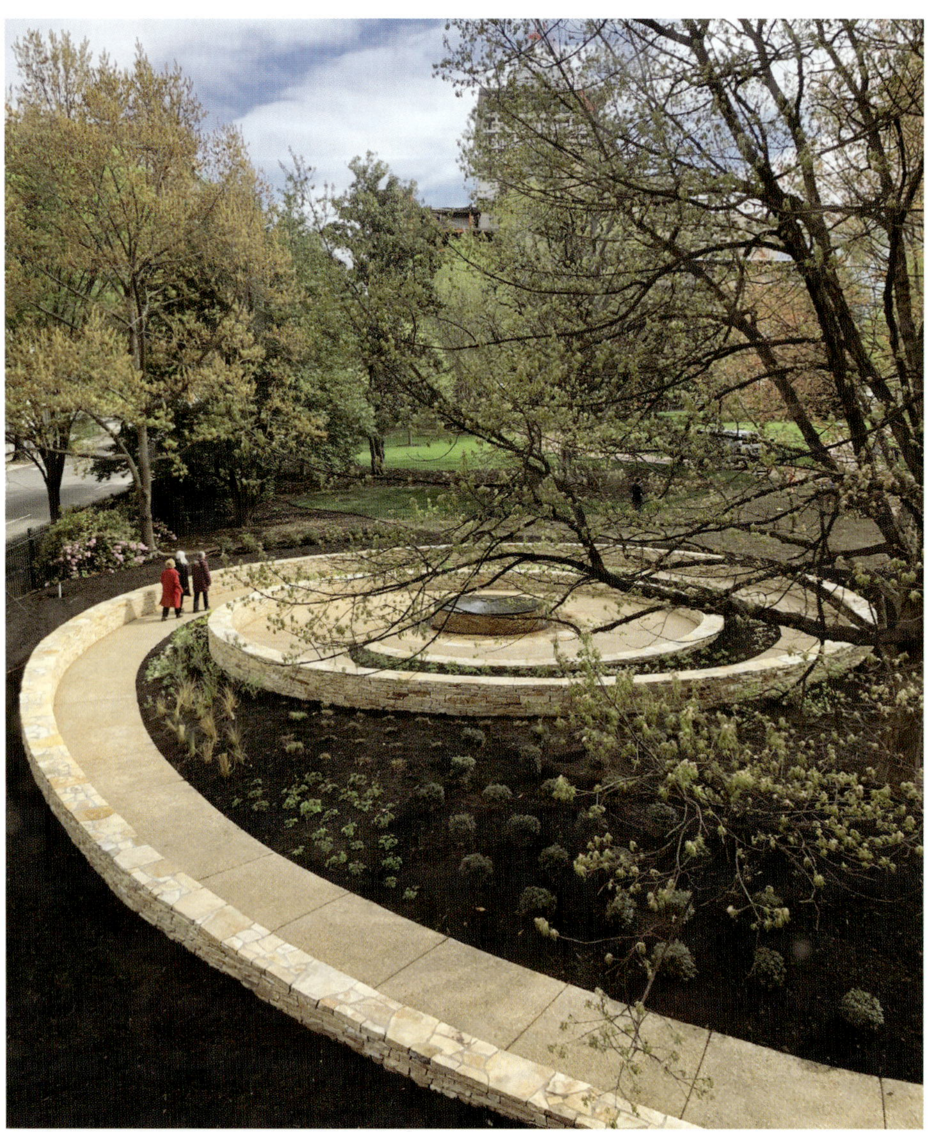

4.14 Alan Michelson (Mohawk, b. 1953)
Mantle (2018)
Stone, earth, concrete, plants, fountain, 4,200 square feet
Courtesy of the artist. Photograph by Justin Gunther.
Capitol Square Park, Richmond, Virginia

Not content to memorialize human history alone, Michelson has packed *Mantle* with references to natural history as well. His project description notes that "mantle" is also a term for a section of the earth's crust (a shrewd gesture to the "center of the earth") and that the spiral path of the monument "rises out of and returns to the earth."[86] Moreover, *Mantle* incorporates life-sized cast images of corn, squash, and bean plants embedded along the edges of the reflecting pool at the work's center, much like the plants and animals of the extinct ecosystem of Collect Pond embellished *Earth's Eye* in Manhattan twenty-five years earlier.[87] Finally, Michelson describes the spiral form of the monument as being inspired by the shell of a still-living but truly ancient sea creature, the chambered nautilus.

Of all of *Mantle*'s allusions to the landscape, natural history, and geological time, perhaps none is more profound than its affinity to Smithson's monumental earthwork, *Spiral Jetty*, constructed in the Great Salt Lake in Utah in 1970. Though earthworks emerged out of the minimalist art movement of the 1960s, these monumental land-based structures have long been suspected of harboring greater symbolic meaning than their geometrically determined, gallery-based counterparts.[88] In the case of *Spiral Jetty*, Smithson expanded on the basic polyhedral vocabulary of minimalism to include what he considered an equally "primary" structure, the spiral. As a devotee of the natural sciences, Smithson regarded the spiral as perhaps *the* fundamental shape of life—it was the form of galaxies and DNA, of fractals and fingerprints. Projecting *Spiral Jetty* into the Great Salt Lake allowed Smithson to reach back deep into geologic time, to the very origins of life in a salty sea. Michelson's adoption of the spiral form in *Mantle* acknowledges all of this cosmic history, merging it seamlessly with human history and cultural memory.

Finally, according to Michelson, *Mantle* also draws on ancient traditions of contemplation itself: the spiraling path is meant to inspire reflection, as landscaped labyrinths have for thousands of years. Yet *Mantle* is not just a space for passive remembrance, and Michelson is not content to merely document or commemorate vanished peoples and ecosystems. His intention is to foster the renewal of Native life in the Virginia capital, beginning with the restoration of the Native habitat: *Mantle* is surrounded by groves of replanted crepe myrtle and American holly, chestnut, oak, and magnolia trees. As visitors to *Mantle* move deeper into the earth along the spiraling path of the monument, they are immersed in the sights and sounds and smells of a living, breathing natural environment. Michelson writes that *Mantle* "requires the visitor to neither look up nor look down, but invites one to enter—from the east—and participate in it. It is not conceived as a static monument to be venerated but an active one to be experienced by moving off the everyday grid and into the American Indian circle."[89] In this last respect, *Mantle* demonstrates the unique ability of contemporary landscape sculpture and installation art to move beyond the visual into the realm of fully haptic experience.

CHAPTER FIVE

The Embodied Landscape

There is no such thing as a landscape without human figures, whether or not figures exist there.

CHARLES HARRISON

I HAVE DELAYED DISCUSSION OF THE FIGURE IN NATIVE AMERICAN LANDSCAPE representation for this final chapter, though by now it is obvious that the body permeates every aspect of this book, from the shift in attention of contemporary landscape theory away from the tacit acceptance of a disembodied eye to consideration of the whole phenomenological self; to recognition of the painting as a stand-in for the body of the artist, especially in WalkingStick's and Lavadour's work; and to contemplation of the way that the body of the viewer is interpellated by landscape installations. One reason for avoiding the figure until now is that there is a tendency among viewers and scholars to allow the landscape to slip silently into the background once our attention is drawn to the figural or narrative content in a work of art. Another compelling reason to have kept this topic in reserve stems from the recognition of the pivotal role that the presence (or absence) of the figure has played in European representations of the Native landscape, especially those traditions that Mitchell refers to as being "intimately bound up with the discourses of imperialism."[1] On the one hand, a landscape that is absent inhabitants may seem to be more accommodating to potential settlement, but on the other hand, a landscape totally devoid of human occupation may seem dauntingly inhospitable. A "solution" to this problem in many European depictions of the colonial periphery was to acknowledge Indigenous occupation of the land but to diminish that presence by shrinking the figures to insignificant scale or, alternatively, to so romanticize the figures as to consign them to an ineffectual, premodern state.[2] Clearly, none of these approaches to the figure would be acceptable in Native portrayals of the landscape.

WalkingStick, who has abandoned and returned to the figure more than once in her painting career, comments that the struggle to divest her figures from "the romantic thing that always attaches to them in nineteenth-century paintings" led her to avoid direct references to the body in her diptych paintings in the 1980s and 1990s.[3] In the late 1990s, however, WalkingStick spent extended periods of time teaching in Rome, and figures began to resurface in her work there. She writes of this moment: "The move to figures seemed inevitable, although I hadn't depicted humans in my paintings for many years. In fact, their absence had seemed crucial to the significance of the work. It had been the uninhabited landscape I had sought in relation to the eternal."[4] The first figures to (re)enter WalkingStick's uninhabited landscapes—such as the seated form on the far right in *Il Sogno, II* (1998) and the kneeling nude in *Blame the Mountains III* (1998; figure 5.1)—are shown as mere outlines, thus the body is made up of the same substance as the land. Importantly, the body depicted in these paintings is WalkingStick's own: there are no surrogates here, just the artist, joined with the earth. In the case of *Blame the Mountains III*—in which the contour lines of the mountain range and the artist's back and shoulders align—the close association of the body with the landscape exposes the vulnerability of both entities, which allies the work with many of the earlier diptychs, especially *Venere Alpina* (1997). *Venere Alpina*, which pairs an image of a mountain ridge on one side of the diptych with a steel mesh panel that is ripped open to expose glistening red sequins, signifies the desecration of the environment yet also affirms the sacredness of the earth.[5] According to WalkingStick, *Venere Alpina* led her to recognize that her painted landscapes had essentially always been incarnate, a stand-in for her own suffering yet resilient body.

More often than not, the embodied landscapes are also overtly sensual, and the figures that emerged into or out of them in the 2000s were increasingly joyous, as demonstrated by the dancing, cavorting figures of *Gioioso, Variation I* and *Gioioso, Variation II* (both 2001).[6] The flattened silhouettes of these later works recall the figures that populated WalkingStick's paintings nearly thirty years earlier: these were precisely drawn figures arranged in compressed, antinatural spaces. Looking back on the period roughly from 1971 to 1973, the artist recalls that "it was the depiction of space and shape that interested me. I liked the idea of using figures in the painting, but I wanted to make a contemporary statement about figures in space."[7] Thus the nude forms in *Me and My Neon Box* (1971) and *April Contemplating May* (1972) are reduced to silhouettes to emphasize the flatness of the space they inhabit and to underscore their modernity.[8] Moreover, WalkingStick manipulated the color fields to interrupt the temptation to read the compositions as other than compressed: the negative spaces formed between the figures become abstracted shapes in their own right, confusing the relationship between figure and ground. Despite

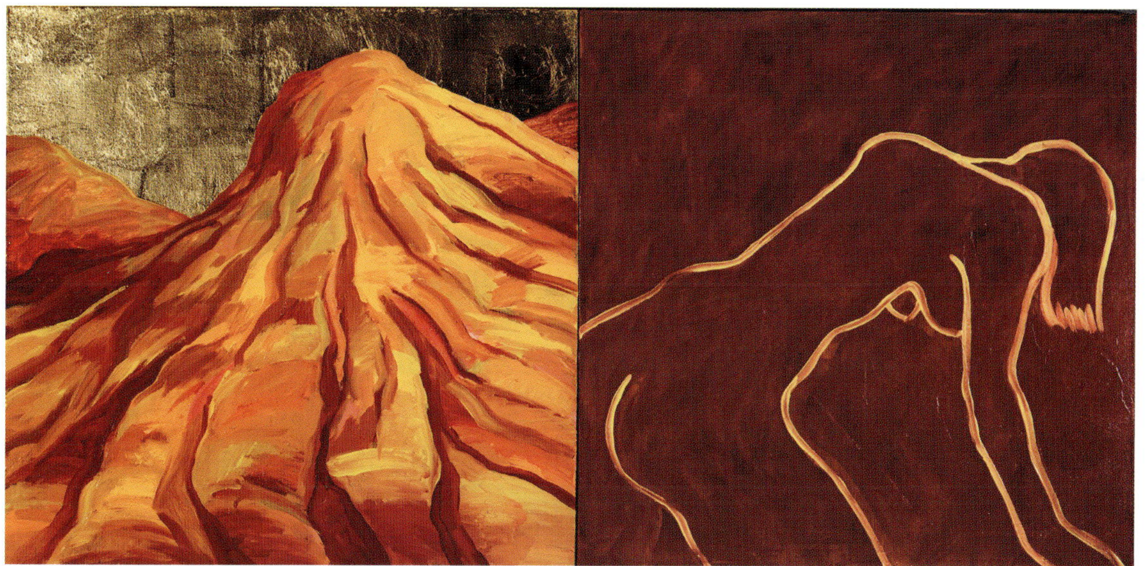

5.1 Kay WalkingStick (Cherokee, b. 1935)
Blame the Mountains III (1998)
Oil and brass leaf on canvas, 32 × 64 inches
Copyright Kay WalkingStick. Courtesy of the artist.
Collection of Allentown Art Museum

the spatial ambiguities and the paucity of detail in these paintings, there is nothing generic or impersonal about the figures, which are again based on the artist's own body. That the bodies in question are sensual, even sexual bodies is made clear by the shading of the genitalia. As WalkingStick put it, "There is a joyousness in their nakedness, rather than nudity. They are enjoying their bodies. A lot of that early work was really about feminism and my own recognition of my own sexuality."[9]

When WalkingStick entered graduate school at Pratt in 1973, her attention shifted to more devout forms of abstraction, and the figure disappeared from her work. Yet the sensuality remained, transferred from the subject matter into the substance of the paintings. With the addition of wax, the previously thin acrylic paint became denser and more lustrous, and her surfaces grew more visceral and expressive. "It made this lovely surface," WalkingStick recalls, "I just fell in love with the surface. I had always loved paint, this physical, joyous thing."[10] By the time WalkingStick began applying layers of material to her canvases with her bare hands, the surface and its substrates had become the focus of the work, and the landscape was poised to emerge, ostensibly free of the figure. That landscape held center stage for nearly two decades, but in retrospect it is plain to see why WalkingStick would characterize the return to the figure in 2000 as “inevitable”: the body has always been present in her paintings. Early on, the figures were overt, though enticingly mingled with the flattened planes of indistinct interior spaces; subsequently, they were subsumed into the material of the minimalist paintings. Finally, the figure resurfaced, now absolutely integral to the landscape. In its mature form, the figural landscape conveys WalkingStick’s holistic view of life, the body, and art: “One of the subjects of my paintings has always been the unity of humans. The figure makes this more explicit, this shared human experience in this wonderful body we all have. The figure, the body in my paintings, has become a unifying force.”[11]

The reconciliation of the figure and the landscape that WalkingStick achieved has remained elusive to other Native artists, including Lavadour. Like WalkingStick, Lavadour embraced the figure early in his career: he found it essential to conveying what he wanted to say about difficult topics such as sex and death, alcohol addiction, loss, and the darker side of life on the reservation.[12] Rather quickly though, despite the favorable reaction such images garnered in the art press, Lavadour became disenchanted with the figure and with narrative content in his art. He turned instead to the landscape, in a measured course of change that is reminiscent of WalkingStick’s experience. In a review of Lavadour’s work at the Cliff Michel gallery in Seattle in 1990, the art critic Lyn Smallwood remarked: “In the mid-’80s, Lavadour was painting human figures in a furiously swiped-out expressionist style. Gradually the backgrounds seem to have assumed more interest for him, and he began suppressing the figures. But . . . the human figures did not go away. They seem instead to have escaped into the earth, occasionally breaking out in ghostly heads and torsos adrift among the peaks, or in rocks laid bare like gnashing teeth. Lavadour’s land is, then, possessed by restless spirits.”[13]

Lavadour’s willingness to let the figures disperse into the earth only to reappear as ghostly fragments draws its inspiration from both Native and non-Native sources. Countless Indigenous creation stories, including one involving Coyote that Lavadour specifically relates to his work, revolve around the notion that the ancient earth was shaped by animate forces that remain visible to this day in particular landscape features.[14] The uncanny way that bodies seem to meld with the elements in Lavadour’s paintings is also indebted to an iconic American landscape painter, Albert Pinkham Ryder, whose allegorical seascape *The Flying Dutchman* (1887) Lavadour viewed in 1986.[15] Though the bones, skulls, and ghostly specters faded from Lavadour’s images after 1991, they have never been fully vanquished: two skulls, one human and one animal, feature prominently in the monumental composition *Naming Tanager* (2001). In that composition, the skulls allude to another set of creation stories, the sweat lodge ceremonies in which all living creatures (including the Western Tanager) received their names.[16] For the most part, Lavadour’s figures did not make the transition from conveying pain and anguish to embodying joyous, sensual energy the way that WalkingStick's did, and the dark psychology that cleaved to them was increasingly out of sync with the artist's more optimistic worldview, and with his ethics of painting. As an adherent of the Bahá'í faith, Lavadour believes that the purpose of art is to edify humanity: "I want art to be fruitful, I want it to be uplifting, I want it to be somehow expanding perceptions. . . . I want it to be humanitarian."[17] To this end, Lavadour has embraced his role as a conduit of energy and creative force. The body—his body—is essential to the work, but it is felt rather than seen.

PLACES OF EMERGENCE

Jeffrey Gibson (Mississippi Band of Choctaw/Cherokee), whose fanciful landscapes were featured in the National Museum of the American Indian exhibition *Off the Map: Landscape in the Native Imagination* in 2007, has been explicit in chronicling the emergence of human figures in his already richly representational paintings. Gibson, who was educated at the School of the Art Institute of Chicago and the Royal Academy of Art in London, remarks that he was wary of introducing the figure into the fertile environments of such paintings as *Camouflage* (2004) and *The First Principle* (2004) because "the Native experience is that an occupied landscape is destined to become imbalanced and ultimately dystopic."[18] Even without the figure, Gibson's lush tropical paradises are simultaneously alluring and disquieting. *Camouflage*, a 30-by-31-inch oil painting on board, evokes a watery blue idyll, with its saturated blue and green washes literally flooding the canvas. An accretion of pigmented silicone beads drip, flow, and very nearly crawl across the painted surface of the work, enticing and entangling the viewer in a torrent of tropical kitsch. *Camouflage* is deceptive, however; its very title suggests that something ominous lurks in the dense foliage. This sense of foreboding is heightened in the slightly larger *The First Principle*, which Gibson says represents his attempt to imagine "what creatures might be able to survive" in his dark gardens. In the 46-by-56-inch painting, Gibson allows us a glimpse into a small clearing in which an enigmatic object resembling a nest is suspended in a network of vines. Radiating outward from this static core is a swirl of brightly colored forms that resemble yet never fully coalesce into the flora and fauna of the rainforest. The question of what creatures might endure here goes unanswered: Gibson remarks that he is still not sure whether the proto-organisms that surround the clearing "emanate from the nest or are threatening to devour it."[19]

For nearly a year after he created *Camouflage* and *The First Principle*, Gibson forestalled the entrance of fully fleshed life-forms into his imaginary landscapes, but like WalkingStick he concedes that the move to the figure was inevitable. *Natura Non Facit Saltum* (2005; figure 5.2) and *Realms of Fin, Feet and Wing* (2005) attest to Gibson's conviction that life evolves, albeit slowly. (*Natura Non Facit Saltum* reminds us that "nature makes no great leaps.")[20] The inexorable drift toward the figure in the landscape finally culminated in Gibson's works of late 2005, including *The Urge That Binds*, *The Infinite Third Dimension*, *All That Matters*, and *State of Emergency*, as well as *Psychic Roots*—paintings that embrace the full continuum of human sexuality as a foundational condition of the utopian ideal. Though there is no pictorial record to show that the entrance of the figure into Gibson's landscapes caused them to become "imbalanced and ultimately dystopic" as the artist had feared, it is nevertheless clear that Gibson remained uneasy about their presence. To accompany the suite of landscape paintings from this period that were exhibited in *Off the Map*, Gibson created an entirely new work, the enticingly titled *Submerge* (2007), which may or may not have included figures. We will never know because the artist obscured most of the surface of the canvas with a thick film of black spray paint, leaving us only a glimpse of the landscape and whatever might have existed within it.

The turn toward working with spray paint was an important one for Gibson: he experimented with the medium over the next few years in the series of untitled works on paper collectively referred to as the *Red Black White* series (2007) and in many related paintings on canvas in 2008 including *Singular* and *Surveillance*. All of the compositions after *Submerge* juxtapose layers of acrylic or oil paint laid down in clean-edged and precise vertical, horizontal, and diagonal lines and spray paint applied in broad, loose gestures that feel almost like acts of vandalism. Writing about Gibson's work for the Eiteljorg Fellowship for Native American Fine Art in 2009, Jimmie Durham likened these striped works to musical compositions, acknowledging their rhythmic and improvisational qualities. What is harder to determine is whether the works have any lingering connection to the lush primordial landscapes that predate them. The impressive size and horizontal orientation of *Submerge*, at 7 by 10 feet, implies at least a vestige of connection to landscape representation that the striped paintings do not share. On the contrary, the resolutely human scale of *Surveillance* (with a height of 60 inches, or 5 feet) combined with the strong vertical composition of the image hint at an indistinct figure that is both veiled and literally watched over.[21] In every case there is a notable shift in the character of the figure and its surroundings away from a predominantly natural, primordial, or even Edenic environs to a contemporary urban one. Using the quintessential urban art medium—Day-Glo spray paint—Gibson infuses the linear grids of works like *Metropolis* (2007) with the rebellious energy of graffiti and in the process raises a host of thorny issues regarding privacy and individual freedom in civil society (e.g., in *Surveillance*, *Singular*, and *Wrapped and Bound*).

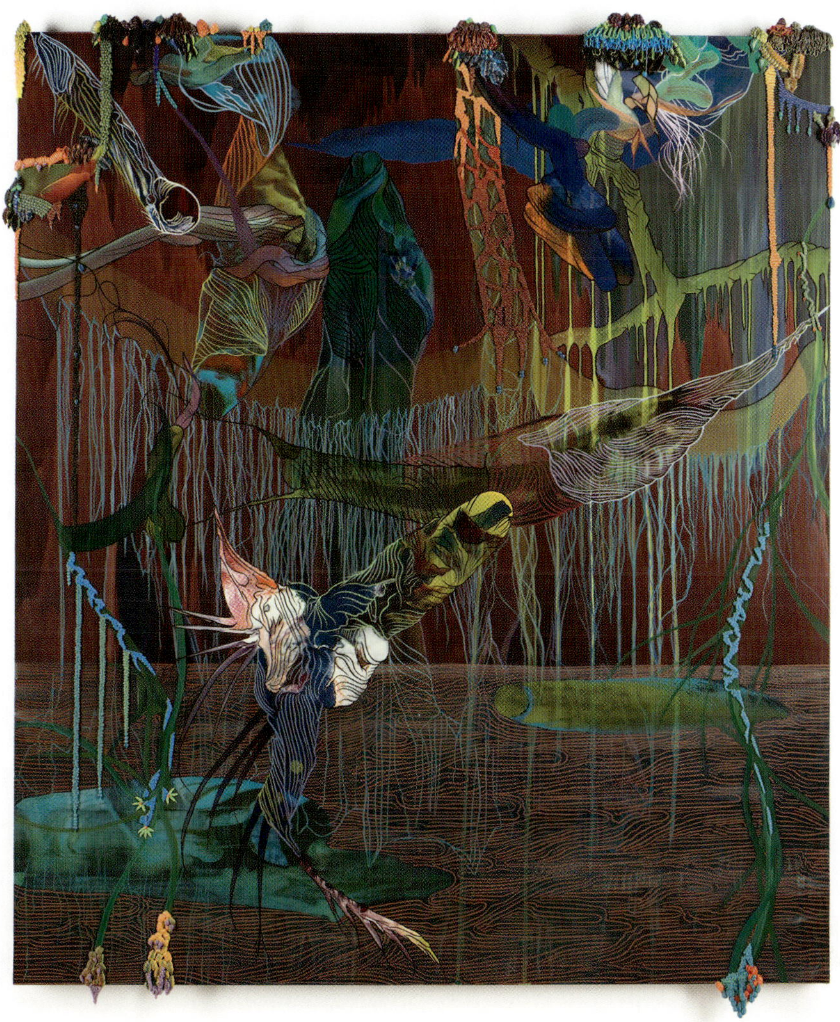

5.2 Jeffrey Gibson (Choctaw/Cherokee, b. 1972)
Natura Non Facit Saltum (2005)
Oil and pigmented silicone on board, 30 × 31 inches
Courtesy of the artist
Collection of the artist

The shift in Gibson's milieu from the mythical wilds to the metropolis is also indicated in the wry title given to the artist's solo show at the National Academy Museum in New York City in 2013: *Said the Pigeon to the Squirrel*. The title substitutes the denizens of the city for the anthropomorphized creatures of the forest, desert, and mountains that populate Indigenous creation stories.[22] The works in this exhibition are even further removed from the natural worlds of Gibson's earlier paintings in the degree to which they are abstract, non-gestural, and highly disciplined. The fifty-five-part drawing *Infinite Sampling* (2010), for example, is a nearly obsessive investigation into the limits of geometric abstraction, particularly its capacity to deny representation. Gibson remarks, "I feel like it's such an image saturated world . . . that I made a conscious decision to focus on the formal elements that construct image, and hold them at this point before they become image."[23] Accompanying this retreat from representation is an expanding interest in material. *Infinite Sampling* incorporates graphite, watercolor, acrylic paint, tape, and thread, and the paintings from the same period boast a range of materials drawn from traditional Native American art practices, including deer hide and sinew.[24] In the latter examples, Gibson plays with both the form and function of traditional Plains parfleches, rawhide containers typically painted in bright geometric designs that also appear in Kay WalkingStick's landscape paintings in this same period. The term "parfleche," which means "to turn away arrows" in French, was incorrectly applied to the storage containers in the nineteenth century because they were made of the same material as the rawhide shields used by Plains warriors. Gibson riffs on this moment of cultural misunderstanding in a series of hide-wrapped and painted ironing boards, which he refers to as *Shields* (2012).[25]

SKIN

Whether stretched over found objects like antique mirrors and ironing boards, or minimalist boxes and fluorescent light fixtures, animal skin as Gibson uses it evokes the body in fascinating ways, just when the landscape as subject has seemingly disappeared from the work.[26] A view of Gibson's exhibitions between 2012 and 2014 gives the impression that the body simply walked off the canvas into real space, morphing into sculptural forms. Perhaps an argument could be made that the same thing had happened to his landscapes a few years earlier, that they too had spilled out of the frame and into the gallery in works such as *The Becoming* (2006) and *Promise* (2007).[27] The gradual transition in Gibson's work from painting to sculpture and installation alters our understanding of the figure and the environment in ways that are somewhat different than what we have seen so far. For WalkingStick and Lavadour, both the painting and the landscape are extensions of the artist's own body; for Michelson and other sculptors and installation artists, the body that figures most prominently in the artistic equation is the viewer's body, cast into a physical relationship with the environment. In Gibson's work, the sculpted form represents neither the artist nor the viewer; rather, the body is distinct from and external to both. Consider, for example, Gibson's account of the genesis of the series of embellished vinyl punching bags that includes *Deep Blue Day* (2014;

figure 5.3), *The Quiet One* (2012), *Atomic* (2013), and *Storyteller* (2014), to name but a few. Gibson had been exercising with a physical trainer, kick-boxing against a heavy Everlast bag. He recalls, "I began to appreciate the bag itself as a form hanging from the ceiling, formally, but also as a stand-in for a body. . . . The bodily-ness of the bag interested me."[28] Gibson's hanging sculptures become bodies in dialogue with ours. And they are kinetic, swinging freely from the ceiling when pushed; even when they are not touched directly, the tin jingles and fringe attachments sway and rustle with passing air currents.[29] The kinetics are crucial to understanding these works, which are embellished with glass beads, shells, and recycled wool and shawl fragments—materials typically associated with powwow dance regalia. Like dancers or boxers, they *move*.

Gibson's material citation of jingle dresses in particular and his selection of titles such as *Tomboy* (2012), *American Girl* (2013), and *She Walks Lightly* (2013) indicate that in these pieces, the body of the other is not only a gendered body but is more often than not coded as female.[30] This is an uneasy association, given that the female forms in question here continue to function as punching bags, but I do not believe that the works signify aggression toward women. On the contrary, as a gay man, Gibson has repeatedly stated his interest in pushing the limits of gender and sexual expression; in 2014 he added the presumably self-referential *New York City Boy* and *People Like Us* to the growing compendium of Everlast sculptures.[31] Rather, like the earth as depicted in WalkingStick's *Venere Alpina*, Gibson's corporeal forms are lovingly embroidered, consecrated bodies that prove their resilience under duress.

The implied association of the canvas with the afflicted body allies Gibson's work (and WalkingStick's) with other contemporary Indigenous art projects, such as Nadia Myre's *The Scar Project* (2006–13). Myre, the creator of *For Those Who Cannot Speak*, has been exploring the expressive capacity of the canvas as a surrogate skin for more than a decade. Each of the more than 1,400 individual 10-inch-square canvases included in *The Scar Project* bears a "wound" that is incompletely mended. Each represents a real or metaphorical, physical or psychic injury suffered by Myre or one of the thousands of Americans, Canadians, and Australians invited to participate in her public art projects. These collaborative events are typically held in museum or gallery settings where Myre provides raw stretched canvases to visitors and asks them to render an impression of a scar that is illustrative of their lived experience. She also asks them to write a narrative of their injury, and these explanations are frequently exhibited alongside the works. For Myre, the series is about trauma, longing, and loss, as well as about healing. Reflecting on the series at its completion, she remarked: "Each scar canvas and its accompanying story is unique and tells an individual narrative, yet bringing them together in an installation serves to highlight common threads of experience—hurt, healing and forgiveness."[32] Gibson's punching bag sculptures share the bodily connotations, evidence of trauma, and bold suture lines borne by Myre's canvases.

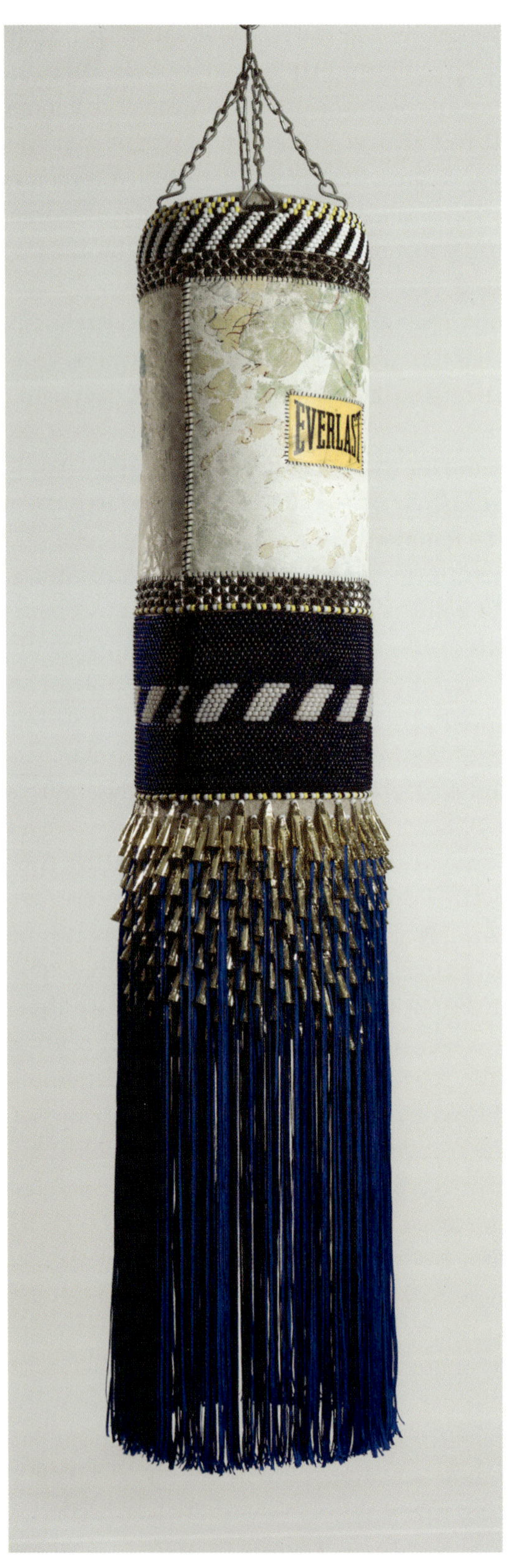

5.3

Jeffrey Gibson (Choctaw/Cherokee, b. 1972)
Deep Blue Day (2014)
Vinyl punching bag, recycled wool blanket, artist's own repurposed painting, steel studs, tin jungles, nylon fringe, artificial sinew, 49½ × 16 inches
Courtesy of the artist
Collection of the artist

And they too stress resilience, drawing on the symbolic power of the jingle dance to promote healing.[33]

The landscape as subject is difficult to locate in either of these series, but intriguingly, many of Gibson's works, including the aptly titled *Deep Blue Day*, incorporate fragments of his repurposed landscape paintings. For Myre, the connection between the landscape and the scarred body is finally made explicit in *Landscape of Sorrow* (2008; figure 5.4). In this composite work, produced midway through *The Scar Project*, six cotton canvases, 6 by 84 inches and stitched by the artist, are exhibited together, forming a double horizon line more than twenty feet long. The similarity of this format to the Two Row Wampum is not incidental: Myre created a number of beaded versions of wampum belts in the early 2000s, and in this work the symbolism of the river as a site of intercultural negotiation is interwoven with that of a desecrated landscape *and* a desecrated body. According to curator Anne Ellegood, *Landscape of Sorrow* refers to the overwhelming accumulation of scars rendered in *The Scar Project*, "but their elongation and movement across multiple canvases plays with scale and perspective, shifting the scars from the site of the body to the surface of the earth. These scars on the landscape represent the environmental damage inflicted by humans and underscore the fact that it is not only the human body that is vulnerable."[34] Once again, there is a strong resonance with Walking-Stick's *Venere Alpina*, but Myre's rapidly accumulating experience with *The Scar Project* also led her to recognize that loss of connection to the land is one of the deep traumas that resonate through Indigenous lives.[35]

There is perhaps no more poignant illustration of this resonant grief than Cree artist Kent Monkman's multimedia installation at the Denver Art Museum, *Lot's Wife* (2012; figure 5.5), which presents us with the ethereal specter of a figure gazing longingly at a distant landscape. The work references the most famous exile in history, the biblical figure of Lot's wife, who was said to have been turned into a pillar of salt for the sin of looking back at her homeland as she and her family were led from the city of Sodom. Though it is commonly assumed that Lot's wife was punished for disobeying the word of God, Monkman disagrees, insisting instead that "she was punished for remembering. . . . We're not supposed to look back and remember where we are from."[36] For Monkman, the story is both universal and personal: *Lot's Wife* memorializes his own great-grandmother, Caroline Everett, a citizen of the Cree Nation who was forced to relocate off-reserve from her home on the Red River in Manitoba in 1907. That very landscape, the Red River as it flows south from Lake Winnipeg, is shown in the video image projected in the installation, accompanied by an audio track of bird songs and other ambient noise from the natural environment. The beauty of the image underscores the poignancy of the loss suffered by Everett, by Monkman, and, by inference, by generations of Indigenous people. Echoing Myre, Monkman refers to the land as "the site of our conflict, *and* our connection."[37]

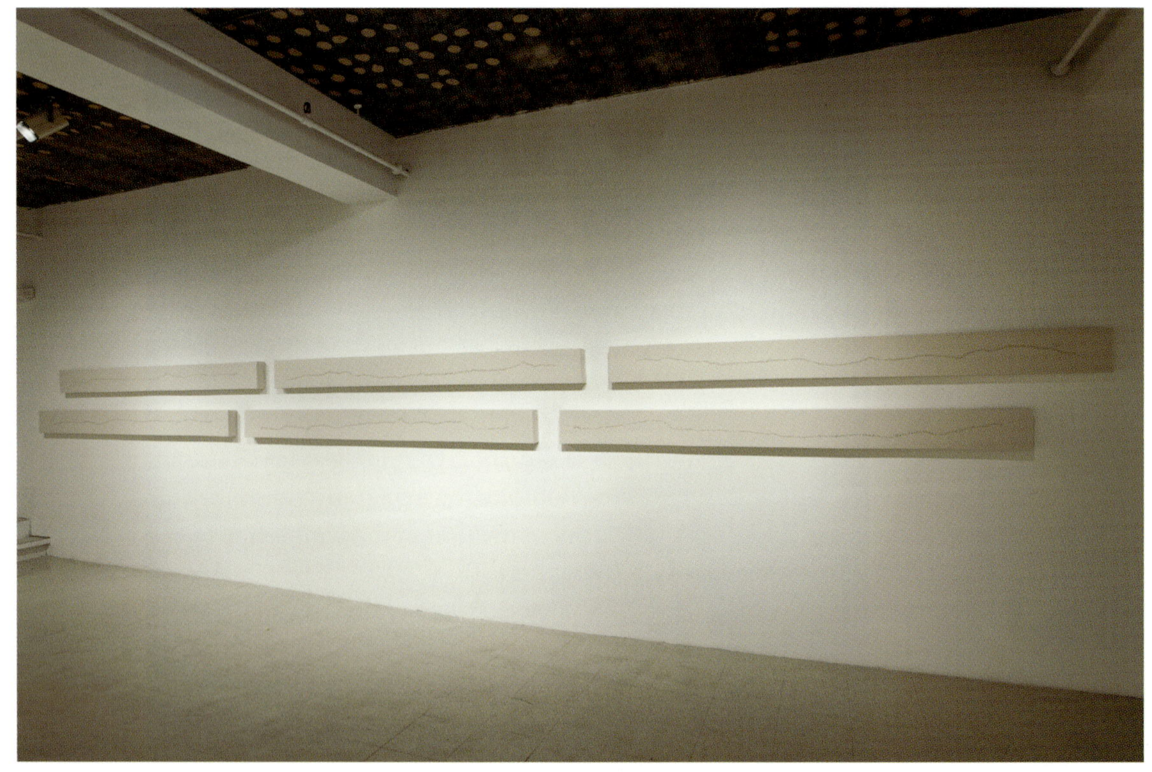

5.4 (*above*) Nadia Myre (Algonquin, b. 1974)
Landscape of Sorrow (2008)
Canvas, cotton thread, six elements, each 6 × 90 inches
Copyright Nadia Myre. Courtesy of Art Mûr Gallery, Montreal.
Photograph by Brian Gardiner

5.5 (*facing page*) Kent Monkman (Fisher River Band Cree, b. 1965)
Lot's Wife (2012)
Fiberglass, Styrofoam, wood, taxidermy deer, artificial grass, and video projection, 96 × 96 × 96 inches (sculptural element); 108 × 192 inches (video projection)
Installation view, Denver Art Museum
Courtesy of the Denver Art Museum. Gift from Vicki and Kent Logan, 2013.71A-J.

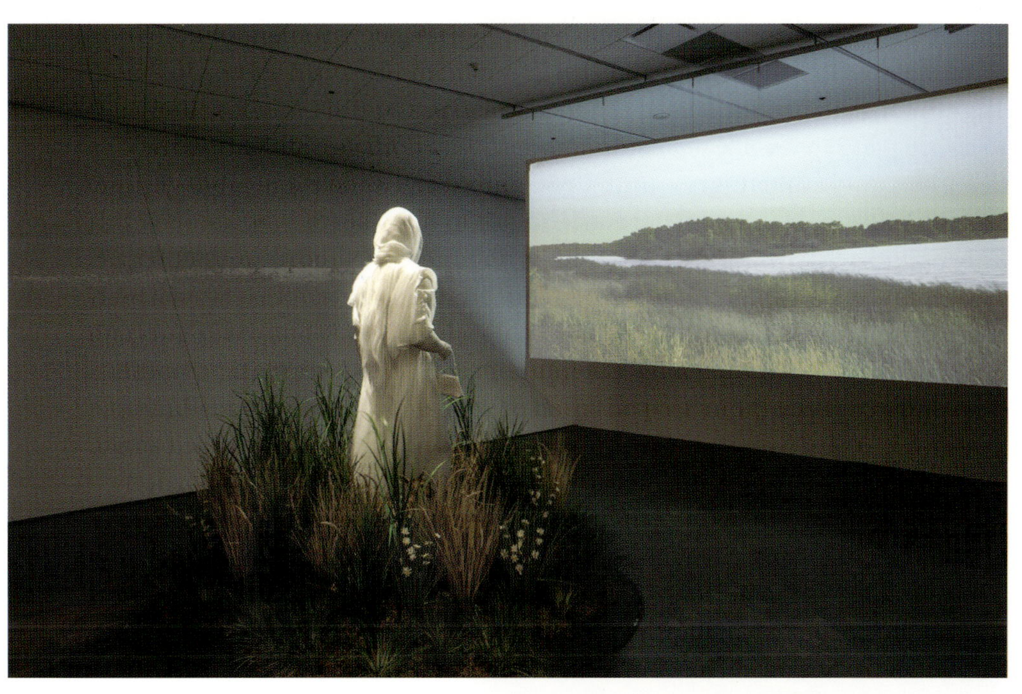

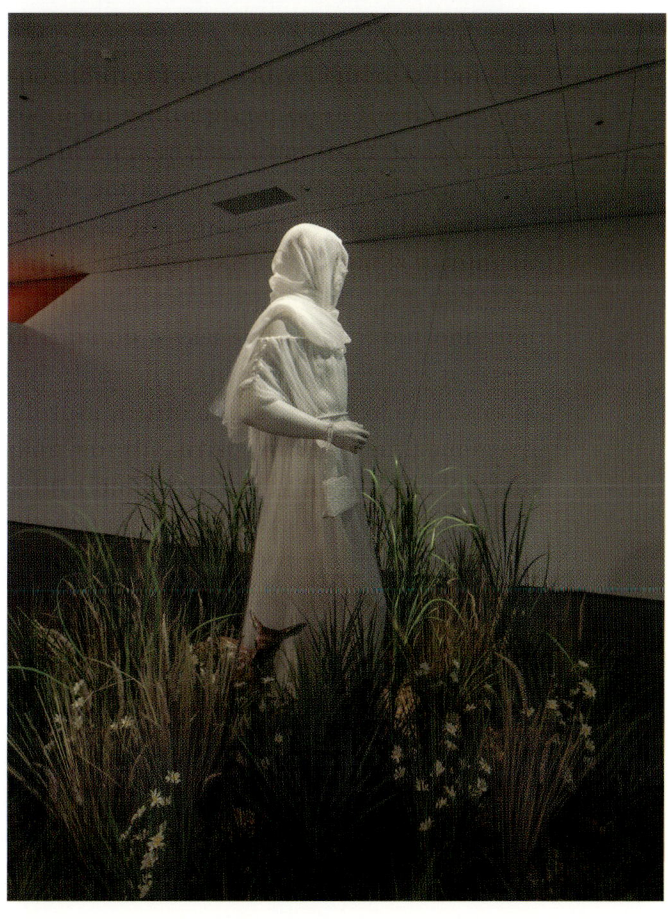

MIMESIS

But what are we to make of the three-dimensional landscape that Monkman presents to us in *Lot's Wife*? The quiet naturalism of the video image is not sustained in the small patch of prairie that Monkman crafted out of plastic and Styrofoam and wood. Amid the artificial grasses and flowers, we find the unmistakable signs of kitsch taking root: a taxidermy fawn shelters behind the figure, her ears back as if startled by the appearance of the real landscape before them, her hooves anchored in a bed of landscaping supply store peat moss, shredded bark, and plastic sheeting.[38] Reigning over all of this is the 6-foot-tall ghostly white figure, constructed not of salt but of fiberglass. Clad in a diaphanous off-the-shoulder dress and headscarf, clutching a dainty purse, the figure is certainly feminine, but it is not wholly (or only) female: discreetly but imperfectly concealed beneath the sheer fabric of the dress is a distinctly masculine body. If this is not Caroline Everett, then it stands to reason that it is instead her great-grandson, Monkman himself. But this too is only partially correct: the figure represents Monkman's alter ego, the flamboyant Miss Chief, who has been a recurring presence in Monkman's art since the early 2000s.

If it can be said that the figure in Gibson's landscape paintings emerged from the canvas into three dimensions, the same must be said for Monkman's alter ego. Miss Chief made her debut on the canvas as a subversive insertion into Monkman's majestic landscape paintings—such as *Portrait of the Artist as Hunter* (2002) and *Trappers of Men* (2006; figure 5.6)—and migrated from there into increasingly performative territories and media such as photography, film, video, video installation, and live performance. The story of Miss Chief's genesis has been recounted many times, with each subsequent version serving to further burnish her legend.[39] Yet every version emphasizes a few crucial aspects of Miss Chief's persona: her identity as a queer, transgender, or explicitly two-spirited figure; her fabulous wardrobe of feather headdresses, beaded sashes, bone breastplates, loin cloths, stiletto heels, or fetish boots—much of it inspired by the entertainer Cher's "Half-Breed" persona of the early 1970s, and her empowered and subversive sexuality.[40] Miss Chief's flamboyant personality and camp sensibility are so insistent that one critic was inspired to refer to her as a "Postindian Diva Warrior."[41]

As is befitting a diva, Miss Chief's presence was announced well before she finally took the stage in a painting: only her name appeared on the canvas of *Ceci n'est pas une pipe* (2001), in the form of her initials, S.E.T., inserted in the place usually reserved for the artist's signature. These initials, which appear as the signature on several of Monkman's works, is a shortened form of Miss Chief's full name, Miss Chief Share Eagle Testickle. Although Monkman postponed Miss Chief's entry into the pictorial space in *Ceci n'est pas ne pipe*, her spirit can be felt in the sexually explicit and explosively radical image of an

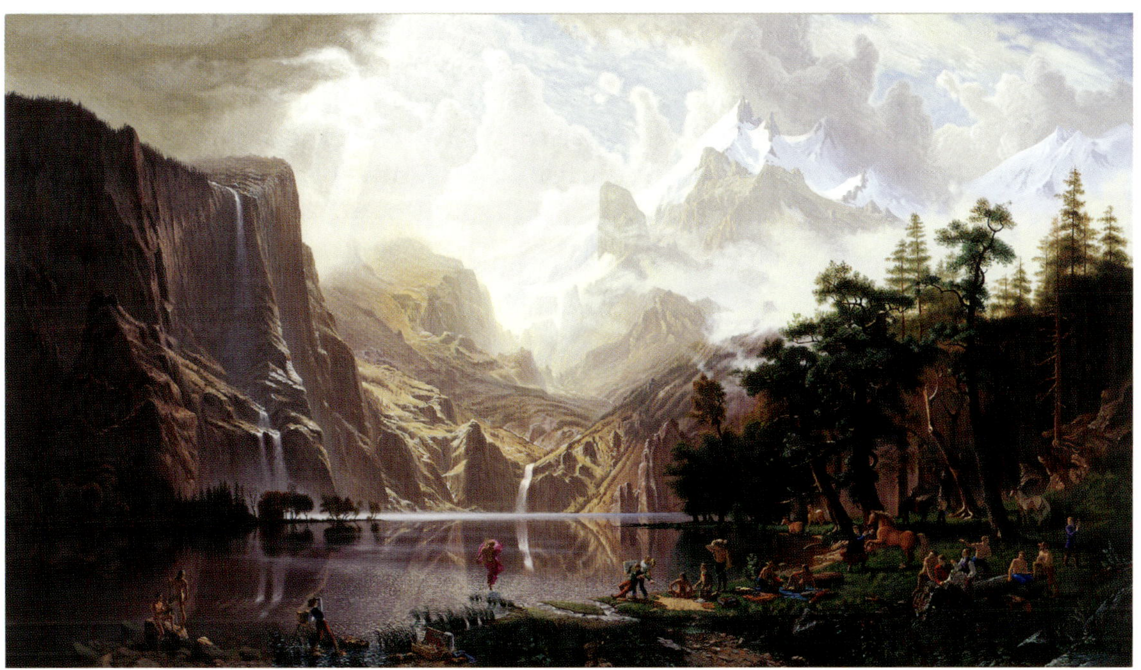

5.6 Kent Monkman (Fisher River Band Cree, b. 1965)
Trappers of Men (2006)
Acrylic on canvas, wood frame, 103 × 163½ inches
Copyright Kent Monkman. Courtesy of the artist.
Montreal Museum of Fine Arts. Purchase, Horsley and Annie Townsend bequest, anonymous gift, and gift of Dr. Ian Hutchison, inv. 2006.87

Indian warrior mounting a bare-bottomed cowboy against the backdrop of an idyllic nineteenth-century Western landscape. Perhaps Monkman signed Miss Chief's name in order to distance himself from the radical subject matter of the image or even from the wry pun of the painting's title; if so, his reluctance to claim marquee space for both himself and his alter ego was short-lived. *Portrait of the Artist as Hunter* establishes the synonymy between the artist and his subject. Monkman, Miss Chief, the artist, and the hunter are all conflated in a singular figure—this time clad in an eagle feather headdress, pink sash, and stiletto heels—that charges into the frame from the lower left in hot pursuit of a cowboy who flees before her. The scene that unfurls around these characters is notably anachronistic: a buffalo hunt plays out across verdant plains worthy of a nineteenth-century landscape painting, with Indians and wild-eyed animals thundering through the composition under gathering storm clouds. As John Mix Stanley, Paul Kane, or George Catlin might have painted it in the 1830s or 1840s, the hunt is at once a timeless scene and an elegy for the past:

in their hands, such images suggested that the Indians and their way of life were destined to go the way of the buffalo, with only the painter left to mark their passing. The nostalgia of such images is thoroughly trounced in *Portrait of the Artist as Hunter*, however, by the appearance of both Miss Chief and her quarry. Modernity bursts onto the scene in the form of an overtly queer camp sensibility, riding close on the heels of the cowboy who wears chaps but no trousers and the Indian warrior who takes careful aim at his naked buttocks with her drawn bow.

As *Trappers of Men* attests, *Portrait of the Artist as Hunter* was not the last of Monkman's inspired recreations of canonical nineteenth-century European representations of the North American West. For more than a decade, Monkman has reproduced paintings by Stanley, Catlin, Kane, and Albert Bierstadt nearly verbatim, yet always with a subversive twist that exposes the romanticism of the originals. More often than not, Miss Chief is the instrument of disruption, and this is especially true in paintings that parody Catlin, whom Monkman singles out as a voice of "authority" in constructing the narratives of the West. Monkman writes, "The reason I respond to these artists is because I think their work *is* important. It's worth examining that whole period of art, so purely one-sided, like a big cover-up of what was really happening."[42] The cover-up that Monkman consigns to Catlin in particular effects the erasure of alternate forms of gender and sexuality in Native cultures, including the two-spirit and berdache traditions.[43] Noting that Catlin encountered and made sketches of many individuals who might now be described as third-gender during his travels but that he denigrated those traditions in his journals and rarely translated those sketches into finished paintings, Monkman asks what other histories were "obliterated" by Catlin and his European contemporaries. In Monkman's view, the entry of Miss Chief into a landscape limned by Catlin, Kane, or any of the other "authorities" who shaped the mythology of the West represents a correction of the historical record.[44]

Monkman's engagement with Catlin runs deeper than with the others named here, in part because it was in Catlin's work that he first recognized the current of conceit or self-absorption that so often mingles with romantic ideals.[45] Not only did Catlin's predilection for insinuating himself into his paintings give Monkman "permission" to do the same as Miss Chief, but Monkman recalls that it provided him with the inspiration for crafting Miss Chief's proper name: "I chose the name [Share] after Cher, but Eagle Testickle was intended to sound like egotistical so it was that whole idea of self-aggrandizement and self promotion that I saw in the original artists."[46] Monkman's parodic assumption of Catlin's egocentric position is archly illustrated in *Artist and Model* (2003), a painting that, like *Portrait of the Artist as Hunter*, is signed S.E.T. The composition of *Artist and Model* is loosely based on Catlin's self-portrait in the act of painting the Mandan chief Mato-tope in the 1830s, though Monkman takes considerable artistic license with the figures.[47] Miss Chief occupies the artist's position on the right, standing at her easel with a brush in her hand. She wears her signature attire, but in this rendition, her long, trailing eagle feather headdress and erect bearing ally her visually with the Mandan chief depicted in Catlin's version. To further complicate the perceived dichotomy between the primitive and the modern, Miss Chief brandishes a bow and arrow and a Louis Vuitton arrow quiver, and she renders her subject in a pictographic style on a birchbark canvas. The subject of Miss Chief's painting and, it would seem, her desire is a pastiche of Western lore—a cowboy photographer whose large-format camera lies broken at his feet. He is bound to a tree, stripped naked except for his cowboy boots and hat, and pierced with pink-feathered arrows that we must assume were shot from Miss Chief's bow. According to Shirley Madill, Monkman "makes clear that behind each colonial artist's claim of scientific objectivity lurks an explosive mix of fear and lust for the 'other.'"[48]

One final divergence of *Artist and Model* from Catlin's version regards the physical setting in which the action occurs. The densely wooded landscape that Miss Chief and her model occupy is hardly characteristic of the northern plains: the view from their promontory encompasses an endless expanse of low mountains unfurling along a bucolic river valley. It would seem that Monkman has transported his characters from Catlin's West to Cole's East—a move that, while impressive in geographic scope, is less of a leap in ideological terms. In Monkman's view, Catlin and Cole were kindred spirits in the sense that both produced paintings that "were like billboards urging, 'Come occupy this empty real estate.'"[49] Although this statement is more easily applied to Catlin's landscape paintings than to the self-portrait that inspired *Artist and Model*, it reveals an important organizing principle for Monkman, namely that while the specifics of Miss Chief's actions confront any number of representational tropes, her very existence in the landscape disrupts the rhetoric of settler colonialism.

While Miss Chief is capable of making a quantum leap into nearly any setting, it is clear that the mythologies of the American West exert a strong pull on Monkman. The 7-by-12-foot acrylic painting *Trappers of Men*, for example, depicts a luminous and sublime Western landscape replete with cascading waterfalls, rugged cliffs, and storm-shrouded peaks. In the foreground, a serene mountain lake adjoins a small patch of alpine meadow ringed by great gnarled pines and redwood trees. The landscape is a nearly exact copy—lovingly drawn by hand, brushstroke for brushstroke—of Bierstadt's 6-by-10-foot oil painting *Among the Sierra Nevada Mountains, California* (1868). Concerning his faithful emulation of another artist's work, Monkman explains, "For me, it's about following a tradition in painting that has existed for centuries in which painters make copies of master paintings and learn through that process. So what I'm doing is taking the most spectacular landscapes that I can find and painstakingly reproducing them in a way that conceptually reclaims those landscapes."[50] Elsewhere, Monkman adds that through this labor-intensive process he also aims to usurp the authority of the originals.[51] Where *Trappers of Men* diverges from Bierstadt's prototype is in its depiction of the inhabitants of the landscape: the only fauna that populate *Among the Sierra Nevada Mountains, California* are a small group of deer and a brace of ducks. As diminutive as the animals in Bierstadt's painting are, they serve both to underscore the vast scale and relative emptiness of the landscape and to enhance the dramatic contrast between stillness and turbulent movement in the image. Monkman's painting is also largely devoid of figures, at least in spatial terms: roughly 85 percent of his composition is devoted to the landscape features. Nevertheless, the nearly two dozen figures packed into the foreground rival the drama of the landscape behind them.

At center is Miss Chief herself, shown blowing in off the surface of the lake like a campy New World version of Botticelli's *Venus*, her blonde locks billowing in the wind.[52] Miss Chief's sudden appearance startles an odd assortment of characters who have gathered along the lakeshore to transact their business. Robust, bare-chested mountain men trade their wares with equally strapping young Native men, while alongside them the explorers Lewis and Clark pause to consult their map—they may be strangers to the land but certainly not to the mythos of the American West. To the left of center along the water's edge, one of the preeminent architects of Western lore, the photographer Edward Curtis, is interrupted in the act of staging a portrait of a pair of nearly naked Indian men, one of whom prepares to don a wig and eagle feather that Curtis has no doubt supplied to him. Curtis's status as a maker of images—and mythologies—is echoed in the figures that occupy the shoreline to the right of center: the Dutch modernist painter Piet Mondrian faints in the arms of Jackson Pollock at the sight of Miss Chief's sudden apparition. Seated below these two is the Lakota artist Lone Dog, painting his winter count while Catlin busily records *his* likeness. The endlessly self-referential cycle of artists chasing one another's representational tails within the painting radiates outward from the canvas to encompass the artist's own irreverent acts of usurpation. And, as is the case with so many other acts of drag or camp impersonation, there is much at stake here: according to Monkman, his appropriation of images such as Bierstadt's allows him to "investigate the relationship of sexuality to conquest, xenophobia, and imperialism."[53]

While Monkman speaks of colonized identities in particular, the central figure in his revelatory dramas, Miss Chief, has expressed her own set of concerns. Speaking as an artist rather than as a subject and as a time traveler of evident skill, Miss Chief detailed her efforts to intervene in the colonialist rhetoric of early landscape traditions in an "interview" with Cathy Mattes in

2008: “Well, the Europeans in North America, they had really pillaged our society. They had stolen our land. They created this whole document called ‘art history’ around their exploits here in North America. . . . I felt that borrowing from their landscape paintings would be a way of reclaiming some of the land they had stolen from us. Their version of history was one-sided. So I, being a very fair and equal person, took it upon myself to balance the equation.”[54]

In this wonderfully convoluted passage we confront the full complexity of Monkman’s artistic strategy: in the guise of his alter ego, Monkman declares himself both image and maker, victim and aggressor, libertine and moralist. As we pause to consider exactly how Monkman’s progression from mimicry to mastery enables him to reclaim the ideological territories that were once the exclusive domain of Bierstadt, Cole, Catlin, or Kane, it is important to recognize that Monkman rarely alters the *landscape* in his inspired recreations of their paintings. As Gerald McMaster notes, “what we don’t see, but what is entirely implied” in Monkman’s work “are the changes in the land brought about by colonization.” Instead, we encounter an unscathed paradise that is “wild with abandon.”[55] In *Portrait of the Artist as Hunter, Artist and Model, Trappers of Men*, and a host of other canvases, it is the figures that intrude and steal the show. *Charged Particles in Motion* (2007) is an excellent case in point. This 4-by-6-foot painting is an imaginative pastiche of not just one but two source paintings: Bierstadt’s *Yosemite Winter Scene* (1872) and Kane’s *Scene from the Northwest: Portrait of John Henry Lefroy* (aka *The Surveyor*, 1845–46).[56] The landscape is pure Bierstadt, majestic and serene, and in the prototype it is entirely devoid of humans or other fauna. The figural group is pure Monkman, albeit inspired by Kane’s canonical portrait of the British colonial administrator Henry Lefroy. In Monkman’s version, a Louis Vuitton dogsled bearing a fur-clad Miss Chief and drawn by six snow-white huskies runs roughshod over Lefroy’s motley crew of a poodle and two retrievers. Lefroy himself lies face down in the snow in Miss Chief’s wake. Despite Monkman’s careful reproduction of details such as the shape of Lefroy’s loaded toboggan and the adornments of his red leggings, snowshoes, and decorative rifle cover—the scene is not so much lifted from Kane’s portrait of *The Surveyor* as it is a virtuoso rebuttal of the laudatory rhetoric of territorial exploration and expansion.

Thus, despite the artist’s own assertion that the figures are secondary in his paintings (he claims, “I paint the narrative in last so I have a couple of months to imagine what it’s going to be”), they alone cause the disruption in the colonialist narrative.[57] Not only does their presence contradict what Lawrence Buell has called “the aesthetics of the not-there,” but they seem curiously anachronistic, as if they had wandered into the frame from the wrong century.[58] In a recorded interview with Monkman, filmmaker David Furnish noted this effect, describing the incongruities of Monkman’s work: “What I find so striking . . . is it has a very old-fashioned, burnished, comforting quality to it.

At the heart there's a depiction of what you would initially interpret to be a classical scene, but when you look closely you see something completely modern and surprising within that environment. It's that juxtaposition of what appears to be a painting that could have been hanging on someone's wall for a hundred years, and yet it has this incredible jolt of modernity whacked right into the middle of it."[59]

We might ask: what is so "modern" about Monkman's figures? Mondrian and Pollock notwithstanding, most of them do "belong" in the old West. It must be their sensibility or, more explicitly, their sexuality that lends them their air of modernity. Consider the provocatively titled *History Is Painted by the Victors* (2013; figure 5.7), in which soldiers from Custer's Seventh Cavalry cavort on the shores of yet another Bierstadt lake.[60] Sharp-eyed viewers will recognize the figural groupings as imported from the works of Thomas Eakins. Miss Chief, on the other hand, is seen recording their likeness using a distinctly Indigenous representational style (as she did in *Artist and Model*), in this case employing the conventions of Plains ledger drawings. Underscoring the irony of Monkman's title, the scene reproduced on Miss Chief's easel within the painting is an exploit from the Battle of the Little Bighorn, which has yet to occur in the temporal rift of the scenario.[61] Unaware of the fate that awaits them in Montana, Custer's company is glimpsed at ease in their mountain surroundings—they swim, box, wrestle, and otherwise remain faithful to Eakins's vision. It is left to Monkman and to the figure of the artist in their midst to lay bare the latent homoeroticism of Eakins's studies of the male nude. Clad only in thigh-high red vinyl fetish boots, Miss Chief provides the "jolt of modernity" that Furnish has led us to anticipate in Monkman's work.

Yet Monkman insists that his figures are *not* modern at all; rather, he claims that they have always existed, submerged in the current of colonialist histories: "This whole body of work is about revisiting these early images that represent the very safe and secure foundation of the mythology about the exploration of the West. When you look at those paintings as an aboriginal person, you realize how subjective they are. So when I make these paintings I'm not necessarily repainting history, but I'm nudging people toward seeing that there are these big missing narratives."[62] In Monkman's view, the willful blindness of nineteenth-century observers extends to twenty-first-century audiences as well. He notes that just as Catlin suppressed evidence of Native peoples' contemporaneity in the nineteenth century, there is today "a reluctance to accept aboriginal identity in its current state."[63] The continuing denial of Native "modernity" on the part of citizens of settler nations may be regarded as an extension of the tenets of Manifest Destiny, now mobilized to resist the claims of Indigenous sovereign nations demanding the restoration of their aboriginal lands.

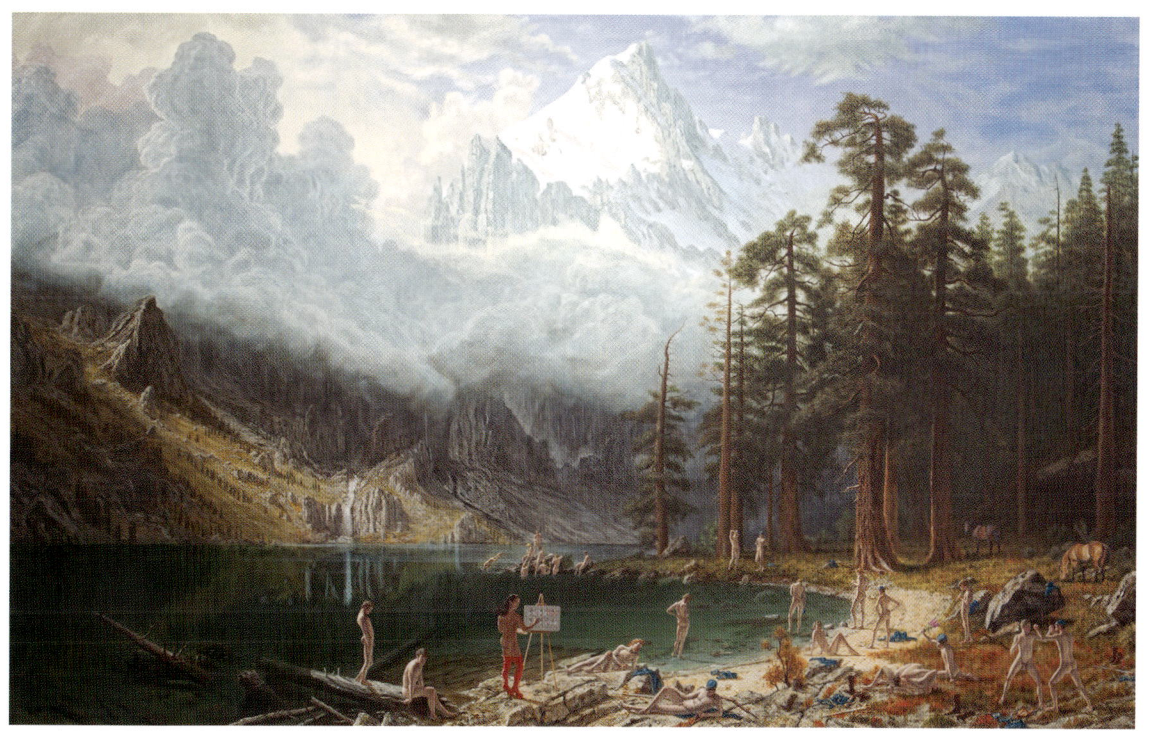

5.7 Kent Monkman (Fisher River Band Cree, b. 1965)
History Is Painted by the Victors (2013)
Acrylic on canvas, 72 × 113 inches
Denver Art Museum
Courtesy of Denver Art Museum. Gift from Vicki and Kent Logan, 2016.288

COMPRESSION

The particular phenomenon that Monkman is describing—the tendency of viewers to regard images of Indians in a technological present as anomalies—was the subject of Philip Deloria's important study *Indians in Unexpected Places*, published in 2004. Contemplating Walter Ferguson's 1904 photograph *Geronimo at the Wheel*, which pictures the Apache warrior in top hat behind the wheel of a Cadillac, Deloria wrote that the shock of such images for twentieth-century audiences was that they ran counter to the "American narrative which held that Indian people, corralled on isolated and impoverished reservations, missed out on modernity—indeed almost dropped out of history itself."[64] To test this hypothesis, in 2014 Monkman reversed the temporal paradigm of his paintings, importing Miss Chief into a resolutely contemporary—and urban—setting. *The Chase* (2014), which shows Miss Chief hunting buffalo from astride a motorcycle, capitalizes on what Deloria termed "automotive unexpectedness." It is also an indirect reference to the fact that shortly after Ferguson took his famous photograph, Geronimo was released from house arrest at Fort Sill long enough to take part in a Wild West show spectacle promoted as "The Last Buffalo Hunt," in which Indians chased a herd of buffalo around a rodeo ring in a car.[65] For Monkman, *The Chase* combats the amnesia of a modern culture that is still beholden to mythologies codified a century ago, one that "freezes Aboriginal people in time."[66]

While the narrative of *The Chase* reaches back more than a century, it is clear in this image and the suite of paintings that it belongs to that Monkman has begun to mine artistic sources closer to our own time. Among the herd of stampeding buffalo in *The Chase*, five hybrid creatures stand out as strangely compressed, their bodies fractured into multiple planes. There is no other word to describe them than "Picasso-esque." *The Chase* signaled a new direction in Monkman's work, relocating his character-driven dramas to a contemporary, urban environment and broadening his field of vision to encompass the entire history of Western art, from Lascaux to Tintoretto, Picasso to Henri Moore. The fidelity of these works to their purported sources is drastically reduced, however, and in Monkman's telling the "Casualties of Modernity" are victimized by the history of representation as much as by any other force.[67] The modernist flattening of pictorial space is mobilized here "as a metaphor for how Indigenous cultures got flattened during the last 120 years."[68] For this reason the victims are almost exclusively female, assaulted first by modernist forms of representation—their bodies are fractured and flattened cubist forms—and then again by the mechanized violence of contemporary culture. In the aptly titled *Death of the Female* (2014; figure 5.8), a group of young men in street clothes rush to the aid of a nude figure that has been either run down or dumped in the street by a muscle car driven by a bull (possibly a reference to Picasso's *Guernica*).

Despite the presence of a quattrocento angel hovering overhead and a group of Plains Indian warriors looking on, the setting of *Death of the Female* is far from allegorical. Monkman explains the migration of his characters into this gritty inner-city environment: "My earlier work . . . focused on the historical narratives between settler culture and Native American people. I wanted to re-stage some of these scenes in urban environments, because a lot of Indigenous people live in cities. In Canada, more than half are living in cities. And a lot of urban environments are places where Native people once inhabited."[69] The setting for Monkman's *Urban Res* (the title selected for the exhibition of these works in 2014) is the north end of Winnipeg, one of the poorest, most crime-ridden cities in Canada.[70] Monkman grew up in this neighborhood, home to the country's largest population of Indigenous residents; here he exploits the brutal circumstances of contemporary life on the

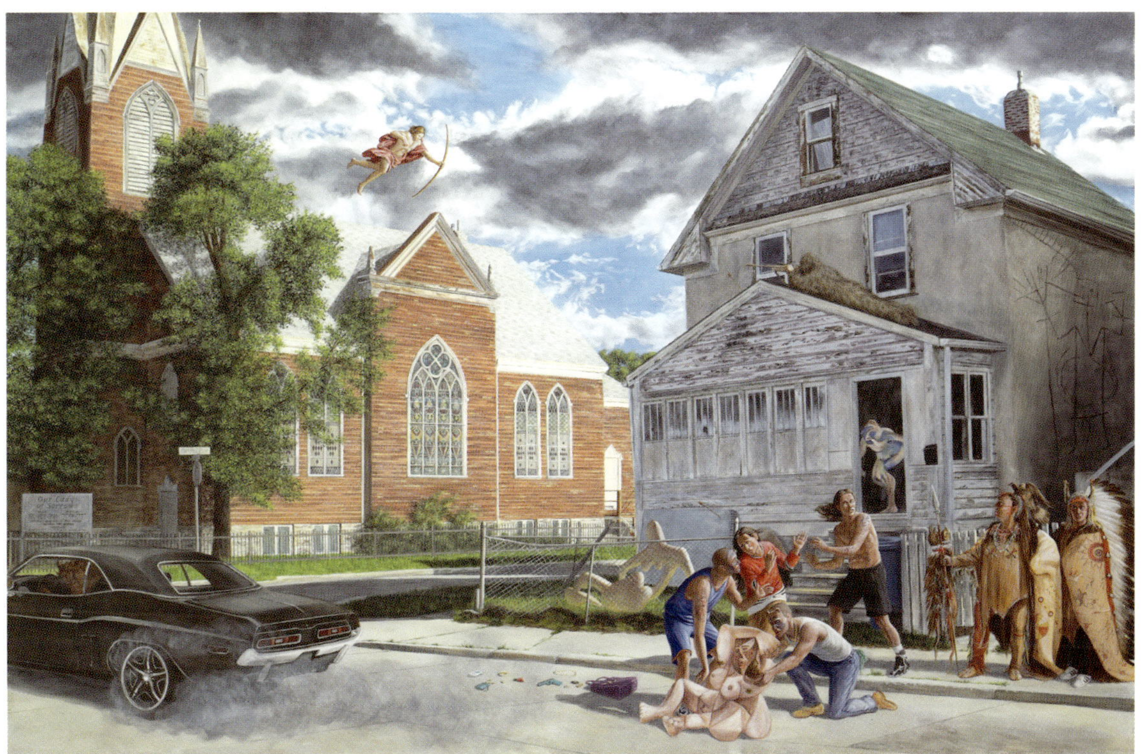

5.8 Kent Monkman (Fisher River Band Cree, b. 1965)
Death of the Female (2014)
Acrylic on canvas, 84 × 126 inches
Copyright Kent Monkman. Courtesy of the artist.
Collection of the artist

"urban res" to stress both the displacement and resilience of Native peoples. One reviewer of the exhibition astutely observed, "What is absent from these works is a sense of home, or a place that feels safe from the outside world. The violence of contemporary life permeates everything."[71]

This is especially evident in *Struggle for Balance* (2013), in which the by-now-familiar female casualty and mourners are caught up in a maelstrom of rioting and gun violence. As flames and smoke billow from a fire-bombed SUV, even the angels fall prey to an enormous bald eagle. Other animals appear in the margins of the scene: a bear escapes the mayhem on the left, while on the right a deer lies dead in the road, yet another casualty of this urban cataclysm. In Monkman's world, humans and animals (as well as a host of fantastical creatures drawn primarily from the history of painting) appear as both victims and aggressors, casualties and survivors. All are metaphors for an Indigenous culture under siege yet somehow perseverant. In this respect,

Monkman's paintings may be considered visual manifestations of Indigenous survivance: the community rallies in the face of literally unimaginable adversity. "Survivance," Vizenor wrote, "is an active sense of presence, the continuance of native stories, not a mere reaction, or a survivable name. Native survivance stories are renunciations of dominance, tragedy and victimry."[72]

Miss Chief is notably absent from the majority of the paintings in *Urban Res*, save for her cameo appearance in *The Chase*. In the larger context of the exhibition, however, she could not be missed. In *Bête Noire* (2014; figure 5.9), a life-sized diorama installed at the end of the gallery, Miss Chief appears astride her Indian motorcycle, arms outstretched, honoring the spirit of the buffalo that she has slain with her fluorescent pink arrows. She is a striking spectacle in her constructed world, suspended between two and three dimensions,

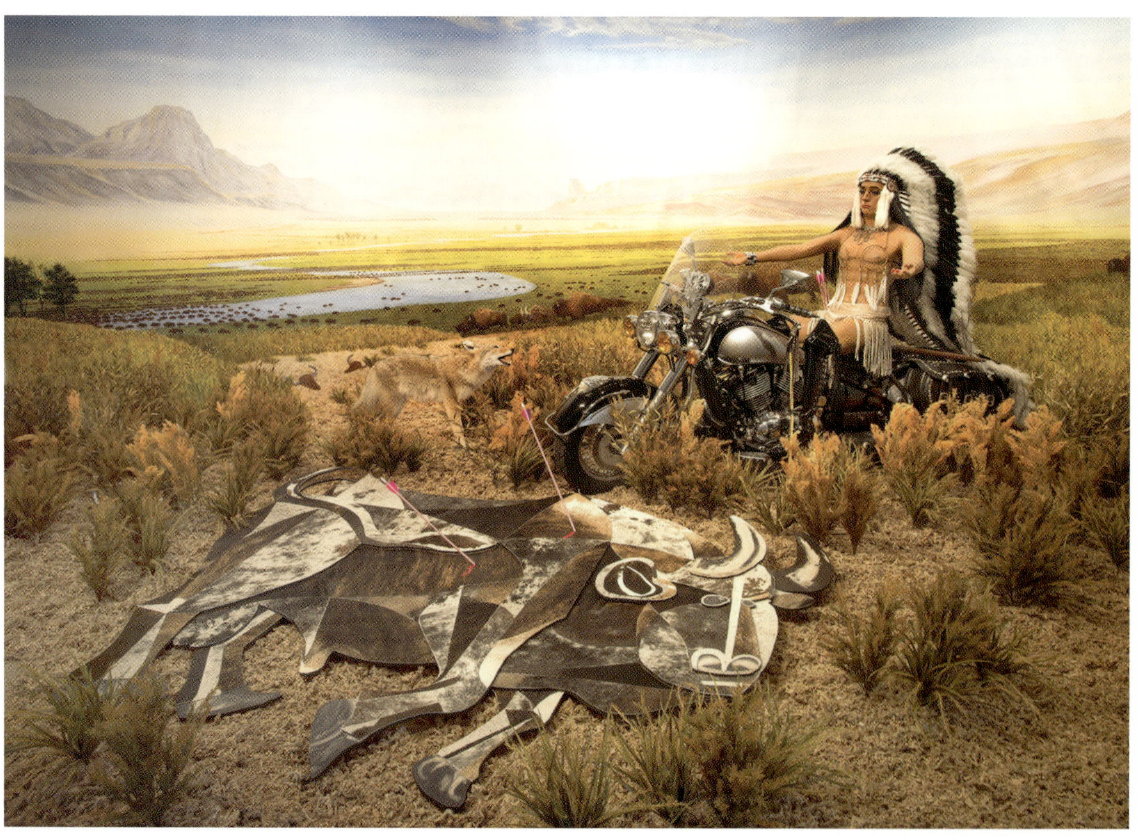

5.9 Kent Monkman (Fisher River Band Cree, b. 1965)
Bête Noire (2014)
Acrylic on canvas, mixed media, 192 × 192 × 120 inches
Installation view, Sargent's Daughters, New York
Copyright Kent Monkman. Courtesy of the artist.

between representation and flesh, between modernity and romanticism, between the past and the present. The title of the work is a double entendre: literally translated as "black beast," it may refer to the unfortunate creature in the foreground, flattened in good cubist fashion, but the term is more commonly understood to indicate an anathema or a pet peeve. In this regard it may refer to Monkman's frustration with representation itself. He recalls viewing the dioramas of Indian peoples in the Manitoba Museum as a child growing up in Winnipeg: "There were these life-size dioramas where Native Americans were frozen in time, in some idyllic pre-contact state. This is what we were supposed to be. And then I'd step out onto the streets and see skid row and the fall-out of colonization."[73] The works collected under the banner of *Urban Res* are Monkman's rejoinder to that failure of representation that squeezed and then froze time, that denied Indians entry into a technological present but nonetheless consigned them to a ruinous, postindustrial future.

Jonathan Katz argues that this dislocation of history and modernity, nature and culture, is precisely what drew Monkman to the romantic landscape tradition in the first place. He writes that

> Romantic landscape painting, the nostalgia-dipped genre that Kent Monkman appropriated and rode to early artistic success, arose at a moment of crisis. . . . Vast swaths of canvas were enlisted to perform an act of transubstantiation, reintegrating man and nature in a seamless unity at the very moment that unity began to fray, recasting a language of exploitation and conquest into images of Arcadian fullness and plentitude. Throughout the nineteenth century, landscape's central claim to our sympathies lay in this act of remembering a lost totality, restoring the unity of the human and the nonhuman under the rule of nature.[74]

Katz notes, however, that Monkman's paintings produce exactly the opposite effect, tearing at the fabric of that supposed integration of man and the environment. He wryly observes that Monkman's "torrid mini-dramas[,] . . . always set on the margin of a gigantic, overwhelming and self-reifying Nature, nonetheless triumph over it, recasting the vast wilderness into a stage set for a vastly more compelling human drama that draws its power from its refusal to act 'naturalized.'"[75] This is a fair assessment, especially given Monkman's early training as a set designer with Native Earth Performing Arts in Toronto. No matter how magnificent these sets are, they seem to signal the demotion of the landscape from a primary to at best a secondary object of our regard. Once we catch sight of Monkman's transgressive, intriguing, entertaining cast of characters, we simply don't see the landscape any longer. It disappears from our view and, by extension, our consciousness.

Must we conclude, however, that in taking center stage, the figures "triumph over" the landscape? Or that, as Katz put it, Monkman's work "posits culture *as* nature"? I would argue against this interpretation and suggest instead that for Monkman the question is very much unresolved. Recall that in *Trappers of Men*, for example, the two figures that have been transported into the scene from the modern era signify two strikingly different perspectives on the subject: Mondrian famously turned his back on nature, while Pollock even more famously declared himself to *be* nature. It is true that in Monkman's work there is no seamless integration of nature and culture, nor even of the figure and the landscape. Time and again his paintings render the collision of these forces, yet in every instance the brunt of the impact is borne by the figure, while the landscape emerges unscathed. Make no mistake: Monkman's landscapes are landscapes of trauma, but the trauma belongs to the realm of culture; it is the trauma of colonization, cultural compression, and historical amnesia.[76]

It is also and especially the trauma of spatial dislocation. Two of the more puzzling examples of geographical conflation in Monkman's work occur in *Pity* (2013; figure 5.10) and *Lamentation* (2013), scenes in which young Native American men confront the "Casualties of Modernity" in the shadow of the European Alps. The landscapes are cribbed from Bierstadt again—from *Sunrise on the Matterhorn* (1875)—and might even be regarded as Monkman's tribute to the homeland of his predecessor. More likely they are a veiled reference to Bierstadt's tendency to depict the landscapes of the North American West in the guise of the Alps: Bierstadt is said to have figuratively moved mountains, to have inserted the Matterhorn in his sketches of the Rocky Mountains. If this is the case, then Monkman's paintings call out not only Bierstadt's artifice but also his failure of vision, his inability to see the landscapes before him. Perhaps Bierstadt's blindness is analogous to our own, if in the face of Monkman's human dramas the landscape has tended to slip from our sight. I suggest that Monkman recognizes this dilemma, for in his curiously affective installations—including *Lot's Wife* and *Bête Noire*—he implores us to look back, to look again. In the full-scale diorama entitled *The Collapsing of Time and Space in an Ever-Expanding Universe* (2011), Miss Chief is figured as an aging diva alone with her faithful animal companions in her Paris apartment, listening to her one-hit record ("Dance to Miss Chief") and longing for her lost youth.[77] Given the temporal disjunction of the subject and the actual location of the installation in a medieval château in France, the diorama is aptly titled; what is especially remarkable about the piece is the placement of one of Monkman's own landscape paintings outside of the apartment window.[78] This is the landscape that Miss Chief gazes at through her tears, the past that she longs for. The irony is that we, an audience educated *by* Monkman, have come to understand that Miss Chief's grief, her nostalgia, is for both a past and a place that never existed, that was as fictive as Bierstadt's Rockies. Yet still we mourn.

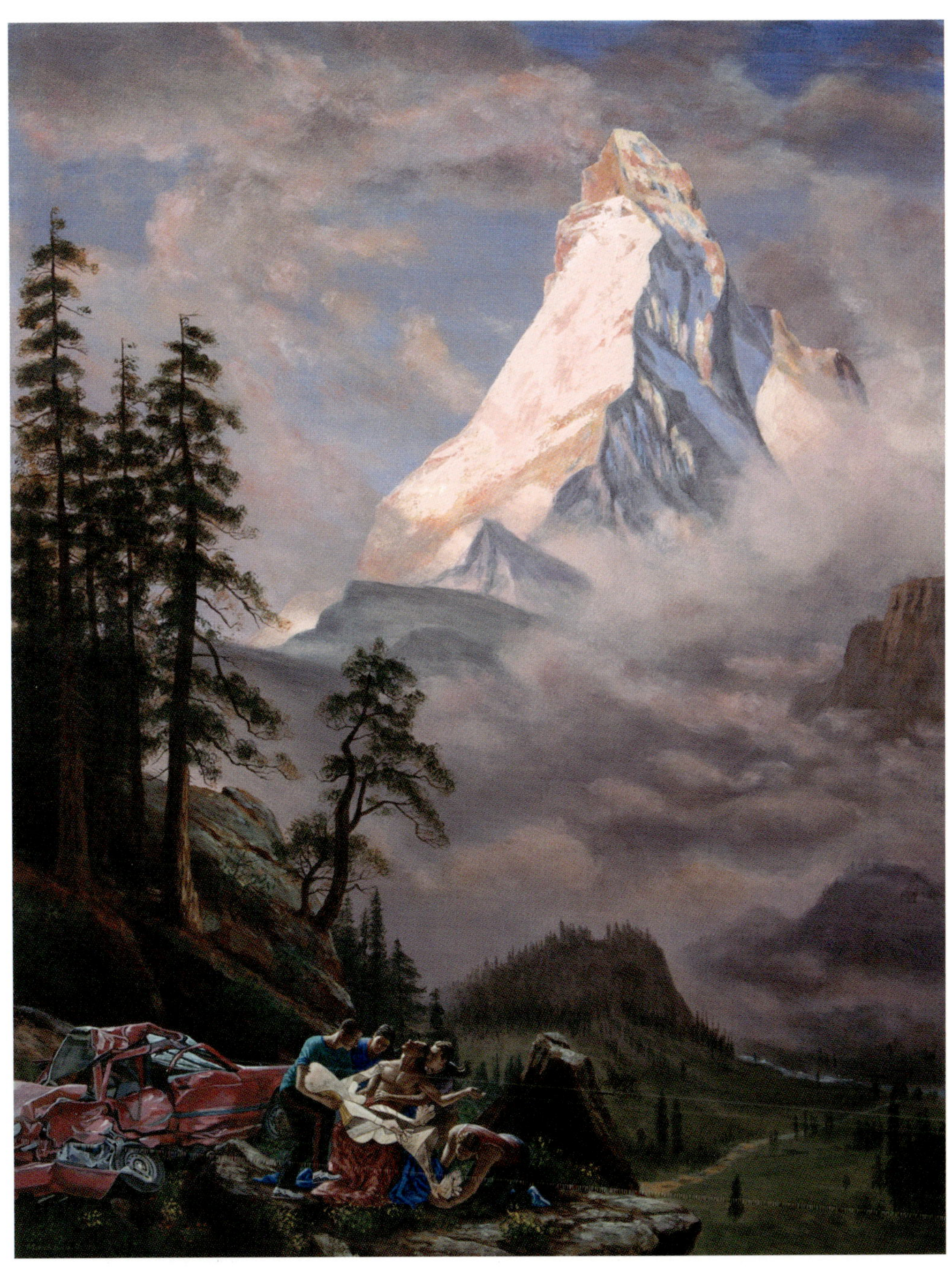

5.10 Kent Monkman (Fisher River Band Cree, b. 1965)
Pity (2013)
Acrylic on canvas, 48 × 36 inches

Collection of the artist

RELATIONAL BODIES

In the suspended present of *The Collapsing of Time and Space in an Ever-Expanding Universe*, the fate of the "trackless forests" of Miss Chief's youth is not revealed; however, it is probably no accident that Monkman chose to depict in the painting within the diorama a scene of buffalo grazing on the banks of a placid river.[79] In the pictorial language of the Western landscape tradition, the American bison is the ultimate nostalgic emblem because the species was driven to the brink of extinction, a subject that Monkman confronted head-on in the full-scale installation *The Rise and Fall of Civilization* at the Gardiner Museum in Toronto in 2015. In that more recent installation, the figure of Miss Chief watches in sad resignation as the last bison are driven over a buffalo jump (a 9-foot-tall cliff in the exhibition). According to the Gardiner Museum's program notes, the pile of smashed ceramics that the artist installed at the base of the cliff contrast the eons-long history of sustainable hunting practices of Indigenous people with the catastrophic slaughter brought about by European settlers.[80] Thus, in addition to dramatizing the impact of settler colonialism on Indigenous lifeways, Monkman's *The Rise and Fall of Civilization* raises the level of concern expressed by Gibson and others at the beginning of this chapter: that a landscape inhabited by humans is one that is destined to become dystopic. In the second decade of the twenty-first century, the global discourse on climate change has brought new urgency to forms of artistic expression (and practice) that document or ideologically resist the devastating impact of humans on the earth's climate and environment. Viewed in this context, Monkman's demonstration of human culpability in the extinction of a species documents the rise not only of civilization but of the Anthropocene—the present geological epoch defined by the effect of human activity on the planet.

In 2013, in a special issue of the journal *Third Text* titled "Contemporary Art and the Politics of Ecology," scholars Jessica Horton and Janet Catherine Berlo make a compelling case for the primacy of contemporary Indigenous art—especially works that evoke the Indigenous landscape—in the growing compendium of "eco-aesthetic" practices.[81] Tracing the ascendancy of a strain of anthropological and visual criticism that addresses the "modern" divide between humans and nonhumans, culture and nature, Horton and Berlo note that the "ecological promise of these 'new materialisms' is to invite a dialogue among a wider host of agents, imagining a profoundly relational world in which humans interact with, rather than act upon, others."[82] According to Horton and Berlo, these "new materialisms" are not new at all but have deep roots in Indigenous intellectual traditions, and they are on full display in the ecologically based works of Indigenous artists who "grant environmental entities the agency to push back, to punish or reward human activity, to remind people of their precarious position in a relational world where allies are essential to flourishing."[83] Nature's retributions are the implied subject of three of the works that Horton and Berlo discuss: Jimmie Durham's series of installations in which airplanes and automobiles are crushed by enormous boulders, Diné photographer Will Wilson's visions of environmental apocalypse in the series *Auto-Immune Response* (2005), and Anishinaabe performance artist Rebecca Belmore's *Fountain*, exhibited at the 2005 Venice Biennale.[84] In the latter two examples, Horton and Berlo argue, humans and the environment—especially Indigenous peoples and lands—share a common fate as victims of environmental violence.[85]

Less visible in the works that Horton and Berlo analyze in this article are the "non-human allies"; nevertheless, such creatures are well represented in the many depictions of the landscape that we have investigated in this chapter. In Monkman's *Struggle for Balance*, for example, bears, eagles, and deer struggle to survive alongside humans; in *Lot's Wife*, a fawn shelters in the shadow of the exiled figure. In *The Collapsing of Time and Space in an Ever-Expanding Universe*, Miss Chief's "faithful animal companions" accompany her in two temporal scenarios: Miss Chief and her horse mingle harmoniously with the buffalo herd in the nostalgic landscape, and in the diorama, a coyote and beaver are the cohabitants of Miss Chief's boudoir. Nor can we discount the relational presence of the land itself in the larger corpus of Indigenous landscape representation. Lavadour and WalkingStick both pay homage to the creative and spiritual forces of nature in their paintings; Devine's *Letters from Home* address geological features as sentient beings; Myre's *Landscape of Sorrow* configures the earth as a suffering body.

The most iconic example of Indigenous land art that literally addresses the earth as an animate being is Rebecca Belmore's *Ayum-ee-aawach Oomama-mowan, Speaking to Their Mother* (1991–96; figure 5.11), a mixed media sculpture created in the wake of a land dispute that escalated into crisis at a Mohawk community near Oka, Quebec, in 1990. Between July and September of 1990, hundreds of members of the Akwesasne, Kanesatake, and Kahnawake Mohawk communities and their Indigenous allies engaged in a seventy-eight-day standoff with the Royal Canadian Mounted Police in an effort to block the private development of a golf course on sacred land. The protest and the international news coverage it generated were not unlike the events that transpired during the Dakota Access Pipeline protest movement in South Dakota in 2016–17, except that tragically, the clash at Oka resulted in a loss of human life. Watching these tragic events unfold and frustrated by the failure of the mainstream media to accurately represent the perspective of the protestors at Oka, Belmore took it upon herself to construct, with the aid of her fellow artists in residence at the Banff Center for the Arts in 1991, a massive wooden amplifier for a megaphone more than six feet high and twelve feet long. Her intention was not to address the protestors, the media, or the police, but to speak directly to the land itself: for the next five years, Belmore transported her apparatus to sites of environmental conflict in every corner of Canada to foster communication between the earth and its people.

One of the first installations of *Ayum-ee-aawach Oomama-mowan, Speaking to Their Mother* was at the Wiggins Bay logging blockade in northern Saskatchewan, where the megaphone was positioned on a hillside across from a parcel of forest that had recently been clear-cut. According to Stó:lō sound and performance scholar Dylan Robinson, protestors and Cree tribal members used the megaphone to speak to the earth in their Indigenous languages.[86] Belmore recalls her own first experience of speaking through the megaphone in Banff: "I felt really humble. I felt so small . . . and I felt my place as a human being as part of the land."[87] Robinson and others have noted that even as the original "audience" for the work was the earth itself, the temptation to use the device to address other humans, especially those in power, was overwhelming. In

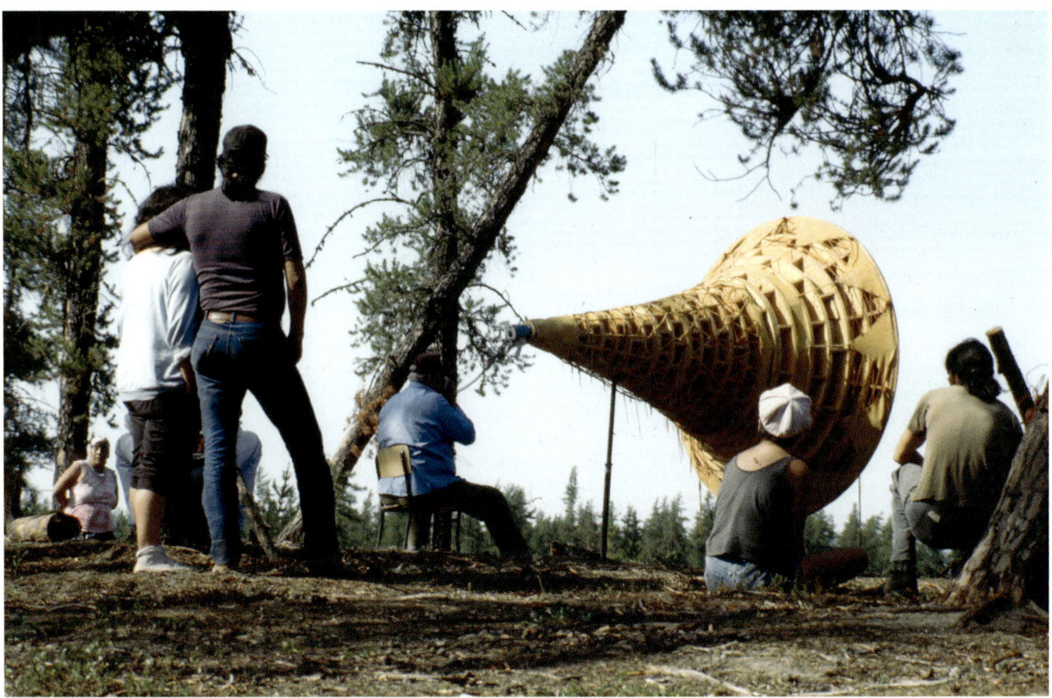

5.11 Rebecca Belmore (Anishinaabe, b. 1960)
Ayum-ee-aawach Oomama-mowan, Speaking to Their Mother (1991–96)
Wood megaphone, 72 × 144 inches
Gathering, logging blockade, North of Meadow Lake, Saskatchewan, 1992
Courtesy of Walter Phillips Gallery, Banff Centre for Arts and Creativity
Photograph by Michael Beynon. Purchased with the support of the York Wilson Endowment Award, Canada Council for the Arts. Accession no. P08 001 S

its five-year run, *Ayum-ee-aawach Oomama-mowan, Speaking to Their Mother* was utilized in public parks opposite government buildings and in front of the Canadian prime minister's residence, and in 1996 it was installed on Parliament Hill in Ottawa to enable members of the Assembly of First Nations to symbolically address the gathering of Canada's first ministers.

The twin desires to "speak to power" and to the earth also underscore the performative interventions of Tahltan artist Peter Morin. In *Cultural Graffiti: A Tahltan Indian Declares War on the British Monarchy* (figure 5.12)—a series of subversive speech acts performed by Morin and witnessed by Robinson in London in 2013—Morin sought to address the "foundations of empire" in as direct a manner as possible. Over a two-week period in June of 2013, Morin traversed the city of London, singing to the bases of buildings and monuments that are directly implicated in the history of British colonialism. According to Robinson, Morin visited two kinds of sites: the first were "the support structures of colonial power and monarchy," such as the Houses of Parliament, the Canada Gate at Buckingham Palace, the Magna Carta monument, and the statue of Queen Victoria at the University of London. Lying face down on pavements, steps, or plinths, Morin sang into the earth, informing the British ancestors that they had failed to eradicate Indigenous people. The artist described his thoughts to Robinson: "walk up to the gate . . . use your voice to write on the gate. the words 'we are still here. we remain. we are still vibrant, you did not win . . . anything. today. you lose everything.'"[88] A second set of sites selected by Morin included "lesser-known Indigenous monuments and sites of Indigenous presence in London, including Pochahontas's grave."[89] At those sites, Morin sang songs to commemorate the lives of Indigenous people who were effectively taken from their homeland.[90]

For Robinson the most important aspect of Morin's and Belmore's speech acts is their ability to "carry our cultural knowledge into the present" and to do so in a way that honors and strengthens the relationships between the living and the dead, the people and the land, humans and nonhumans.[91] He writes, "As song acts and oratory acts, they continue the work that our songs and oratory do in ceremonial context—they communicate with our ancestors, honor our families, and affirm sovereign rights."[92] Thus it becomes clear that in the case of *Ayum-ee-aawach Oomama-mowan, Speaking to Their Mother*, the "work" is not the constructed object itself but the ceremonial acts it engenders. This was evident to Belmore early on in the project: "the art object itself was simply a tool" for directing attention to the land and for situating the body—all bodies—in relationship to the earth.[93] As Cree scholar Gerald McMaster put it, "The work's efficacy is that it brings to our attention the continued belief in the relationship of humanity to the rest of nature. Belmore created an opportunity for everyone to speak without prejudice, fear, or embarrassment to the universe, because at the moment of enunciation,

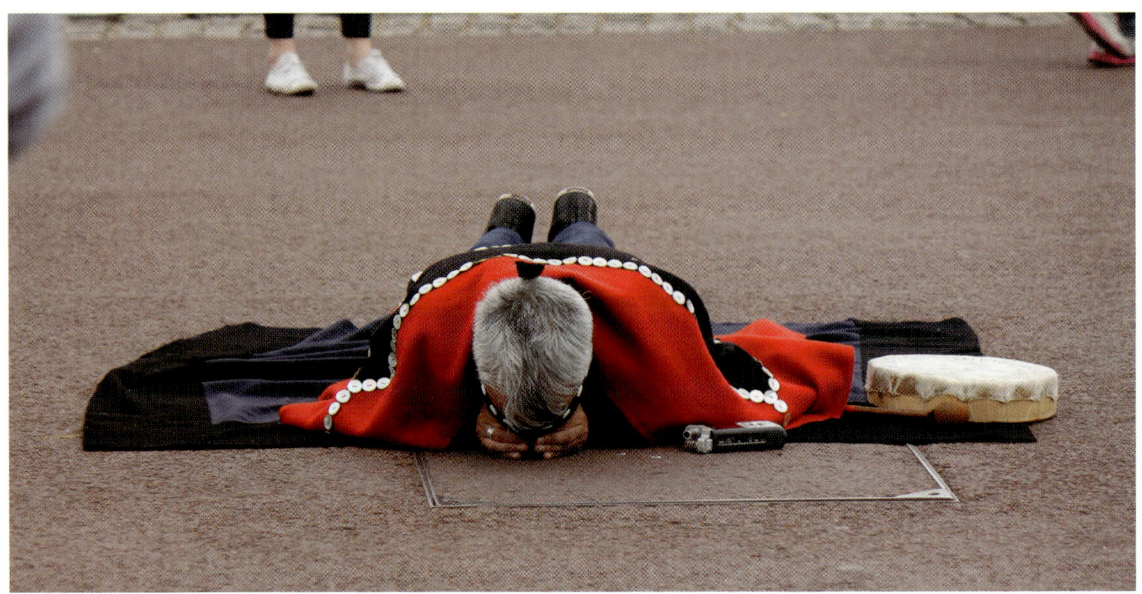

5.12 Peter Morin (Tahltan, b. 1977)
Cultural Graffiti: A Tahltan Indian Declares War on the British Monarchy (2013)
Performance documentation, London
 Photograph by Dylan Robinson.

everything and everybody—the animals, the grass, the wind, the rocks, the sun, the mountains—are witnesses to the address."[94]

The essentially relational aesthetics that inform Morin's and Belmore's art practices course through the majority of the land-based installation and performance works that we have already encountered in this study—especially those that incorporate the human voice.[95] Consider the rather surprising example of Postcommodity's *Do You Remember When?*, a work in which humans are visually absent yet aurally represented in the form of recorded Indigenous voices (in Arizona the sound of Pee Posh social dance songs and in Sydney the utterances of Aborigines calling to the animals of the local ecosystem). Those voices do not emanate from the microphone that hangs over the open pit in the floor; rather they emanate from speakers hidden *beneath* the earth. The hanging microphone that feeds out through a series of speakers in the ceiling is live, picking up the ambient sounds in the room: the sounds of visitors walking and talking or simply breathing. Even the previously recorded songs are picked up and fed back into the environment in a kind of feedback loop that unites all of the humans and nonhumans, present and past, in a vast web of relationships. In a final poignant gesture, Postcommodity affixed a microphone to the excised slab of concrete that rests on the plinth—as a minimalist form it is arguably the most inanimate object in the room—in order to amplify its resonant frequency. In this way the very substance of the earth joins the conversation, and this is a critical contribution of *Do You Remember When?*: the work reminds us that we must learn to *listen* as well as to speak.

This is a lesson that Belmore also learned, in part through her experience watching others interact with *Ayum-ee-aawach Oomama-mowan, Speaking to Their Mother*. In an interview with Cynthia Nixon in 2017, Belmore recalled that the most moving iterations of the speeches she witnessed over the years were those that produced an echo in the landscape. She told Nixon that when the sound bounced off landscape features or buildings, "You'd kind of be confronted with your own self in relation to the land, you know? It's this relationship between the land and yourself."[96] When the opportunity arose for Belmore to revisit the work in 2017 as part of the same *LandMarks* 2017 series of installations in Canada's national parks that included Michael Belmore's *Coalescence*, discussed in the preceding chapter, Belmore sought to formulate a work that could reproduce that accidental effect. She created *Wave Sound* (2017; figure 5.13), an object of similar form to *Ayum-ee-aawach Oomama-mowan, Speaking to Their Mother* but of inverse function: a device not for speaking but for listening.

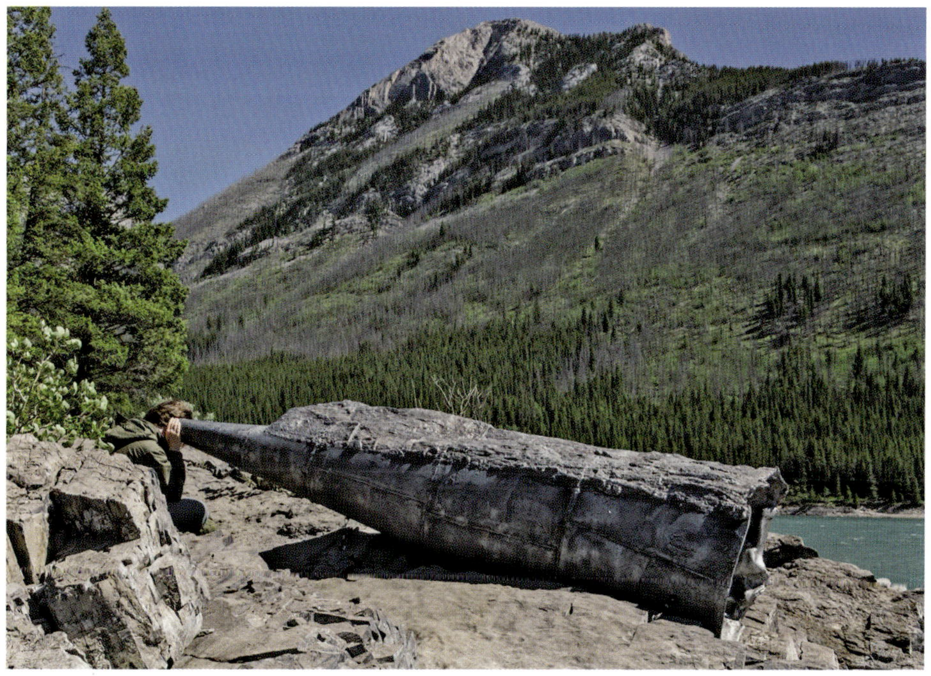

5.13 Rebecca Belmore (Anishinaabe, b. 1960)
Wave Sound (2017)
Aluminum with imprint of stone, 108 inches long, mouth 42 × 41 inches
Installation view, Green Point, Gros Morne National Park, Canada
Courtesy of the artist

For a few weeks in July of 2017, separate iterations of *Wave Sound*—cast aluminum funnels bearing a lithic imprint of the associated landscape—were installed in Banff, Pukaskwa, and Gros Morne National Parks.[97] The conical apparatuses of *Wave Sound* are smaller than the monumental megaphone that preceded them, and their more intimate scale is reflected in the choice that Belmore made to mount them as close to the earth as possible. In order to bring their ears to the level of the funnel, users are obliged to lower themselves to the ground, to kneel or lie on the surface of the earth as they listen to the sounds of waves crashing on a beach or wind moving across a glacier. "I think it is really about taking a moment to sit on the earth itself," the artist explains. "That's really what I'm after in terms of this idea that as human beings we are connected to the earth."[98] Like *Do You Remember When?* before it, *Wave Sound* reminds us that our physical and cultural survival depends on our capacity to unearth and to heed place-based knowledge. Fortunately, we have the work of Indigenous artists to guide us.

NOTES

INTRODUCTION

1 From April 2016 to February 2017, thousands of Native activists and their allies blocked construction of the pipeline, which poses a dire threat to the water supply of the Standing Rock Sioux and an estimated 8 million people living in the Missouri River watershed. If completed, the DAPL will desecrate scores of Indigenous sacred, historical, and cultural sites along its intended 1,172-mile route.

2 The idea for the mirror shield project originated with Luger, who posted do-it-yourself instructions for making the shields on Vimeo in the fall of 2016. With the help of Wakemup from All My Relations Gallery in Minneapolis and Jack Becker of Forecast Public Art, more than five hundred shields were assembled and brought to Oceti Sakowin camp, where *Mirror Shield Project: Water Serpent Action* was performed and filmed. See Regan, "The Standing Project Turns DAPL Protest into an Art Form."

3 Cannupa Hanska Luger, artist's website, www.cannupahanska.com/mniwiconi. See Joyce, "Artists Join the Fight to Protect Standing Rock."

4 For more on art associated with the NoDAPL movement, see Horton, "Drones and Snakes."

5 The most ubiquitous symbol of NoDAPL protest art is a black serpent, thus this performance references the river, the oil fields, and the pipeline itself.

6 Krauss, "Sculpture in the Expanded Field," 30.

7 Krauss, "Sculpture in the Expanded Field," 33.

8 Gerald Vizenor defines "survivance" as "an active form of presence" and a renunciation of "dominance, tragedy and victimry" (*Manifest Manners*, vii).

9 Indigenous visual sovereignty may also be considered a form of strategic resistance to the imposition of colonialist thought, culture, or representation. See Rickard, "Sovereignty." See also Raheja, "Reading Nanook's Smile."

10 Jolene Rickard, "Beyond Jimmie Durham: Contemporary Native American Art and Identity," remarks at a public forum moderated by Kathleen Ash-Milby, Whitney Museum of American Art, November 16, 2017.

11 Mitchell, "Imperial Landscape," 9.

12 I use the term "Native American" to refer to Indigenous people of both the United States and Canada.

13 I use the term "decolonial" (in place of "postcolonial") to indicate an active or present state of the dissolution of colonial structures and processes. A related form of this term, "decoloniality," refers to an active state of resistance, or what Latin American theorist Walter Mignolo has called "epistemic disobedience." In Mignolo's view, decoloniality is distinct from decolonization: the latter is more strictly associated with political and historical movements, and the former refers (like Indigenous sovereignty) to a vast array of cultural expressions and even habits of mind. Mignolo, *Darker Side of Western Modernity*, 122–23.

14 Mitchell, "Imperial Landscape," 5.

15 Mitchell, "Preface," xii.

16 Robinson, "Public Writing, Sovereign Reading."

CHAPTER ONE: THE LAY OF THE LAND

Epigraph: Mitchell, "Imperial Landscape," 5.

1 Rushing, "What the Ground Says," 75.

2 For images of Lavadour's paintings not illustrated here, see the artist's pages at PDX Contemporary Art, http://pdxcontemporaryart.com/james-lavadour.

3 Dobkins, *James Lavadour*, 3. I am indebted to Dobkins for her many insightful writings on Lavadour's work and for accompanying me to the artist's studio on the Confederated Tribes of the Umatilla Reservation in March 2014.

4 Lavadour, artist's statement in Nemiroff, Houle, and Townsend-Gault, *Land, Spirit, Power*, 177.

5 Interview with Lavadour by the author, March 1, 2014.

6 Halper, *James Lavadour*, 15.

7 Longfish and Randall, "Contemporary Native American Art."

8 Dobkins and Ash-Milby describe these works in similar terms. See Ash-Milby, "Imaginary Landscape."

9 Ash-Milby, "Imaginary Landscape," 29.

10 Mejia, "Contemporary North American Indigenous Artists."

11 Morgan, "Kay WalkingStick," 12.

12 Kay WalkingStick, presentation at the National Conference of the Women's Caucus for Art, San Francisco, 1989. Cited in Abbott, *I Stand in the Center*, 269.

13 Abbott, *I Stand in the Center*, 273.

14 WalkingStick, quoted in Abbott, *I Stand in the Center*, 274.

15 Morgan, "Kay WalkingStick," 12.

16 Abbott, *I Stand in the Center*, 274.

17 Artist's statement in Spang and Redcorn, *Indian Time: Art in the New Millennium*.

18 WalkingStick, "Native American Art in the Postmodern Era," 17.

19 Artist's statement in Spang and Redcorn, *Indian Time: Art in the New Millennium*, n.p.

20 Rushing, "What the Ground Says," 78.

21 Mitchell, "Introduction," 1.

22 Cosgrove, *Social Formation and Symbolic Landscape*, 15.

23 Mitchell, "Introduction," 1. Mitchell's argument is slippery here: in defining the modernist approach, he alludes more to the *production* than the *reception* of landscape

at midcentury when he speaks of "the evacuation of verbal, narrative, or historical elements and the presentation of an image designed for transcendental consciousness." His reference at this juncture is to Ernst Gombrich, *Norm and Form: Studies in the Art of the Renaissance* (Chicago, University of Chicago Press, 1966), yet his description readily evokes the art practices of the abstract expressionists and the art criticism of Clement Greenberg. See Greenberg, "Modernist Painting."

24 Bermingham, *Landscape and Ideology*, 119–20.

25 Located in the collection of the Philadelphia Museum of Art.

26 Many of the landscape scenes that Thomas Cole depicted in his paintings were chosen expressly for their significance in the American Revolutionary War. Fort Putnam was strategically situated across the Hudson River from West Point and figured prominently in Benedict Arnold's conspiracy to surrender American military assets to the British. See Effman, "Thomas Cole's *View of Fort Putnam*."

27 Bermingham, "System, Order, and Abstraction," 84.

28 The panopticon is a penitentiary design first proposed in the eighteenth century that allows a single guard to watch all of the prisoners at once from a centralized viewing platform. The panopticon's success as a disciplinary apparatus relies on shielding the prisoners' view in such a way that they cannot know when or whether the guard is looking at them. See Foucault, *Discipline and Punish*.

29 Mitchell, "Introduction," 1–2.

30 Mitchell, "Introduction," 1.

31 Adams, "Competing Communities," 66.

32 Bunn, "'Our Wattled Cot,'" 127.

33 Mitchell, "Imperial Landscape," 5.

34 Mitchell's use of the term "imperialism" instead of "colonialism" is indebted to Edward Said, who is also a contributor to the second edition of *Landscape and Power*. Elsewhere, Said wrote that "the term 'imperialism' means the practice, the theory and the attitudes of a dominating metropolitan center ruling a distant territory; 'colonialism,' which is almost always a consequence of imperialism, is the implanting of settlements on distant territory. . . . In our time, direct colonialism has largely ended; imperialism, as we shall see, lingers where it has always been, in a kind of general cultural sphere as well as in specific political, ideological, economic, and social practices." Said, *Culture and Imperialism*, 9.

35 Mitchell, "Imperial Landscape," 9.

36 It should be noted that Mitchell's essay is unique in this regard: other authors in the collection maintain some degree of focus on the individual when they consider exactly how landscapes construct the position of the viewer. "Commanding a view," "occupying an Olympian position," "inviting entry"—all of these terms imply a singular perspective.

37 Mitchell, "Introduction," 3–4. This supposition is reiterated and refined as Thesis 8: "Landscape is an exhausted medium, no longer viable as a mode of artistic expression. Like life, landscape is boring. We must not say so." The statement's inclusion on the list of theses imbues it with some irony, if not skepticism on Mitchell's part. Mitchell, "Imperial Landscape," 5.

38 Harrison, "The Effects of Landscape," 204.

39 Mitchell, "Introduction," 3.

40 Mitchell, "Imperial Landscape," 9.

41 Mitchell, "Preface to the Second Edition," vii.

42 For more on Foucault's theory of power and agency and especially his assertion that power is distributed throughout the social body, see Foucault, *History of Sexuality*, especially part 4, chapter 2, "Method."

43 Mitchell, "Preface," viii. Here Mitchell refers specifically to the work of the French philosophers Michel de Certeau and Henri Lefebvre and to geographers J. B. Jackson and David Harvey. He does not specifically cite Maurice Merleau-Ponty, but it is clear that his thinking is also indebted to the author of *Phenomenology and Perception* (1945).

44 Mitchell, "Preface," ix.

45 Mitchell, "Preface," ix.

46 Mitchell, "Preface," x. Mitchell grants that his "dialectical triad" of space, place, and landscape corresponds roughly to Henri Lefebvre's "triadic conceptual organization" of perceived, conceived, and lived space. See Mitchell, "Preface," xi–x.

47 Mitchell, "Preface," xii.

48 The Art Seminar series is sponsored by the University of College Cork, Burren College of Art (both in Ireland), and the University of Chicago. The purpose of the seminars is to address "some of the most challenging subjects in current writing on art." The proceedings of the landscape seminar, the sixth in the series, were published as *Landscape Theory*, ed. DeLue and Elkins, in 2008, with the addition of several responding essays.

49 DeLue, quoted in DeLue, Elkins, et al., "Art Seminar," 92.

50 Dubow, quoted in DeLue, Elkins, et al., "Art Seminar," 104.

51 Marshall, "Toward Phenomenology,"197.

52 See Marshall, "Toward Phenomenology."

53 Elkins, quoted in DeLue, Elkins, et al., "Art Seminar," 88.

54 De Lue, "Elusive Landscape and Shifting Grounds," 11.

55 Collectively, this group of exhibitions heralded installation art as a fundamental medium of Native American contemporary art practice. See Martin, "Adjacencies and Distances."

56 Editors' statement in McMaster and Martin, *Indigena*, 15–16.

57 Editors' statement in Nemiroff, Houle, and Townsend-Gault, *Land, Spirit, Power*, 12–13. For more on the themes of the quincentennial response shows and on individual works in the *Land, Spirit, Power* exhibition that addressed the subject of land, see Montiel, "After Columbus."

58 Smith, "Curator's Statement," in *Our Land/Ourselves*, vi–vii.

59 Lowe, paraphrased from quote in Nemiroff, Houle, and Townsend-Gault, *Land, Spirit, Power*, 185.

60 Lavadour, artist statement in Nemiroff, Houle, and Townsend-Gault, *Land, Spirit, Power*, 177.

61 The United Nations Economic and Social Council convened the first meeting of the working group in 1982, charging it with the mandate "to formulate new international standards regarding the rights of Indigenous peoples." See Roulet, *Human Rights and Indigenous Peoples*.

62 The UN Draft Declaration on the Rights of Indigenous Peoples was adopted by the UN Sub-Commission on the Prevention of Discrimination and Protection of Minorities in August of 1994. The final declaration was adopted by UN General Assembly Resolution 61/295 on September 13, 2007.

63 UNDRIP Article 26 (2).

64 UNDRIP Article 25.

65 Gottman, *Significance of Territory*, 15.

66 UNDRIP Article 28 (1) stipulates that Indigenous peoples have the right to "redress, by means that can include restitution or, when this is not possible, just, fair and equitable compensation, for the lands, territories and resources which they have traditionally owned or otherwise occupied or used, and which have been confiscated, taken, occupied,

used or damaged without their free, prior and informed consent." For more on the history and implementation of the UNDRIP, see Echo-Hawk, *In the Light of Justice*.

67 The United States has not legally endorsed the provisions of the UNDRIP, despite President Barack Obama's announcement in December 2010 that the United States had "changed its position" on the declaration. See United States Department of State archived content, "Diplomacy in Action: UN Declaration on the Rights of Indigenous Peoples Review," https://2009-2017.state.gov/s/tribalconsultation/declaration/index.htm.

68 Aspects of culture are fundamental to the provisions of the UNDRIP as well: Article 8 (1) stipulates that "indigenous peoples and individuals have the right not to be subjected to forced assimilation or destruction of their culture."

69 Warrior, *Tribal Secrets*, 124. Warrior's application of the term (and the concept) is both an extension and a critique of legal scholar Vine Deloria Jr.'s groundbreaking study *The Nations Within: The Past and Future of American Indian Sovereignty* (with Clifford Lytle; New York: Pantheon Books, 1984). For more on the evolution of the concept of sovereignty from a strictly legal-political principle to an intellectual ideology, see Cobb, "Understanding Tribal Sovereignty."

70 Rickard, "Diversifying Sovereignty," 81.

71 Rickard, "Visualizing Sovereignty," 467.

72 Rickard, "Sovereignty," 51.

73 Rickard, "Sovereignty," 51.

74 The film was written, directed, acted, filmed, and produced by the majority Inuit production company Igloolik Isuma Productions, Inc.; it was released in 2000. Raheja, "Reading Nanook's Smile," 1162. See also Raheja, "Visual Sovereignty."

75 Raheja, "Reading Nanook's Smile," 1165.

76 Raheja, "Reading Nanook's Smile," 1180 (emphasis added). Raheja calls for "a reading practice for thinking about the space between resistance and compliance wherein Indigenous filmmakers and actors revisit, contribute to, borrow from, critique, and reconfigure ethnographic film conventions" (1161).

77 Rickard writes, "Growing up, I assumed that everybody knew that Native people used a number of strategies to survive, ranging from traditional governments to spiritual political movements. . . . It's still how people talk in our communities, mostly playing down our resistance to the state" ("Sovereignty," 54).

78 Rickard, "Sovereignty," 54. See also Rickard, "Visualizing Sovereignty."

CHAPTER TWO: THE EMERGENT TRADITION OF NATIVE AMERICAN LANDSCAPE PAINTING

1 See Toedtemeier and Laursen, *Wild Beauty*, 9.

2 Interview with Lavadour by the author, March 1, 2014.

3 Morgan, "Kay WalkingStick," 13.

4 Morgan, "Kay WalkingStick," 13.

5 Ash-Milby, "Imaginary Landscape," 26. Emphasis added.

6 Abbott, *I Stand in the Center*, 274.

7 Abbott, *I Stand in the Center*, 275.

8 Raheja, "Reading Nanook's Smile," 1161.

9 Raheja, "Reading Nanook's Smile," 1165.

10 Interview with WalkingStick by the author, January 2, 2014.

11 See Peck, *Thoreau's Morning Work*, 25.

12 The first major dam project in the gorge was the Bonneville Dam, constructed in 1938. Since then, eight more hydroelectric dams have been erected on the Columbia River, leaving only an estimated fifty miles of free-flowing water between the Bonneville Dam and the Canadian border. Toedtemeier and Laursen write in *Wild Beauty* that the Columbia River basin is one of the most altered ecosystems in the United States.

13 See Rojas-Burke, "Sonar Shows Celilo Falls."

14 Quoted in Halper, *James Lavadour*, 15. Lavadour has noted elsewhere that working monochromatically allows him to isolate aspects of particle behavior without being distracted by color or color theory. See Mejia, "Contemporary North American Indigenous Artists."

15 Lavadour engaged in conversations with a physicist while attending a printmaking residency at Rutgers University in 1995. Dobkins and Lavadour, *James Lavadour*, 3–4. See also Rushing, "What the Ground Says," 78.

16 Dobkins and Lavadour, *James Lavadour*, 2.

17 Interview with Lavadour by the author, March 1, 2014.

18 Mejia, "Contemporary North American Indigenous Artists."

19 Abbott, *I Stand in the Center*, 273.

20 Abbott, *I Stand in the Center*, 273.

21 Quoted in Waller, *Homage to the American Elm*.

22 Interview with WalkingStick by the author, January 2, 2014.

23 In November 2015 a retrospective exhibition of Kay WalkingStick's career as an artist opened at the Smithsonian National Museum of the American Indian in Washington, DC. Between 2015 and 2018, *Kay WalkingStick: An American Artist* traveled to five other major exhibition venues in the United States. All of WalkingStick's paintings that are discussed in chapter 2 are illustrated in the companion catalog for the exhibition: Ash-Milby and Penney, *Kay WalkingStick*. Portions of this chapter were previously published in Morris, "What Lies Beneath."

24 The work on paper that made up the left side of *Death of the Elm* is no longer extant, but WalkingStick still has the painting that was the right panel of the diptych. Communication with the author, March 10, 2018.

25 WalkingStick recalls that one of the reasons she had to double-layer her canvases during this period was so that she could gouge more deeply into the material. The horizontal line in *Montauk I* was created with a screwdriver. Interview with WalkingStick by the author, January 2, 2014.

26 Interview with WalkingStick by the author, January 2, 2014.

27 Abbott, *I Stand in the Center*, 274.

28 WalkingStick says, "I saw myself as a modernist. I didn't see myself as an abstract expressionist or a conceptualist. I saw myself as a modernist." Among many others, WalkingStick cites the influence of Ad Reinhardt, Mark Rothko, Jasper Johns, Brice Marden, Helen Frankenthaler, and Sam Gilliam. Interview with WalkingStick by the author, January 2, 2014.

29 Interview with WalkingStick by the author, January 2, 2014.

30 WalkingStick says, "It was always important to me to be recognized as a Native person. It was also important to be understood as a New York artist, one who was working in the mainstream" (interview with WalkingStick by the author, January 2, 2014). For more on the American Indian Movement, see Smith and Warrior, *Like a Hurricane*. For more on the development of art in relation to the American Indian Movement, see Horton, *Art for an Undivided Earth*.

31 Interview with WalkingStick by the author, January 2, 2014.

32 Chief Joseph's band of the Nez Perce was trying to join with Sitting Bull's Hunkpapa

Lakota band in Canada, but after three months of evading the U.S. Army, they were finally forced to surrender on October 5, 1877, at Bear Paw, Montana Territory, just forty miles south of the border. WalkingStick says she was "was very taken with the story of that exodus, so I did the NMAI [National Museum of the American Indian] painting *Homage to Chief Joseph* that led directly to the *Chief Joseph* series. . . . I got more involved in the story itself and the tragedy of it, how he never went home again. It was a tragic loss. . . . I've dealt with it a number of times" (interview with WalkingStick by the author, January 2, 2014).

33 Interview with WalkingStick by the author, January 2, 2014.

34 Welish, "Susan Hoeltzel, Kay WalkingStick and David Frumer," 128.

35 WalkingStick plotted her designs on graph paper before transferring them to the painting or drawing surface. Interview with WalkingStick by the author, January 2, 2014.

36 Krauss, "Grids," 50, 54n1. The essay illustrates works by Jasper Johns, Agnes Martin, and Robert Ryman, but Krauss is addressing the phenomenon of the use of grids much more broadly, mentioning the work of Piet Mondrian, Ad Reinhardt, Frank Stella, Sol LeWitt, Andy Warhol, Chuck Close, and others.

37 Interview with WalkingStick by the author, January 2, 2014. Agnes Martin worked almost exclusively in a square format.

38 Krauss's argument in "Grids" is part of a larger dialogue on the flatness and "objecthood" of modernist painting that began with Greenberg's essay "Modernist Painting." Greenberg wrote, "Realistic, illusionist art had dissembled the medium, using art to conceal art. Modernism used art to call attention to art. The limitations that constitute the medium of painting—the flat surface, the shape of the support, the properties of pigment—were treated by the Old Masters as negative factors that could be acknowledged only implicitly or indirectly. Modernist painting has come to regard these same limitations as positive factors that are to be acknowledged openly."

39 Krauss, "Grids," 52. Krauss's use of the term "materialism" indicates the physical properties of the medium and should not be confused with acquisitiveness.

40 Interview with WalkingStick by the author, January 2, 2014.

41 Phillips, "New York Reviews," 236.

42 Castle wrote that the works "have the quality of imporing touch." Castle, "Kay Walking-Stick at Bertha Urdang," 147.

43 Interview with WalkingStick by the author, January 2, 2014.

44 Perlman, "New York Reviews," 165.

45 Interview with WalkingStick by the author, January 2, 2014.

46 Krauss, "Grids," 50.

47 Krauss, "Grids," 50; emphasis added. In the "temporal" sense, the grid is considered the "emblem of modernity" because it is ubiquitous in the present but appeared "nowhere at all in the art of the last [century]" (52).

48 Abbott, *I Stand in the Center*, 273.

49 WalkingStick quoted in Morgan, "Kay WalkingStick," 12.

50 Krauss, "Grids," 60, 60–61.

51 Krauss, "Grids," 61.

52 Krauss, "Grids," 64.

53 Krauss's primary example of an artist whose work exhibited both centrifugal and centripetal tendencies is Piet Mondrian; however, she locates the two distinct approaches in separate canvases rather than in a single work. Her secondary examples of artists who "think about the grid in both ways at once"—Joseph Albers, Ellsworth Kelly, and Sol LeWitt—would seem to support this reading, given that all worked in series.

54 Malarcher, "The Meanings of 'Duality.'"

55 Morgan, "Kay WalkingStick," 12.

56 Interview with WalkingStick by the author, June 8, 2006. WalkingStick had explored this theme at least once before in *Fear of Non-Beings* (1974), which is in a series of works she calls the *Beings and Non-Beings*. According to WalkingStick, the series was inspired by her decision to "deal with" her feelings about the death of both of her parents in the late 1960s. Interview with WalkingStick by the author, January 2, 2014.

57 For an artist who had for decades been committed to affirming the physical and material aspects of painting, WalkingStick's exploration of the immaterial represented a momentous shift in her approach.

58 Interview with WalkingStick by the author, June 8, 2006. The painting is in the collection of the Pinacoteca di Brera, Milan.

59 This 20-by-40-inch charcoal drawing may be considered a sketch or study for the diptych paintings of the same period: the waterfall element of *Is That You?* is nearly identical to the one featured in *Loss*.

60 For further analysis of this series, see Seppi, "Metaphysics and Materiality," 119ff.

61 In Euclidean geometry the ellipse is associated with both circles and cones; in optics it can be defined as a circle seen from an oblique angle; in astronomy it is associated with orbital paths.

62 Interview with WalkingStick by the author, June 8, 2006.

63 Excerpt from WalkingStick's artist statement at Hillwood Art Museum, *Kay WalkingStick Paintings: 1974–1990* (New York: Long Island University, 1991), cited in Archuleta, "Kay WalkingStick," 23.

64 Morgan, "Kay WalkingStick," 12–13.

65 WalkingStick, "Native American Art in the Postmodern Era,"16–17.

66 Morgan, "Kay WalkingStick," 13.

67 Abbott, *I Stand in the Center*, 279.

68 In addition to WalkingStick, Native American artists who participated in *The Decade Show* include G. Peter Jemison, George Longfish, James Luna, Jaune Quick-to-See Smith, and Richard Ray Whitman. See the digital archive of the New Museum, archive.newmuseum.org.

69 Nemiroff, Houle, and Townsend-Gault, *Land, Spirit, Power*, 213–14.

70 The copper plaque is a duplicate of one incorporated in WalkingStick's mixed media sculpture, *Tears* (1991), which was exhibited in the *Submuloc Show/Columbus Wohs*. In her artist's statement in that catalog, WalkingStick writes, "My anger is profound. We are all angry and heartsick" (Smith, *The Submuloc Show/Columbus Wohs*, 66).

71 In 1992 WalkingStick also produced an illustrated book, *The Wizard Speaks, the Calvary Listens, December 29th 1890*. Only four panels long, the book contains images referencing the massacre at Wounded Knee, South Dakota, in 1890 and text reproduced from a contemporaneous editorial written by L. Frank Baum in which he advocates for the extinction of all Indians. See Valentino, "'Mistaken Identity,'" 70–72.

72 Morgan, "Kay WalkingStick," 13.

73 See Seppi, "Metaphysics and Materiality," 150.

74 There are three other works in the *Four Directions* series, all from 1994–95: *Four Directions: The Void Within*; *Four Directions: Stillness*; and *Four Directions: Vision*. Many other diptychs from this period feature the equilateral cross, yet one of the *Four Directions* series does not. In *Four Directions: The Void Within*, a diamond shape replaces the cross, perhaps to better convey the idea of a void.

75 Seppi, "Metaphysics and Materiality," 150. Seppi cites WalkingStick's personal papers, dated 1994.

76 WalkingStick considers reverence for the earth as sacred to be a commonality of Native cultures.

77 Seppi, "Metaphysics and Materiality," 151.

78 Seppi, "Metaphysics and Materiality," 151.

79 Krauss, "Grids," 54. Krauss is being intentionally ironic here: she argues in this essay that the infusion of modernist works with religious connotations was an open secret.

80 The notion that Indigenous art is naturally imbued with spirituality is not uncontroversial. See the critical response to the *Magiciens de la Terre* exhibition at the Pompidou Center in Paris in 1989.

81 WalkingStick remarks, "I am a Christian, but I pray to the four directions" (quoted in Seppi, "Metaphysics and Materiality," 153). Following a period of religious study in Rome, WalkingStick converted to Catholicism in 2000 (184).

82 In the early diptychs, WalkingStick used abstraction to mitigate the illusionist qualities of the landscape paintings. Here the roles seem to be reversed: the introduction of the landscape imagery alters our perception of the abstract elements.

83 WalkingStick, "Native American Art in the Postmodern Era," 17.

84 The left-right reversal of the abstraction and landscape panels is somewhat atypical of WalkingStick's diptychs, but it is not absolutely unique. *The Abyss* (1989) and many of the diptychs painted after 2001 exhibit this orientation.

85 Morgan, "Kay WalkingStick," 13.

86 This diptych is uncharacteristically small: it is only 15 ½ by 31 inches, indicating that it may be considered a study for future works.

87 *Continuum 12 Artists* was a series of solo exhibitions by twelve artists held at National Museum of the American Indian George Gustav Heye Center in New York City as a prelude to the opening of the NMAI on the Washington Mall in Washington, DC, in 2004. The series was curated by Truman Lowe and ran from 2003 to 2005. WalkingStick was the second artist in the series; her work was on view from April to August 2003. For a complete list of artists and their works, see National Museum of the American Indian exhibition archive, www.nmai.si.edu/exhibitions/continuum.

88 Of the relationship between the charcoal sketch and the fully realized oil painting, WalkingStick notes that "changes in my art work are usually seen first in my drawings. For instance, in 2002, I was making works on paper from a single viewpoint, yet single image landscape didn't appear in my paintings until 2006" (artist's statement, www.kaywalkingstick.com).

89 The cost of these materials accounts for the relatively small size of the diptychs, which are either 12 by 24 inches or 24 by 48 inches. Only *Autumn's End* is larger (32 by 64 inches); it is embossed with aluminum foil.

90 In "Modernist Painting," Greenberg argued that "all recognizable entities (including pictures themselves) exist in three-dimensional space, and the barest suggestion of a recognizable entity suffices to call up associations of that kind of space. The fragmentary silhouette of a human figure, or of a teacup, will do so, and by doing so alienate pictorial space from the literal two-dimensionality which is the guarantee of painting's independence as an art."

91 Artist's statement, www.kaywalkingstick.com.

92 Conversely, the joining of the landscape and the pattern may establish the primacy of land in Native American art. Many of the patterns are regarded as symbolizing land in other media such as weaving and ceramics.

93 Interview with WalkingStick by the author, January 2, 2014.

CHAPTER THREE: BEYOND THE HORIZON

Epigraph: Quoted in Nemiroff, Houle, and Townsend-Gault, *Land, Spirit, Power*, 107.

1 Smith, "Curator's Statement," vi.

2 Morrison's position as a central figure in the development of both American and Native American modernist painting has been firmly established by Anthes, in *Native Moderns*, and Rushing and Makholm, *Modern Spirit*.

3 Morrison, *Turning the Feather Around*, cited in Anthes, *Native Moderns*, 108.

4 Morrison, *Turning the Feather Around*, cited in Anthes, *Native Moderns*, 108.

5 Morrison, *Turning the Feather Around*, cited in Rushing and Makholm, *Modern Spirit*, 29. Rushing and Makholm write that the lines are "simultaneously a critical formal element, a symbol, and [Morrison's] logo" (39). Anthes notes that David Penney had earlier compared "the horizon line that is common in all of Morrison's work after the mid-1940s to the signature motifs of the non-Native painters of the New York school, such as Barnett Newman's instantly recognizable 'zips' or Adolph Gottlieb's 'bursts'" (Anthes, *Native Moderns*, 112).

6 Morrison, *Turning the Feather Around*, cited in Rushing and Makholm, *Modern Spirit*, 41.

7 Cited in Rushing and Makholm, *Modern Spirit*, 28.

8 For more on the genesis of Morrison's collages and his relationship with Louise Nevelson, see Rushing and Makholm, *Modern Spirit*, 26ff.

9 Cited in Anthes, *Native Moderns*, 111.

10 Earlier works were composed of driftwood from the Atlantic shore; later ones incorporated wood from Lake Superior and elsewhere. Friends and colleagues of Morrison are quick to reminisce about contributing wood to his collection. See Kay WalkingStick's foreword, "A Special Visit with George Morrison," in Rushing and Makholm, *Modern Spirit*, ix.

11 Anthes, *Native Moderns*, 112.

12 Morrison was awarded a Fulbright Fellowship to study in Paris and Aix-en-Provence, France in 1952. See Netha Anita Cloeter, "George Morrison Chronology," in Rushing and Makholm, *Modern Spirit*, 149ff.

13 Anthes cites Morrison's autobiography: "'I could never have done this kind of abstraction in Minneapolis,' he wrote, 'Never, never, never.'" Anthes, *Native Moderns*, 110.

14 Anthes, *Native Moderns*, 111.

15 Anthes, *Native Moderns*, 111.

16 Morrison cited in Anthes, *Native Moderns*, 111. Morrison is referring in part to joining the American Indian Movement, which was then forming in Minneapolis.

17 For an in-depth consideration of Morrison's Native American identity and its impact on both the production and reception of his work, see Rushing and Makholm, *Modern Spirit*, 43ff.

18 Penney, "George Morrison," 22. Also cited in Anthes, *Native Moderns*, 112.

19 Morrison was diagnosed with Castleman's disease, a lymphatic system disorder, in 1985. He sought treatment through both Western and traditional medicine and in 1986 was given his Ojibwe names, "Standing in the Northern Lights" and "Turning the Feather Around," as part of his healing ceremonies.

20 Rushing and Makholm, *Modern Spirit*, 41.

21 Rushing and Makholm, *Modern Spirit*, 41.

22 Smith, "Lie That Blinds," 78.

23 Smith, *Our Land/Ourselves*, v–vi. Penney's later description of Morrison's landscapes as being reflective of an "internalized" experience of place derived from "an inner state" of contemplation would seem to align with this perspective as well, though Penney's emphasis is on the conceptual nature of Morrison's work rather than on his status as an insider.

24 See Roberts, "Conflict of the Spirit."
25 Kastner, *Jaune Quick-to-See Smith*, 28.
26 Kastner, *Jaune Quick-to-See Smith*, 29.
27 Kastner, *Jaune Quick-to-See Smith*, 30.
28 Kastner, *Jaune Quick-to-See Smith*, 30–31.
29 Duncan, "Sites of Representation," 40.
30 The etymology of the word "landscape" is endlessly contested. For a brief synopsis of the many possible meanings of the term, see Olwig, "The 'Actual Landscape.'"
31 Olwig, "The 'Actual Landscape,'"63–164.
32 The *Oxford English Dictionary* defines "perspective" as "the true understanding of the relative importance of things; a realistic sense of proportion."
33 Interview with Lavadour by the author, March 1, 2014. This story of flying over the Grand Canyon is also mentioned in Halper, *James Lavadour*, 19.
34 Halper notes that in 1986 Lavadour began mixing his paint with large quantities of the synthetic resin medium Rapid Set to create "a more fluid, malleable surface for recording his gestures"(*James Lavadour*, 19).
35 Interview with Lavadour by the author, March 1, 2014.
36 Mejia, "Contemporary North American Indigenous Artists"; punctuation added.
37 Some early landscapes contained figures but not in a conventional sense: often the figures were ghosts or skeletons that hovered above or were embedded within the earth. See Halper, *James Lavadour*.
38 Interview with Lavadour by the author, March 1, 2014.
39 Both *Nest of Suns* and *Sunflower* (1999) measure 72 by 96 inches; Dobkins likens this arrangement to the "Plateau star," a motif found in traditional Plateau weaving. Dobkins and Lavadour, *James Lavadour*, 6. For the quotation, see Mejia, "Contemporary North American Indigenous Artists."
40 The 1995 residency at Rutgers was Lavadour's second; the first was in 1990, when Lavadour learned printmaking under the tutelage of master printer Eileen Foti. See Dobkins and Lavadour, *James Lavadour*, 3–4. See also Rushing, "What the Ground Says," 78–80.
41 Lavadour's fascination with the terminology of fluid dynamics can be gleaned from his selection of the title *Fingering Instabilities* for an exhibition of his work at Portland's PDX Gallery in 2014.
42 Dobkins writes that Lavadour "understands painting to be not merely similar to forces that shape the earth but a physical force governed by the same natural laws" (*James Lavadour*, 2).
43 Smallwood, "Review," 168.
44 Quoted in Gibson, "James Lavadour," 45.
45 Interview with Lavadour by the author, March 1, 2014.
46 Mejia, "Contemporary North American Indigenous Artists"; punctuation added.
47 Dobkins and Lavadour, *James Lavadour*, 5. Dobkins notes that *Ice* and *Hollow*, both from 2007, demonstrate Lavadour's technique of applying a layer of mica particles to enliven the washes of thinned white paint.
48 Dobkins and Lavadour, *James Lavadour*, 4.
49 Interview with Lavadour by the author, March 1, 2014. Lavadour's use of the term "architectural" is not to be taken literally, though he sometimes refers to "doors and windows and platforms" in his paintings. The term is a metaphor for an armature—or structure—that organizes space.
50 Interview with Lavadour by the author, March 1, 2014.
51 Interview with Lavadour by the author, March 1, 2014.

52 Interview with Lavadour by the author, March 1, 2014.

53 Lavadour notes that "the grid is not necessarily a literal line; it could be a back wall in this thing that kind of creates space" (interview with Lavadour by the author, March 1, 2014).

54 Krauss, "Grids," 50.

55 Krauss, "Grids," 50. Lavadour regards the prototypical modernist grid as "a sterile structure; nothing can grow on it" (interview with Lavadour by the author, March 1, 2014).

56 Jackson, *A Sense of Place, A Sense of Time*, 154.

57 Glowen, "Review," 177. Lavadour notes in his artist's statement in the *Land, Spirit, Power* catalog that he also has worked in the areas of education, alcohol and drug treatment, housing, economic development, and natural resources management. Since 1990 he has been the driving force behind Crow's Shadow Institute for the Arts, a printmaking workshop on the Umatilla Reservation.

58 Interview with WalkingStick by the author, January 2, 2014.

59 In the conventional language of digital printing, "landscape" format refers to the horizontal orientation of a page versus the vertical portrait orientation.

60 Mejia, "Contemporary North American Indigenous Artists."

61 Jackson, *A Sense of Place, A Sense of Time*, 154.

62 See Crandall, "Anything That Moves." See also Crandall, "Embedded Reporters, Predator Drones, and Armed Perception."

63 In a recent essay in *Art in America*, Horton considers the use of UAVs (unmanned aerial vehicles) by both protestors and state police during the Dakota Access Pipeline protests. She writes of the UAVs operated by protestors: "The drones of NoDAPL represent a complex scenario in which technologies with violent origins are bent to the work of 'survivance' by the populations they were designed to control" (Horton, "Drones and Snakes," 104).

64 It is interesting to note that Lavadour's flight over the Grand Canyon in a small plane in 1987 would have afforded him an aerial view rather than an in-canyon perspective.

65 Artists who have worked with the Walla Walla Foundry include Marie Watt, Kiki Smith, Jim Dine, Maya Lin, Jenny Holzer, Jeff Koons, and Richard Prince. See the "Portfolio" section of the Walla Walla Foundry website, https://wallawallafoundry.com.

66 Interview with Lavadour by the author, March 1, 2014. For a brief description of the process, and images of both the original black and white painting and the finished sculptures, see the videotaped interview, "James Lavadour at PDX," March 28, 2012, https://vimeo.com/39369277.

67 Interview with Lavadour by the author, March 1, 2014.

68 Each edition comprises three separate pieces: 13 by 24 by 18 inches; 5 by 27 by 27 inches; and 2 by 4 by 25 inches. *Red River* is installed outside the Oregon Department of Transportation headquarters in Salem, Oregon, as part of the department's public art program.

69 Interview with Lavadour by the author, March 1, 2014.

CHAPTER FOUR: CENTERING

1 Postcommodity member Kade Twist, quoted in San Francisco Art Institute's Graduate Lecture Series, February 28, 2017.

2 Judd, "Specific Objects."

3 The title of the work refers to a time before the present, when all land was Native land. The work underscores both the presence and absence of aboriginal peoples with the inclusion of a sound component (of aboriginal songs and prayers).

4 Installation art was not common in Native American art until roughly 1990. In that year, the Heard Museum's *Shared Visions: Native American Painters and Sculptors in the Twentieth Century* exhibition included James Luna's installation *The Creation and Destruction of an Indian Reservation* (1990). When the quincentennial exhibitions opened two years later, they featured many installations, in part because the large venues provided ample space and support for them. See Morris, "Introduction to Sculpture," and Martin, "Adjacencies and Distances."

5 Ortel, *Woodland Reflections*, 98. Ortel writes of *Ottawa*, "Although not strictly speaking site-specific—it has subsequently been shown in various locations—this work was also made in response to a particular place" (98).

6 Ortel, *Woodland Reflections*, 98.

7 See Ash-Milby, "HIDE," 27–29.

8 Holubizky, "Michael Belmore," 73.

9 *LandMarks* 2017/*Reperes*2017 featured the work of twelve contemporary artists who were invited to create "multidisciplinary art projects inspired by nature" in Canada's national parks and historic sites. The exhibition was organized by Toronto-based Partners in Art with support from the Canadian government, in honor of the 150th anniversary of Canada's Confederation. *LandMarks* 2017 culminated in June 2017 with a series of public events, but Belmore's *Coalescence* will remain in situ.

10 See the *Coalesence* project pages in the *LandMarks* 2017 web archive, https://landmarks2017.ca/info/michael-belmore/coalescence/.

11 Houle, "Bonnie Devine," 38.

12 See Ash-Milby, "Alan Michelson."

13 Thoreau, *Walden*. Michelson's engagement with Thoreau continued into 2007 with his installation *A Closer View* for Wave Hill in the Bronx. The sound installation reflected on Thoreau's acts of civil disobedience. For more on Thoreau's night in Concord jail and its relevance to the shaping of his thoughts on nature, see Solnit, *Storming the Gates of Paradise*.

14 Everett, "Alan Michelson." Robert Smithson (1938–73) was born in Rutherford, New Jersey. He studied at the Art Students League of New York from 1955 to 1956 and was a member of the minimalist movement of the 1960s. He is best known for his large-scale earthwork *Spiral Jetty* (1970). Smithson's non-sites (begun 1968) are key works in the history of both minimalism and earth art.

15 Smithson, "Earth,"160.

16 Owens has argued that Smithson's non-sites are relegated to being "a vacant reflection of the site." He writes, "Whenever Smithson invokes the notion of the center, however, it is to describe its loss"("Earthwords," 122).

17 In essence, *Do You Remember When?* encompasses both the site (the hole in the floor, the "raw reality—the earth") and the non-site (the excised slab, the "abstraction") in a single work, placing them in close proximity to one another.

18 For detailed analysis of Postcommodity's participation in the 2012 Sydney Biennale, see Watson, "'Centering the Indigenous.'"

19 Artist collective statement on the "*Do You Remember When?*" pages of the Postcommodity website, http://postcommodity.com/DoYouRememberWhen.html.

20 Watson reaches a similar conclusion. He writes that "the Indigenous sense of land is recovered and asserted, involving both a common respect for Indigenous sovereignty and an ethical focus on human-environment reciprocity" ("'Centering the Indigenous,'" 142).

21 Digital video with sound, 19:24, original instrumental score by Michael J. Schumacher, first exhibited at State University of New York at Stony Brook, 2006.

22 Personal communication, January 6, 2009. For more on panoramas, see Oettermann, *The Panorama.*

23 Personal communication, January 6, 2009.

24 Everett, "Alan Michelson," 32.

25 Michelson in McMaster, "Alan Michelson," 44. Joseph Conrad's short novel *Heart of Darkness* (1899) has been described as "a thematic exploration of the savagery-versus-civilization relationship, and of the colonialism and racism that make imperialism possible" (Wikipedia.org/Heart_of_Darkness).

26 Smithson, "Monuments of Passaic."

27 According to Smithson's partner Nancy Holt, this "new consciousness" underscored the creation of the sites and non-sites in the following year (Holt, "Biographical Note," 5).

28 Smithson, "Monuments of Passaic," 54.

29 Owens seems to have extracted the phrase "entropy made visible" from Smithson's own writings. See Owens, "Earthwords." In an interview with Alison Sky, Smithson described entropy as "a condition that's moving towards a gradual equilibrium" (Sky, "Entropy Made Visible," 189).

30 For detailed discussion of the circumstance of the work's commissioning by the General Services Administration's Art in Architecture program, see Morris, "Running the Medicine Line."

31 The sculpture can be likened to a stained glass window: it was fabricated in Munich using a process by which the ten panels of eight-millimeter thick glass were imprinted with images sandblasted through a dot-matrix screen.

32 Cornwall Island (Kawehno:ke) is located within Canada's national boundaries. The Akwesasne Mohawk Nation straddles the U.S.-Canada border. For a map of this territory, see Morris, "Running the Medicine Line."

33 The orientation of this "map" is unusual in that south is positioned at the top. This perspective reflects a Massena-centered view of the river, which in turn reflects the commission of the work by the U.S. government.

34 Lending further critical weight to the project is the uncanny timing of the installation of *Third Bank of the River* at Massena just weeks before the eruption of a serious diplomatic incident between the Mohawk Nation and the Canadian government on the other side of the bridge. With its territories straddling the U.S.-Canada border, the Akwesasne Mohawk Nation had been host to Canada's Border Services Agency (CBSA), allowing that agency to establish a Canadian border crossing station on Cornwall Island. When the CBSA decided in the spring of 2009 that it would begin arming its border agents, the Mohawk Council of Akwesasne objected, viewing the insertion of armed forces as an infringement of their sovereignty. On May 30 the Mohawk Council forced the closure of the border crossing station on Cornwall Island, and six weeks later the CBSA built a temporary crossing on the Cornwall "mainland." See Morris, "Running the Medicine Line."

35 Installed as part of the groundbreaking exhibition *Sakahàn: International Indigenous Art.* The digital print on adhesive film that was exhibited in *Sakahàn* is enlarged from a photograph of a beaded belt also made by the artist.

36 Myre, artist's statement, http://artmur.com/en/artists/nadia-myre/for-those-who-cannot-speak.

37 Mohawk Chief Joseph Brant traveled to London in 1775 to secure an allegiance with the British during the Revolutionary War. The Crown promised the Iroquois land in Quebec in exchange for the Iroquois Confederacy's support against the American colonists. The Haldimand Proclamation was issued by Frederick Haldimand, governor of the province

of Quebec, on October 25, 1784. It granted "the Mohawk Nation and such others of the Six Nation Indians as wish to settle in that quarter to take possession of and settle upon the Banks of the River commonly called Ours [Ouse] or Grand River, running into Lake Erie, allotting to them for that purpose six miles deep from each side of the river beginning at Lake Erie and extending in that proportion to the head of the said river, which them and their posterity are to enjoy for ever."

38 Six speakers were recorded at the Six Nations radio station, CKRZ: Roger Porter, Leona Moses, Tom Hill, Alfred Keye (speaking in Cayuga), Roberta Jamieson, and Amos Keye Jr.

39 Amos Keye Jr., referring to the Grand River, quoted in *TwoRow II* transcript provided by Alan Michelson.

40 Alan Michelson, interview with Raquel Chapa, New York City, October 5, 2005. Available online through New York University's Hemispheric Institute of Performance and Politics.

41 The film dramatizes the plight of poverty-stricken Mohawks from the Saint Regis Reservation near Massena who attempt to smuggle goods across the frozen Saint Lawrence River in December. The film offers an acutely contemporary vision—the "goods" that are smuggled across the border are not contraband cigarettes but illegal immigrants—nevertheless, the navigability of both the river and the border is held to be a foundational condition of Mohawk experience.

42 Codices are illustrated manuscripts from Mesoamerica dating from the fifth to the seventeenth centuries. Many tell of the epic migrations of the Mixtec, Mayan, and Aztec peoples. See Boone, *Stories in Red and Black*.

43 Haozous, remarks at the Photography Institute public lecture series on "Public Art," 1998, www.thephotographyinstitute.org/journals1988.

44 James Earle Fraser's iconic sculpture was first exhibited at the Panama-Pacific International Exposition in San Francisco in 1915.

45 The proximity of the commercial airliners to the skyscrapers in the image was less alarming in a pre-9/11 world, yet Haozous regarded them as "warlike": the searchlights projected into the sky hint at an air raid, and the enormous "U.S." on one of the buildings might be regarded as a military emblem.

46 Haozous's website gives the title as *Otay Mesa Crossing* and does not provide dimensions of the piece or dates of its construction; elsewhere, Haozous recalls the date as 1996. The only published record of the work is in Schroeder, "Official Art, Official Publics." Schroeder's article, drawn from research in the archives of the General Services Administration's Art in Architecture Program, identifies the piece as *Spirit of the Earth*, installed at Otay Mesa in 1994.

47 In this earlier iteration, the landscape is either formed or dominated by Kokopelli, the flute player and fertility figure of ancient Puebloan religion.

48 Schroeder, "Official Art, Official Publics," 261–64.

49 Haozous, remarks at the Photography Institute public lecture series on "Public Art," 1998, www.thephotographyinstitute.org/journals1988.

50 Viewed through the lens of Trump-era border politics, the image suggests a more pointed critique of the desire to allow goods but not people to flow freely across the border.

51 Haozous reprised the use of razor wire on a public monument in 2000 when his monumental *Gate/Negate* was installed near the New Mexico state capitol in Santa Fe.

52 Quoted on the occasion of the installation of the work as part of the Albuquerque Museum's 2018 exhibition *The U.S.-Mexico Border: Place, Imagination and Possibility*. Jackie Kent, "Museum's Newest Installation Highlights Border Tensions," KRQE News, Albuquerque, January 5, 2018.

53 Lippard, "Color of the Wind," 9–10.

54 "We are at a point in Iroquoian society in our relationships to both the U.S. and Canadian governments, where they're wondering when we are going to let go of our borders. I need to do something that reconfirms our borders—the 'borders of sovereignty'—the geopolitical borders that mark our nationhood, our reservation, our self-determination, and our territories" (Rickard, quoted in McMaster, *Reservation X*, 128).

55 Rickard, quoted in McMaster, *Reservation X*, 128.

56 See Morris, "Running the Medicine Line."

57 The provisions of the Jay Treaty were confirmed by the Treaty of Ghent of 1814 but abrogated by the United States Immigration Act of 1924. See Spruhan, "The Canadian Indian Free Passage Right"; and Singleton, "Not Our Borders." Mohawk scholar Audra Simpson's *Mohawk Interruptus* gives perhaps the most comprehensive reading of the cultural complexities of this border zone. Detailing the history and contemporary use of tribally issued passports, Simpson writes that the border to some extent forms the experience of Mohawk identity: "For Iroquois peoples the border acts as a site not of transgression but for the activation and articulation of their rights as members of reserve nations, or Haudenosaunee, or Iroquois Confederacy people. Thus the people who are crossing borders are reserve members or Iroquois before they cross, they are especially Iroquois *as* they cross" (*Mohawk Interruptus*, 116).

58 Rickard has lauded Michelson's *Third Bank of the River* for being a vivid proclamation of Indigenous visual sovereignty ("Visualizing Sovereignty," 469–70).

59 David Winstead, GSA commissioner of Public Buildings Service, quoted in "Thresholds along the Frontier."

60 Postcommodity's interviews with U.S. Border Patrol agents provided some of the impetus for their creation of *Coyotaje* (2017), an installation with video that imagines a border-zone version of the mythical chupacabra. See Puleo, "Artist Collective Postcommodity."

61 In situ October 9–12, 2015. For more on the process of installation, see the feature-length documentary film *Through the Repellent Fence* (2017) by filmmaker Sam Wainwright Douglas.

62 Postcommodity artist collective, description of work, http://postcommodity.com/AVeryLongLine.html and http://postcommodity.com/Repellent_Fence_English.html.

63 For more on these pamphlets and guide books, see Berry and Lewis, *Lives of the Hudson*.

64 Though the experience is of continuous, fluid movement, it is interesting to note that the territory in question is traversed twice. The movement is actually a return, which may be even more analogous to the contemporary border crossing experience of Iroquois people at Massena, Niagara, and other Indigenous territories that straddle the U.S.-Canada border.

65 Krauss, "Sculpture in the Expanded Field." In the essay, Krauss reflected on the effects of removing the pedestal from minimalist and site-specific installations. Looking back to figural sculpture that was erected to commemorate events or mark important historic sites from antiquity to the late nineteenth century, she concluded that the pedestal had helped to define the "logic of the monument"—a logic that rooted sculpture in place. Modernist sculpture, by contrast, defied this logic: in giving up the pedestal, it consigned itself to a condition that Krauss described as "nomadic" or a form of "homelessness."

66 See Berry and Lewis, *Lives of the Hudson*. The exhibition, which explored the past and present of the Hudson River through the multiple perspectives of art, science, and tourism, was on view at the Tang Art Museum from July 18, 2009, through March 14, 2010.

67 Smithson, "Monuments of Passaic," 54–55.

68 Recent scholarship on the art of the 1960s associates much of the art of the era with Hegel's concept of a "bad infinity," characterized by an emphasis on the banal and the endless. See Lee, *Chronophobia*.

69 Michelson, *Shattemuc* wall text, *Lives of the Hudson* exhibition, Tang Art Museum, 2010.

70 Michelson, *Shattemuc* wall text, *Lives of the Hudson* exhibition, Tang Art Museum, 2010.

71 Following the filming of *Mespat*, Michelson increasingly sought out sites of rare beauty and tragedy on the peripheries of New York City. In 2003 he journeyed forty miles north to film the landscape at Indian Point, a nuclear power plant on the banks of the Hudson River. *Twilight, Indian Point*, like the works in the later series *Of Light after Darkness*, records the sun setting in real time and was displayed in a gilded frame.

72 Michelson is not the only contemporary artist to take up the subject of Cole's *The Course of Empire* in their work. The Los Angeles–based painter Sandow Birk (b. 1962), who has created cycles of dystopic "history" paintings in response to contemporary events like the 1992 Los Angeles riots and created sublime vistas of California's thirty-three state prisons (*Prisonation* 2001), painted a five-canvas response to Cole's series entitled *The Rise and Fall of Los Angeles* (1995). Birk's version of the cycle depicts the Los Angeles basin and Hollywood Hills at five "moments" spanning from prehistory to an apocalyptic future.

73 See Wallach, "Cole, Byron, and *The Course of Empire*."

74 Miller et al., *American Encounters*, 257.

75 Artist's website, description of work, www.alanmichelson.com.

76 Between 1895 and 1930 Curtis visited more than eighty Indian tribes in North America in an effort to document Native life and culture before it "disappeared." He made more than forty thousand photographs and ten thousand wax cylinder sound recordings; his twenty-volume series, *The North American Indian*, was published between 1907 and 1930. The passage of Curtis's writings that Michelson excerpted in the titles of his video paintings was published in Tennant, "Work of E. S. Curtis."

77 Owens's characterization of Smithson as a postmodernist is taken up most strongly by Shapiro, *Earthwards*. Roberts launched a strong challenge to this interpretation of Smithson's works in "Landscapes of Indifference."

78 Thomas's family, like Michelson's, is from the Six Nations Reserve. Thomas's series of photographs of the Champlain monument began in 1997 and is ongoing. See Lauzon, "Monumental Interventions." *Buffalo Boy* pictures the Blackfoot artist Adrian Stimson in the guise of his gender-bending alter ego, Buffalo Boy. For more on Stimson, see Ryan Rice and Carla Taunton, "Buffalo Boy: Then and Now," http://indianacts.gruntarchives.org/essay-buffalo-boy-then-and-now-rice-and-taunton.html.

79 Phillips, "Settler Monuments, Indigenous Memory," 284.

80 Phillips, "Settler Monuments, Indigenous Memory," 294. Phillips specifically associates presence with modernity, adding that Thomas and other contemporary Native artists "seek to revise a historical discourse that has silenced Indigenous memory, while countering an art historical discourse that has constructed the Indigenous artist as a primitive, and therefore as outside modernism" (282).

81 Phillips, "Settler Monuments, Indigenous Memory," 300.

82 The tendency to regard Native American art as if it is concerned only with the past is directly countered in the exhibition *Close Encounters: The Next 500 Years*, held at the Plug In Institute of Contemporary Art in Winnipeg, Ontario in 2011. The exhibition brought together "thirty-three international Indigenous artists who reconfigure ways of thinking and being in the future" (Farrell Racette, *Close Encounters*, frontispiece).

83 Cole's *The Course of Empire* may also be interpreted as representing a cycle rather than a rigidly linear sequence. The progression from a "savage" state to high civilization to

decline and desolation is portrayed as an inevitable path of empire, but the implication is that the cycle has been and will be repeated in the course of human history.

84 The design competition for this monument was administered by the Virginia Indian Commemorative Commission, a committee established by executive order of Governor Tim Kaine in 2009. See project description and documentation at http://indiantribute.virginia.gov.

85 The garment has been in the collection of the Ashmolean Museum at Oxford, England, since 1659.

86 Paraphrased in Virginia Indian Commemorative Commission report.

87 *Mantle*'s reflecting pool also includes the names of all the rivers in Virginia that have Native roots. See Jumaa, "Monument Honoring Virginia Native Tribes."

88 *Spiral Jetty* might also be considered an extreme example of a non-site, in that material from the site in Utah was shipped back to New York for display in the Virginia Dwan Gallery to raise money for the project. See Lippard, *Overlay*. For a more recent survey of the land art movement, see Kwon and Kaiser, *Ends of the Earth*.

89 Quoted in Virginia Indian Commemorative Commission report.

CHAPTER FIVE: THE EMBODIED LANDSCAPE

Epigraph: Harrison, "Effects of Landscape," 216.

1 Mitchell, "Imperial Landscape," 9.

2 Morris, "Picturing Sovereignty."

3 Interview with WalkingStick by the author, June 8, 2006.

4 Artist statement, http//www.kaywalkingstick.com.

5 Recall that *Venere Alpina* means "Alpine Goddess." The addition of brass leaf to the left panel of *Blame the Mountains III* is also an allusion to sacred space. See Seppi, "Artist in Italy."

6 Seppi, "Artist in Italy."

7 Interview with WalkingStick by the author, January 2, 2014.

8 In "Modernist Painting" Greenberg wrote that "it is not a principle that Modernist painting in its latest phase has abandoned the representation of recognizable objects. What it has abandoned in principle is the representation of the kind of space that recognizable, three-dimensional objects can inhabit."

9 Interview with WalkingStick by the author, January 2, 2014.

10 Interview with WalkingStick by the author, January 2, 2014.

11 Interview with WalkingStick by author, June 8, 2006.

12 See, for example, Lavadour's *Reservation Voodoo* (1985) in Halper, *James Lavadour*, 18.

13 Smallwood, "Review," 168.

14 See Halper, *James Lavadour*, 12.

15 The legend of the *Flying Dutchman* is itself a maritime ghost story that dates to the eighteenth century.

16 Rushing, "What the Ground Says," 76.

17 Interview with Lavadour by the author, March 1, 2014.

18 Interview with Gibson by the author, June 8, 2006. For more on Gibson's painted landscapes, see Morris, "Places of Emergence."

19 Interview with Gibson by the author, June 8, 2006.

20 Gibson's bestowal of a Latin title here is a deliberate cooption of scientific method. As a student at the School of the Art Institute of Chicago, Gibson worked as an intern at the

Field Museum of Natural History, where he became both fascinated by and critical of the European academic endeavor to name and classify everything in the "known universe" and the tendency to treat all aspects of Native culture, including people, as scientific specimens. See Morris, "Places of Emergence," 55–56.

21 "Surveillance": from French, *sur-*, "over," and *veiller*, "to watch." Observing the grid-like constructions of the *Red Black White* series, Jimmie Durham asks rhetorically whether they may be maps rather than a territory ("Jeffrey Gibson," 66).

22 Price, "Jeffrey Gibson," 19.

23 Price, "Jeffrey Gibson," 20.

24 The painted hide covers are inspired by Plains parfleche designs, which Gibson embraces as a distinctly Indigenous form of abstraction that preceded the modernist aesthetic by nearly a century. See Price, "Jeffrey Gibson," 26–31. For more on the use of hide in contemporary Native American art, see Ash-Milby, *HIDE*.

25 The title and form of these works makes for a tantalizing comparison with Luger's later *Mirror Shields*, created for the NoDAPL movement.

26 Gibson's engagement with minimalist art of the 1960s (cf. Donald Judd's and Robert Morris's boxes and Dan Flavin's fluorescent light sculptures) and the degree to which minimalist art referenced the body is touched upon in Morris, "Introduction to Sculpture."

27 *Promise*, 8 by 8 by 7 feet, installation in *Off the Map*, NMAI 2007. The most striking example is Gibson's *Residual Urge*, a 15-by-7½-by-4-foot accretion of urethane foam, wood, and pigmented silicone that was affixed to the exterior of the Aldrich Museum as part of the exhibition *No Reservations* (2006).

28 Price, "Jeffrey Gibson," 25.

29 The sculptures are occasionally installed near air conditioning vents to exploit this effect. Rosenberg, "Mash-Ups Star in a Homage."

30 Gibson notes that parfleche design and manufacture was the exclusive purview of Plains women in the nineteenth century. See interview with Jonathan F. Walz in conjunction with the exhibition *Tipi Poles Performing as Lines* at Cornell Fine Arts Museum, Rollins College, Florida (2015; available as pdf on the artist's website). Moreover, the gendered associations that tie ironing boards to the domestic sphere and thus to women has led some viewers to regard Gibson's *Shield* paintings as female forms (Waltemath, "Native American Iconography").

31 Interview with Walz, *Tipi Poles as Lines*. The sensual figures that enter into the Edenic landscapes of *State of Emergency* (2005) and *Constellation* (2006) are explicitly male.

32 McLauglin, "Four Questions."

33 The jingle dress and its associated dance stem from the Ojibwe Midewiwin tradition. See Thiel, "Origins of the Jingle Dress."

34 Ellegood, "Nadia Myre," 60.

35 Nadia Myre, artist statement in Ash-Milby, *HIDE*, 110.

36 Milroy, "Kent Monkman." See also Lukavic, "Sovereign."

37 Emphasis added. Litwin, "Landscapes Skewer 'Noble Savage' View."

38 Wendy Red Star's *Four Seasons* series of photographic dioramas work a similar vein of kitsch. Nordstrand refers to Red Star's dioramas as "a hodgepodge of fakery" ("Wendy Red Star," 81).

39 The performative history of Miss Chief is told in Liss, "Kent Monkman, Miss Chief's Return."

40 Cher's status as both a gay icon and a diva is well established in popular culture. Like many of Cher's other signature looks, the "Half-Breed" ensemble was created by celebrity designer Bob Mackie in 1973. For more on Cher's influence on Monkman, see National Gallery of Canada, "Meet the Artist: Kent Monkman," cybermuse.gallery.ca.

41 McIntosh, "Miss Chief Eagle Testickle."
42 Monkman, "Tonto Takes Charge," 24.
43 "Berdache" or "berdash" is a generic term for third-gender individuals in North American Indian tribes. See Will Roscoe, *Changing Ones: Third and Fourth Genders in Native North America* (New York: St. Martin's Press, 1998).
44 Catlin's stated interest was in "describing the living manners, customs, and character of a people who were rapidly passing away from the face of the earth—a dying nation who had no historians or biographers of their own" (cited in McIntosh, "Miss Chief Eagle Testickle," 32).
45 Catlin's infamous traveling exhibition, *Catlin's Indian Gallery*, which consisted of 485 of his paintings and sketches, thousands of his collected artifacts, and a contingent of living Indian people, toured New York, London, and Paris between 1837 and 1846. The entire enterprise, including the *tableaux vivants* that Catlin staged of Indian life, provided the inspiration for Monkman's exhibition *The Triumph of Mischief*, which toured five Canadian cities between 2007 and 2010. See McIntosh, "Miss Chief Eagle Testickle."
46 See Brooks, "Kent Monkman, Aka Miss Chief." Cited in National Gallery of Canada, "Meet the Artist: Kent Monkman."
47 Catlin painted Mato-tope's portrait in 1832; Catlin's self-portrait painting Mato-tope appears at the frontispiece of his book *Letters and Notes on the Manners, Customs, and Conditions of North American Indians*, vol. 1 (London: Wiley and Putnam, 1842).

48 Madill, "Intelligent Mischief," 29.
49 Litwin, "Landscapes Skewer 'Noble Savage' View."
50 Furnish, "Kent Monkman," 137.
51 Monkman, quoted in Davies, "Manned Claims."
52 The pose is reminiscent of Christ's in Michelangelo's painting of the Last Judgment on the altar wall of the Sistine Chapel.
53 Monkman, artist statement, in McMaster, *Remix*, 74. See also, Elston, "Subverting Visual Discourses."
54 Mattes, "Interview with Miss Chief," 108.
55 McMaster, "Geography of Hope," 96.
56 A similar conflation of two different artistic sources, one for the landscape and one for the figures, can be seen in Monkman's *Artist and Model*. Kane's *Scene from the Northwest: Portrait of John Henry Lefroy* may have drawn Monkman's attention because it sold at auction in 2002 for C$5.1 million, the highest price ever paid for a Canadian painting. It is now in the collection of the Art Gallery of Ontario.
57 Monkman, quoted in Furnish, "Kent Monkman," 137.
58 Buell, *Environmental Imagination*, 69.
59 Furnish, "Kent Monkman," 136–37.
60 Bierstadt's 5-by-8-foot oil on canvas *Mount Corcoran* (1876) is a composite representation of a number of different locations Bierstadt visited during his trips to the Sierra Nevada mountains.
61 Interestingly, the Battle of the Little Bighorn was waged in July 1876, at roughly the same moment that Bierstadt was painting his placid depiction of Mount Corcoran. As for Miss Chief, she will eventually tire of her Seventh Cavalry companions: in Monkman's 2015 painting *Expelling the Vices*, Miss Chief is depicted in the same outfit she wears in *History Is Painted by the Victors* whipping the fully clothed soldiers as they pillage the environment for gold and other precious materials.
62 Monkman, quoted in Furnish, "Kent Monkman," 136.

63 Monkman, quoted in Furnish, "Kent Monkman," 137. Monkman remarks, "Catlin and others were obsessed with capturing peoples who wouldn't exist in the future" (quoted in Brooks, "Kent Monkman, Aka Miss Chief").

64 Philip Deloria, *Indians in Unexpected Places*, 6.

65 Philip Deloria, *Indians in Unexpected Places*, 140–43.

66 Timm, "Landscape with Sexy Transvestite," 94–95.

67 The *Casualties of Modernity* series (2012–15) includes multiple paintings, installations, performance works, and even a website for a faux healthcare provider billed as "A leading authority in the diagnosis and forensic analysis of numerous conditions afflicting Modern and Contemporary Art," www.casualtiesofmodernity.com.

68 Nagam and Swanson, "Decolonial Interventions," 32–33.

69 Quoted in Brooks, "Kent Monkman, Aka Miss Chief."

70 *The Urban Res* was exhibited at Sargent's Daughters Gallery in New York City and SITE Santa Fe in New Mexico in 2014. See "Fear, Violence 'Normal' in Winnipeg's North End, Activist Says," *CBC News*, November 26, 2015, www.cbc.ca/news/canada/manitoba/winnipeg-north-end-fear-violence-1.3338067.

71 Vartanian, "Violent History of Kent Monkman."

72 Vizenor, *Manifest Manners*, vii.

73 Brooks, "Kent Monkman, Aka Miss Chief."

74 Katz, "Miss Chief Is Always Interested," 16.

75 Katz, "Miss Chief Is Always Interested," 17.

76 For more on trauma in Monkman's work, see Morris, "Crash."

77 Description of work paraphrased from artist's website, www.kentmonkman.com.

78 See Goddard, "The Artist as Hunter." The twelfth-century Château de Rochechouart houses an archival collection of collage and sound poetry by Raoul Hausmann, the Berlin Dadaist who sheltered near Limoges during World War II.

79 Description of work paraphrased from artist's website, www.kentmonkman.com.

80 "At the Ulm Pishkun Buffalo Jump, one of the largest in the world, a layer of compacted bones thirteen feet deep was found. This compacted bone, much like the bone ash used to make bone china, fills the space below the cliffs and tells the story of thousands of years of sustainable hunting, layer by layer, before the quick destruction of the bison by the European settlers" ("Kent Monkman: The Rise and Fall of Civilization," exhibition brochure posted on "Past Exhibitions" pages of Gardiner Museum website, www.gardinermuseum.on.ca/event/kent-monkman-the-rise-and-fall-of-civilization/).

81 See Demos, "Contemporary Art."

82 Horton and Berlo, "Beyond the Mirror," 17–18.

83 Horton and Berlo, "Beyond the Mirror," 20.

84 Horton and Berlo discuss Durham's *Encore Tranquilité*, exhibited in Paris in 2009. Despite the widespread influence that Durham's artwork and writing have had on contemporary Native American art practices, the artist's claim to Cherokee heritage was definitively denounced by the Cherokee Nation in 2017.

85 Belmore identifies the setting for her video performance—in which she struggles up a sewage-strewn beach to throw a bucket of water or blood on the camera lens—as Iona Beach at the mouth of the Fraser River in Vancouver. The site, Belmore says, is an industrial wasteland just off the runway of the Vancouver International Airport, situated directly across the river from the Musqueam First Nation, where she "think[s] they've had a Longhouse there for at least a thousand years" (Enright, "Poetics of History").

86 See Robinson, "Speaking to Water," 235.

87 Cited in Robinson, "Speaking to Water," 236.

88 Morin, email correspondence with Robinson, original punctuation, cited in Robinson, "Speaking to Water," 229.

89 Robinson, "Speaking to Water," 231.

90 The implicit trauma underlying Morin's choice of subjects in the *Cultural Graffiti* series is one that the artist has addressed at home in Canada as well. In the same year that he symbolically "tagged" the monuments of British colonialism in London, he conducted a series of healing ceremonies to support and honor the work of all those who were then conducting Canada's Truth and Reconciliation Commission hearings on the Indian residential schools.

91 Robinson, "Speaking to Water," 238–39.

92 Robinson, "Speaking to Water," 238.

93 Belmore recalls that when a speaker was using the megaphone, witnesses tended to turn their backs to him or her and look instead out into the landscape. Nixon, "Rebecca Belmore Wants Us to Listen."

94 McMaster, "Towards an Aboriginal Art History," 91–92. See also Horton, "Indigenous Artists against the Anthropocene," 58.

95 Nicholas Bourriard defines "relational aesthetics" as "a set of artistic practices which take as their theoretical and practical point of departure the whole of human relations and their social context, rather than an independent and private space" (Bourriard, *Relational Aesthetics*, 113).

96 Nixon, "Rebecca Belmore Wants Us to Listen."

97 The selection of Banff National Park as one of the sites for the work provided the impetus for *Wave Sound*. On a scouting visit to Banff with *LandMarks* 2017 curator Kathleen Ritter, Belmore was reminded of her experience creating *Ayum-ee-aawach Oomama-mowan, Speaking to Their Mother* twenty-six years earlier. See Nixon, "Rebecca Belmore Wants Us to Listen."

98 Quoted in Nixon, "Rebecca Belmore Wants Us to Listen."

BIBLIOGRAPHY

Abbott, Lawrence. *I Stand in the Center of the Good: Interviews with Contemporary Native American Artists*. Lincoln: University of Nebraska Press, 1994.

Adams, Ann Jensen. "Competing Communities in the 'Great Bog of Europe': Identity and Seventeenth-Century Dutch Landscape Painting." In Mitchell, *Landscape and Power*, 35–76.

Adams, Steven, and Anna Gruetzner Robins, eds. *Gendering Landscape Art*. New Brunswick, NJ: Rutgers University Press, 2001.

Alfred, Taiaiake. *Peace, Power, Righteousness: An Indigenous Manifesto*. Oxford: Oxford University Press, 1999.

Andrews, Malcolm. *Landscape and Western Art*. New York: Oxford Press, 1999.

Anthes, Bill. "Contemporary Native Artists and International Biennial Culture." *Visual Anthropology Review* 25, no. 2 (2009): 109–27.

——. *Edgar Heap of Birds*. Durham, NC: Duke University Press, 2015.

——. *Native Moderns: American Indian Painting, 1940–1960*. Durham, NC: Duke University Press, 2006.

Archuleta, Margaret. "Kay WalkingStick." In *Pathbreakers: The Fellowship for Native American Art 2003*, 13–31. Seattle: University of Washington Press, 2003.

Archuleta, Margaret, and Rennard Strickland, eds. *Shared Visions: Native American Painters and Sculptors in the Twentieth Century*. Phoenix, AZ: Heard Museum, 1991.

Ashcroft, Bill, Gareth Griffiths, and Helen Tiffin, eds. *Key Concepts in Post-Colonial Studies*. London: Routledge, 1998.

Ash-Milby, Kathleen. "Alan Michelson: Landscapes of Loss and Presence." In *We Are Here: The Eiteljorg Contemporary Art Fellowship 2011*, edited by Jennifer McNutt and Ashley Holland, 21–31. Seattle: University of Washington Press, 2011.

——. "Art That Moves." In Ash-Milby, *Transformer*, 3–7.

——. "HIDE." In Ash-Milby, *HIDE*, 15–39.

——, ed. *HIDE: Skin as Material and Metaphor*. Washington, DC: Smithsonian National Museum of the American Indian, 2010.

——. "The Imaginary Landscape." In Ash-Milby, *Off the Map*, 17–45.

——, ed. *Off the Map: Landscape in the Native Imagination*. Washington, DC: Smithsonian National Museum of the American Indian, 2007.

——, ed. *Transformer: Native Art in Light and Sound*. New York: Smithsonian National Museum of the American Indian George Gustav Heye Center, 2017.

Ash-Milby, Kathleen, and Truman Lowe. *Most Serene Republics: Edgar Heap of Birds*. Washington, DC: Smithsonian National Museum of the American Indian, 2007.

Ash-Milby, Kathleen, and David W. Penney, eds. *Kay WalkingStick: An American Artist*. Washington, DC: Smithsonian Museum of the American Indian, 2015.

Belmore, Rebecca. "Making a Garden out of a Wilderness." In Blomberg, *Action and Agency*, 16–19.

Berlo, Janet Catherine, and Jessica L. Horton. "A Gathering Place: Relationality in Contemporary Native Installation Art." In Passalacqua and Morris, *Native Art Now*, 194–215.

Bermingham, Ann. *Landscape and Ideology: The English Rustic Tradition, 1740–1860*. Berkeley: University of California Press, 1986.

——. "System, Order, and Abstraction: The Politics of English Landscape Drawing around 1795." In Mitchell, *Landscape and Power*, 77–101.

Berry, Ian, and Tom Lewis, eds. *Lives of the Hudson*. New York: Prestel Publishing, 2010.

Blomberg, Nancy, ed. *Action and Agency: Advancing the Dialogue on Native Performance Art*. Denver, CO: Denver Art Museum, 2010.

——, ed. *[Re]inventing the Wheel: Advancing the Dialogue on Contemporary American Indian Art*. Denver, CO: Denver Art Museum, 2008.

Boone, Elizabeth Hill. *Stories in Red and Black: Pictorial Histories of the Aztecs and Mixtecs*. Austin: University of Texas Press, 2000.

Bourriard, Nicolas. *Relational Aesthetics*. Dijon, France: Les presses du Reél, 1998.

Bradley, Jessica, and Jolene Rickard. *Rebecca Belmore: Fountain*. Vancouver: Morris and Helen Belkin Art Gallery, 2005.

Brooks, Katherine. "Kent Monkman, Aka Miss Chief Eagle Testickle, Confronts Native American Myths." *Huffington Post*, May 21, 2004.

Buell, Lawrence. *The Environmental Imagination: Thoreau, Nature Writing, and the Formation of American Culture*. Cambridge, MA: Harvard University Press, 1995.

Bunn, David. "'Our Wattled Cot': Mercantile and Domestic Space in Thomas Pringle's African Landscapes." In Mitchell, *Landscape and Power*, 127–73.

Castle, Frederick Ted. "Kay WalkingStick at Bertha Urdang." *Art in America* 72, no. 2 (February 1984): 147–48.

Cobb, Amanda J. "Understanding Tribal Sovereignty: Definitions, Conceptualizations, and Interpretations." *American Studies* 46, no. 3/4 (Fall–Winter 2005): 115–32.

Cosgrove, Denis. *Social Formation and Symbolic Landscape*. Madison: University of Wisconsin Press, 1984.

Cosgrove, Denis E., Rachel Ziady DeLue, Jessica Dubow, James Elkins, Michael Gaudio, David Hays, Róisín Kennedy, Michael Newman, Rebecca Solnit, Anne Whiston Spirn, Minna Törmä, and Jacob Wamberg. "The Art Seminar." Transcript of roundtable discussion. In *Landscape Theory*, edited by Rachel Ziady DeLue and James Elkins, 87–156. New York: Routledge, 2008.

Crandall, Jordan. "Anything That Moves: Armed Vision." *CTheory*, June 15, 1999.

——. "Embedded Reporters, Predator Drones, and Armed Perception." *CTheory*, April 9, 2003.

Crosby, Marcia. "The Multimedia Work of Rebecca Belmore: A Disturbing Uncertainty." In Blomberg, *Action and Agency*, 21–42.

Cruikshank, Julie. *Do Glaciers Listen?: Local Knowledge, Colonial Encounters, and Social Imagination*. Seattle: University of Washington Press, 2005.

Davies, Jon. "Manned Claims, Review of ImagineNative FEST." *Xtra*, October 13, 2005.

Deadman, Patricia. "Nadia Myre." In *Pathbreakers: The Fellowship for Native American Art 2003*, 59–65. Seattle: University of Washington Press, 2003.

Deloria, Philip J. *Indians in Unexpected Places*. Lawrence: University Press of Kansas, 2004.

——. *Playing Indian*. New Haven, CT: Yale University Press, 1999.

Deloria, Vine, Jr., and Clifford Lytle. *The Nations Within: The Past and Future of American Indian Sovereignty.* New York: Pantheon Books, 1984.

DeLue, Rachel Ziady. "Elusive Landscapes and Shifting Grounds." In DeLue and Elkins, *Landscape Theory*, 3–14.

DeLue, Rachel Ziady, and James Elkins, eds. *Landscape Theory*. New York: Routledge, 2008.

Demos, T.J. "Contemporary Art and the Politics of Ecology," *Third Text* 120, no. 1 (January 2013): 1–9.

Denzin, Norman K. *Indians on Display: Global Commodification of Native America in Performance, Art, and Museums*. Walnut Creek, CA: Left Coast Press, 2013.

De Zegher, Catherine, and Gerald McMaster. *The 18th Biennale of Sydney: All Our Relations.* Woolloomooloo, NSW: Biennale of Sydney, 2012.

Dobkins, Rebecca, and James Lavadour. *James Lavadour: The Properties of Paint*. Salem: Hallie Ford Museum of Art, 2007.

Duncan, James. "Sites of Representation: Place, Time and the Discourse of the Other." In *Place/Culture/Representation*, edited by James Duncan and David Ley, 39–56. New York: Routledge, 1993.

Durham, Jimmie. "Jeffrey Gibson: Our Miles Davis." In *Art Quantum: The Eiteljorg Fellowship for Native American Fine Art 2009*, edited by James Nottage, 56–69. Seattle: University of Washington Press, 2009.

Durham, Jimmie, and Jean Fisher. "The Ground Has Been Covered." *Artforum International* 26, no. 10 (Summer 1988): 99–105.

Echo-Hawk, Walter. *In the Light of Justice: The Rise of Human Rights in Native America and the UN Declaration on the Rights of Indigenous Peoples.* Golden, CO: Fulcrum Publishing, 2013.

Effman, Elsie. "Thomas Cole's *View of Fort Putnam*." *Antiques Magazine* 66 (November 2004): 154–59.

Ellegood, Anne. "Nadia Myre: Scarscapes." In Ash-Milby, *HIDE*, 53–63.

Elston, M. Melissa. "Subverting Visual Discourses of Gender and Geography: Kent Monkman's Revised Iconography of the American West." *Journal of American Culture* 35, no. 2 (June 2012): 181–90.

Enright, Robert. "The Poetics of History: An Interview with Rebecca Belmore." *Border Crossings* 24, no. 3 (August 2005): 62–69.

Evans, Lara M. "Setting the Photographs Aside: Native North American Photography Since 1990." In Passalacqua and Morris, *Native Art Now*, 216–23.

Everett, Deborah. "Alan Michelson: Light on Shadowed Ground." *Sculpture* 26, no. 4 (May 2007): 30–35.

Farrell Racette, Sherry, ed. *Close Encounters: The Next 500 Years.* Winnipeg, Manitoba: Plug In Editions, 2011.

———. "'This Fierce Love': Gender, Women, and Art Making." In *Art in Our Lives: Native Women Artists in Dialogue*, edited by Cynthia Chavez Lamar and Sherry Farrell Racette, 27–51. Santa Fe, NM: School for Advanced Research Press, 2010.

Fleras, Augie, and Jean Leonard Elliott. *The 'Nations Within': Aboriginal-State Relations in Canada, the United States and New Zealand.* Toronto: Oxford University Press, 1992.

Foucault, Michel. *Discipline and Punish: The Birth of the Prison.* Translated by Alan Sheridan. New York: Pantheon Books, 1977.

———. *The History of Sexuality, Volume 1: An Introduction*. Translated by Robert Hurley. New York: Pantheon Books, 1978.

Furnish, David. "Kent Monkman: The Canadian Artist Who Is Exploding the Mythology of the West—One Brushstroke at a Time." *Interview* 37, no. 2 (March 2006): 136–37.

Gibson, Daniel. "James Lavadour: Artist of Light." *Native Peoples* 13, no. 6 (September/October 2000): 45.

Glowen, Ron. “Review: James Lavadour at Cliff Michel.” *Art in America* 78 (December 1990): 177.

Goddard, Peter. “The Artist as Hunter: Kent Monkman in France.” *Canadian Art*, August 20, 2014.

Gombrich, Ernst. *Norm and Form: Studies in the Art of the Renaissance*. Chicago: University of Chicago Press, 1966.

Gonzalez, Ray, ed. *Without Discovery: A Native Response to Columbus*. Seattle: Broken Moon Press, 1992.

Gottman, Jean. *The Significance of Territory*. Charlottesville: University Press of Virginia, 1973.

Greenberg, Clement. “Modernist Painting.” *Arts Yearbook* 4 (1961).

Hales, Linda. “At the Border, Creative Crossings.” *Washington Post*, July 29, 2006.

Halper, Vicki. *James Lavadour: Landscapes*. Seattle: University of Washington Press, 2001.

Harrison, Charles. “The Effects of Landscape.” In Mitchell, *Landscape and Power*, 203–39.

High, Steven, and David W. Lewis. *Corporate Wasteland: The Landscape and Memory of Deindustrialization*. Ithaca, NY: Cornell University Press, 2007.

Hill, Greg A., Candice Hopkins, and Christine LaLonde. *Sakahàn: International Indigenous Art*. Ottawa: National Gallery of Canada, 2013.

Hill, Richard William. “Jimmie Durham’s Poles to Mark the Centre of the World.” In Farrell Racette, *Close Encounters*, 32–38.

Holt, Nancy. “Biographical Note.” In *The Writings of Robert Smithson: Essays with Illustrations*, edited by Nancy Holt, 5–6. New York: New York University Press, 1979.

Holubizky, Ihor. “Michael Belmore: Shorelines, Flux, Origins, and Dark Water—The Slowness of Things.” In Ash-Milby, *HIDE*, 67–77.

Hopkins, Candice. “On Other Pictures: Imperialism, Historical Amnesia and Mimesis.” In Hill, Hopkins, and LaLonde, *Sakahàn*, 21–32.

——. “Why Can’t Beauty Be a Call to Action?” In Farrell Racette, *Close Encounters*, 64–75.

Hopkins, Candice, and Lucia Sanroman. Inverted Landscapes.” In *Unsettled Landscapes*, 34–48. Santa Fe, NM: SITE Santa Fe, 2014.

Horton, Jessica L. “Alone on the Snow, Alone on the Beach: ‘A Global Sense of Place’ in *Atanarjuat* and *Fountain*.” *Journal of Transnational American Studies* 4, no. 1 (2012): 1–25.

——. Art for an Undivided Earth: The American Indian Movement Generation. Durham, NC: Duke University Press, 2017.

——. “Art History’s Tangled Legs.” In Ash-Milby and Penney, *Kay WalkingStick*, 145–57.

——. “Drones and Snakes.” *Art in America* 105, no. 9 (October 2017): 104–9.

——. “Indigenous Artists Against the Anthropocene.” In “Indigenous Futures,” edited by Kate Morris and Bill Anthes, special issue, *Art Journal* 76, no. 2 (Summer 2017): 48–68.

——. “Of Mimicry and Drag: Homi Bhabha and Kent Monkman.” In *Theorizing Visual Studies: Writing through the Discipline*, edited by James Elkins, Kristi McGuire, Maureen Burns, Alicia Chester, and Joel Kuennen, 169–91. New York: Routledge, 2013.

Horton, Jessica L., and Janet Catherine Berlo. “Beyond the Mirror: Indigenous Ecologies and ‘New Materialisms’ in Contemporary Art.” *Third Text* 120, no. 1 (January 2013): 17–28.

Houle, Robert. “Bonnie Devine: Land as Metaphor for Survival.” In *We Are Here: The Eiteljorg Contemporary Art Fellowship 2011*, edited by Jennifer Complo McNutt, 33–45. Indianapolis: Eiteljorg Museum of American Indians and Western Art, 2011.

Jackson, John Brinkerhoff. *A Sense of Place, A Sense of Time*. New Haven, CT: Yale University Press, 1994.

Jonaitis, Aldona, and Elizabeth Kalbfleisch. “Native Performance Art: The Medium is Wide Open.” In Passalacqua and Morris, *Native Art Now*, 318–35.

Joyce, Erin. “Artists Join the Fight to Protect Standing Rock.” *Hyperallergic*, November 22, 2016.

Judd, Donald. “Specific Objects.” *Arts Yearbook* 8 (1965).

Jumaa, Yasmine. “Monument Honoring Virginia Native Tribes Awaits Ceremony.” *Chicago Tribune*, March 6, 2018.

Kastner, Carolyn. *Jaune Quick-to-See Smith: An American Modernist.* Albuquerque: University of New Mexico Press, 2013.

Katz, Jonathan. "Miss Chief Is Always Interested in the Latest European Fashions." In Theriault, *Interpellations*, 16–24.

Kramer Russell, Karen, ed. *Shapeshifting: Transformations in Native American Art.* New Haven, CT: Yale University Press, 2012.

Krauss, Rosalind E. "Grids." *October* 9 (Summer 1979): 50–64.

——. *Perpetual Inventory*. Cambridge, MA: MIT Press, 2010.

——. "Sculpture in the Expanded Field." *October* 8 (Spring 1979): 30–44.

Kwon, Miwon. *One Place after Another: Site-Specific Art and Locational Identity*. Cambridge, MA: MIT Press, 2002.

Kwon, Miwon, and Philip Kaiser, eds. *Ends of the Earth: Land Art to 1974*. New York: Prestel Publishing, 2012.

Lauzon, Claudette. "Monumental Interventions: Jeff Thomas Seizes Commemorative Space." In *Imagining Resistance: Visual Culture and Activism in Canada*, edited by J. Keri Cronin and Kirsty Robertson, 79–93. Waterloo, ON: Wilfred Laurier University Press, 2011.

Lee, Pamela. *Chronophobia: On Time in the Art of the 1960s*. Cambridge, MA: MIT Press, 2004.

Lewis, Jason, and Skawennati Tricia Fragnito. "Aboriginal Territories in Cyberspace." *Cultural Survival Quarterly* (Summer 2005): 29–31.

Lippard, Lucy. "The Color of the Wind." In *Our Land/Ourselves: American Indian Contemporary Artists*, edited by Deborah Ward, 7–15. Albany: State University of New York University Art Gallery, 1990.

——. "Double Vision." In *Women of Sweetgrass, Cedar and Sage*, edited by Harmony Hammond and Jaune Quick-to-See Smith, n.p. Phoenix, AZ: Atlatl, 1985.

——. *The Lure of the Local: Senses of Place in a Multicentered Society*. New York: The New Press, 1997.

——. *Overlay: Contemporary Art and the Art of Prehistory*. New York: Pantheon Press, 1983.

Liss, David. "Kent Monkman, Miss Chief's Return: Subverting the Canon through Sublime Landscapes and Saucy Performances." *Canadian Art* 22, no. 3 (October 2005): 79–85.

Litwin, Grania. "Landscapes Skewer 'Noble Savage' View; Native Artist's Alter Ego Shakes Up Historical Scenes—In a Boa and Heels." *Victoria Times Colonist*, June 24, 2010, D10.

Longfish, George, and Joan Randall. "Contemporary Native American Art." *Journal of Arts Management and Law* 18, no. 2 (1988): 20–24.

——. *Contemporary Native American Art: Contradictions in Indian Territory*. Stillwater: Oklahoma State University Department of Art, 1983.

Low, Setha, and Denise Lawrence-Zuniga, eds. *The Anthropology of Space and Place: Locating Culture*. Malden, MA: Blackwell, 2003.

Lukavic, John. *Sovereign: Independent Voices*. Exhibition brochure. Denver: Denver Art Museum, 2013.

Lyons, Scott Richard. "Rhetorical Sovereignty: What Do American Indians Want from Writing?" *College Composition and Communication* 51, no. 3 (February 2000): 447–68.

Madill, Shirley. "Intelligent Mischief: The Paintings of Kent Monkman." In *Kent Monkman: The Triumph of Mischief*, edited by Audrey McClellan, 25–30. Toronto: Museum of Contemporary Canadian Art, 2008.

Majkowski, Tina. "Gypsies, Tramps, Half-Indian, All Queer, and Cher." In Blomberg, *Action and Agency*, 103–25.

Malarcher, Patricia. "The Meanings of 'Duality' in Art." *New York Times*, December 22, 1985.

Marshall, Jennifer Jane. "Toward Phenomenology: A Material Culture Studies Approach to Landscape Theory." In DeLue and Elkins, *Landscape Theory*, 195–203.

Martin, Lee-Ann. "Adjacencies and Distances: Indigenous Installation Art in Canada." In Passalacqua and Morris, *Native Art Now*, 236–61.

——. "Cross Over with Mr. Luna." In *Diversity and Dialogue: The Eiteljorg Fellowship for Native American Art 2007*, edited by James Nottage, 24–32. Indianapolis, IN: Eiteljorg Museum of American Indians and Western Art, 2007.

——. "The Waters of Venice: Rebecca Belmore at the 51st Biennale." *Canadian Art* 22, no. 2 (2005): 48–53.

Mattes, Cathy. "An Interview with Miss Chief Eagle Testickle." In *Kent Monkman: The Triumph of Mischief*, edited by Audrey McClellan, 107–10. Toronto: Museum of Contemporary Canadian Art, 2008.

McIntosh, David. "Miss Chief Eagle Testickle, Postindian Diva Warrior, in the Shadowy Hall of Mirrors." In *Kent Monkman: The Triumph of Mischief*, edited by Audrey McClellan, 31–46. Toronto: Museum of Contemporary Canadian Art, 2008.

McLauglin, Bryne. "Four Questions for Sobey Winner Nadia Myre." *Canadian Art*, December 12, 2014.

McMaster, Gerald. "Alan Michelson: Revealing the Absent Indian." In *New Tribe New York: The Urban Vision Quest*, edited by Gerald McMaster, 38–45. Washington, DC: Smithsonian National Museum of the American Indian, 2005.

——. *Edward Poitras: Canada XLVI Biennale de Venezia*. Hull, Quebec: Canadian Museum of Civilization, 1995.

——. "The Geography of Hope." In *Kent Monkman: The Triumph of Mischief*, edited by Audrey McClellan, 95–102. Toronto: Museum of Contemporary Canadian Art, 2008.

——, ed. *Reservation X: The Power of Place in Contemporary Aboriginal Art*. Seattle: University of Washington Press, 1998.

——. "Towards an Aboriginal Art History." In *Native American Art in the Twentieth Century: Makers, Meanings and Histories*, edited by W. Jackson Rushing III, 81–96. New York: Routledge, 1999.

——. "Under Indigenous Eyes." *Art in America* 105, no. 9 (October 2017): 64–71.

McMaster, Gerald, and Joe Baker, eds. *Remix: New Modernities in a Post-Indian World*. Washington, DC: Smithsonian National Museum of the American Indian, 2007.

McMaster, Gerald, and Lee-Ann Martin, eds. *Indigena: Contemporary Perspectives in Canadian Art*. Vancouver, BC: Douglas and McIntyre, 1992.

Mejia, Anastasia. "Contemporary North American Indigenous Artists: James Lavadour—Walla Walla." Interview transcript, 2011. contemporarynativeartists.tumblr.com.

Mignolo, Walter. *The Darker Side of Western Modernity: Global Futures, Decolonial Options*. Durham, NC: Duke University Press, 2011.

Miller, Angela, Janet C. Berlo, Bryan J. Wolf, and Jennifer L. Roberts. *American Encounters: Art, History, and Cultural Identity*. New York: Pearson, 2007.

Milroy, Sarah. "Kent Monkman: Honouring the Dispossessed." *The Globe and Mail*, October 12, 2012.

Mitchell, W. J. T. "Imperial Landscape." In Mitchell, *Landscape and Power*, 5–34.

——. "Introduction." In Mitchell, *Landscape and Power*, 1–4.

——, ed. *Landscape and Power*. 2nd edition. Chicago: University of Chicago Press, 2002.

——. "Preface to the Second Edition of *Landscape and Power*: Space, Place, and Landscape." In Mitchell, *Landscape and Power*, vii–xii.

Mithlo, Nancy Marie, ed. *Manifestations: New Native Art Criticism*. Santa Fe, NM: Museum of Contemporary Native Arts, 2011.

Monkman, Kent. "Tonto Takes Charge: Kent Monkman on Repainting History." *The Walrus* 5, no. 4 (May 2008): 24.

Montiel, Anya. "After Columbus." *Art in America* 105, no. 9 (October 2017): 86–91.

Morgan, Anne Barclay. "Kay WalkingStick: Interview." *Art Papers* 19, no. 6 (November/December 1995): 12–13.

Morris, Kate. "Art on the River: Alan Michelson Highlights Border-Crossing Issues." *National Museum of the American Indian Magazine* (Winter 2009): 36–40.

——. "Crash: Specters of Colonialism in Contemporary Indigenous Art." In "Indigenous Futures," edited by Kate Morris and Bill Anthes, special issue, *Art Journal* 76, no. 2 (Summer 2017): 70–80.

——. "Introduction to Sculpture, Installation, and Mixed Media." In Passalacqua and Morris, *Native Art Now*, 114–29.

——. "Picturing Sovereignty: Landscape in Contemporary Native American Art," In *Painters, Patrons, and Identity: Essays in Native American Art History in Honor of J. J. Brody*, edited by Joyce Szabo, 187–209. Albuquerque: University of New Mexico Press, 2001.

——. "Places of Emergence: Painting Genesis." In Ash-Milby, *Off the Map*, 46–63.

——. "Reading Between the Lines: Text and Image in Contemporary Native American Art." *American Indian Art Magazine* 34, no. 2 (Spring 2009): 52–59.

——. "'Rising into Ruin': Alan Michelson, Robert Smithson, and the (Post) Modern Landscape." In *Visual Culture of the Ancient Americas: Contemporary Perspectives*, online addenda, edited by Andrew Finegold and Ellen Hoobler. Columbia University Department of Art History and Archaeology, 2017.

——. "Running the Medicine Line: Images of the Border in Contemporary Native American Art." *American Indian Quarterly* 35, no. 4 (Fall 2011): 549–78.

——. "What Lies Beneath: Kay WalkingStick's Sacred Geometries, 1973–1983." In Ash-Milby and Penney, *Kay WalkingStick*, 49–75.

Morrison, George, as told to Margot Fortunato Galt. *Turning the Feather Around: My Life in Art.* Saint Paul: Minnesota Historical Society Press, 1998.

Nabokov, Peter. *Where the Lightning Strikes: The Lives of American Indian Sacred Spaces.* New York: Penguin Books, 2006.

Nagam, Julie, and Kerry Swanson. "Decolonial Interventions in Performance and New Media Art: In Conversation with Cheryl L'Hirondelle and Kent Monkman." *Canadian Theater Review* 159 (Summer 2014): 30–37.

Nemiroff, Diana, Robert Houle, and Charlotte Townsend-Gault, eds. *Land, Spirit, Power: First Nations at the National Gallery of Canada.* Ottawa: National Gallery of Canada, 1992.

Nixon, Lindsay. "Rebecca Belmore Wants Us to Listen to the Land." *Canadian Art*, June 7, 2017.

Nordstrand, Polly. "Wendy Red Star: Beauty and the Blow-Up Beast." In *Art Quantum: The Eiteljorg Fellowship for Native American Fine Art 2009*, edited by James Nottage, 81–93. Seattle: University of Washington Press, 2009.

Oettermann, Stephan. *The Panorama: History of a Mass Medium.* Cambridge, MA: MIT Press, 1997.

Olwig, Kenneth. "The 'Actual Landscape,' or Actual Landscapes?." In DeLue and Elkins, *Landscape Theory*, 158–77.

Ortel, Jo. *Woodland Reflections: The Art of Truman Lowe.* Madison: University of Wisconsin Press, 2003.

Owens, Craig. "Earthwords." *October* 10 (Autumn 1979): 120–30.

Passalacqua, Veronica, and Kate Morris, eds. *Native Art Now: Developments in Contemporary Native American Art Since 1992.* Indianapolis, IN: Eiteljorg Museum of American Indians and Western Art, 2017.

Peck, H. Daniel. *Thoreau's Morning Work: Memory and Perception in A Week on the Concord and Merrimack Rivers, the Journal, and Walden.* New Haven, CT: Yale University Press, 1990.

Penney, David W. "George Morrison." In *Contemporary Masters: The Eiteljorg Fellowship for Native American Fine Art 1999.* Indianapolis, IN: Eiteljorg Museum of American Indians and Western Art, 1999.

——. "Stereo View: Kay WalkingStick's Diptychs." In Ash-Milby and Penney, *Kay WalkingStick*, 83–97.

Perlman, Meg. "New York Reviews: Kay WalkingStick at Bertha Urdang." *ARTnews* 84 (December 1983): 165.

Phillips, Deborah. "New York Reviews: Kay WalkingStick at Bertha Urdang." *ARTnews* 80, no. 6 (June 1981): 236.

Phillips, Ruth B. "Aesthetic Primitivism Revisited: The Global Diaspora of 'Primitive Art' and the Rise of Indigenous Modernisms." *Journal of Art Historiography* no. 12 (June 2015): 1–25.

——. "Settler Monuments, Indigenous Memory: Dis-membering and Re-membering Canadian Art History." In *Monuments and Memory, Made and Unmade*, edited by Robert Nelson and Margaret Olin, 281–304. Chicago: University of Chicago Press, 2003.

Postcommodity Artist Collective (Raven Chacon, Cristóbal Martínez, and Kade L. Twist). "Portfolio." *Art in America* 105, no. 9 (October 2017): 96–103.

Price, Marshall N. "Jeffrey Gibson: Remix and Reconciliation." In *Jeffrey Gibson: Said the Pigeon to the Squirrel*, 15–33. New York: National Academy Museum, 2013.

Puleo, Risa. "Artist Collective Postcommodity on Recovering Knowledge and Making Border Metaphors." *Hyperallergic*, May 4, 2017.

Rader, Dean. *Engaged Resistance: American Indian Art, Literature, and Film From Alcatraz to the NMAI*. Austin: University of Texas Press, 2011.

Raheja, Michelle H. "Reading Nanook's Smile: Visual Sovereignty, Indigenous Revisions of Ethnography, and 'Atanarjuat (The Fast Runner).'" *American Indian Quarterly* 59, no. 4 (December 2007): 1159–85.

——. "Visual Sovereignty." In *Native Studies Keywords*, edited by Stephanie Nohelani Teves, Andrea Smith, and Michelle H. Raheja, 25–34. Tucson: University of Arizona Press, 2015.

Raynor, Vivien. "Where Black is the Primary Color." *New York Times*, February 10, 1980, WC18.

Reed, Joyce Whitebear. *The Post-Colonial Landscape: A Billboard Exhibition*. Saskatoon, Saskatchewan: Mendel Art Gallery, 1993.

Regan, Sheila. "The Standing Project Turns DAPL Protest into an Art Form." *City Pages Minneapolis*, December 22, 2016.

Rickard, Jolene. "Diversifying Sovereignty and the Reception of Indigenous Art." In "Indigenous Futures," edited by Kate Morris and Bill Anthes, special issue, *Art Journal* 76, no. 2 (Summer 2017): 81–84.

——. "The Emergence of Global Indigenous Art." In Hill, Hopkins, and LaLonde, *Sakahàn*, 53–60.

——. "The Local and the Global." In *Vision, Space, Desire: Global Perspectives and Cultural Hybridity*, edited by Elizabeth Kennedy Gische, 59–68. Washington, DC: Smithsonian National Museum of the American Indian, 2006.

——. "Sovereignty: A Line in the Sand." In *Strong Hearts: Native American Visions and Voices*, 51–59. New York: Aperture, 1995.

——. "Visualizing Sovereignty in the Time of Biometric Sensors." *South Atlantic Quarterly* 110, no. 2 (Spring 2011): 465–86.

Roberts, Jennifer. "Landscapes of Indifference: Robert Smithson and John Lloyd Stephens in Yucatan." *The Art Bulletin* 82, no. 3 (September 2000): 544–67.

Roberts, Kathleen. "Conflict of the Spirit." *Albuquerque Journal*, February 4, 2012.

Robinson, Dylan. "Public Writing, Sovereign Reading: Indigenous Language Art in Public Space." In "Indigenous Futures," edited by Kate Morris and Bill Anthes, special issue, *Art Journal* 76, no. 2 (Summer 2017): 85–99.

——. "Speaking to Water, Singing to Stone: Peter Morin, Rebecca Belmore and the Ontologies of Indigenous Modernity." In *Music and Modernity among First Peoples of North America*, edited by Victoria Lindsay Levine and Dylan Robinson, 220–39. Middletown, CT: Wesleyan University Press, 2018.

Rogoff, Irit. *Terra Infirma: Geography's Visual Culture*. New York: Routledge, 2000.

Rojas-Burke, Joe. "Sonar Shows Celilo Falls Are Intact." *The Oregonian*, November 27, 2008.

Rosenberg, Karen. "Mash-Ups Star in a Homage to American Indians: Jeffrey Gibson Injects Visual Pizazz into Found Objects." *New York Times*, July 11, 2013.

Roulet, Florencia. *Human Rights and Indigenous Peoples: A Handbook on the UN System*. International Work Group for Indigenous Affairs Document No. 92. Copenhagen: International Work Group for Indigenous Affairs, 1999.

Rushing, W. Jackson III, "In Our Language: The Art of Hachivi Edgar Heap of Birds." *Third Text* 19, no. 4 (2005): 365–84.

——. "What the Ground Says: The Art of James Lavadour." In *Into the Fray*, edited by James Nottage, 71–81. Indianapolis, IN: Eiteljorg Museum of American Indians and Western Art, 2005.

Rushing, W. Jackson III, and Kristin Makholm. *Modern Spirit: The Art of George Morrison*. Norman: University of Oklahoma Press, 2013.

Ryan, Allan J. *The Trickster Shift: Humour and Irony in Contemporary Native Art*. Seattle: University of Washington Press, 1999.

Said, Edward. *Culture and Imperialism*. New York: Vintage Books, 1993.

Schroeder, Ivy. "Official Art, Official Publics: Public Sculpture Under the Federal Art-in-Architecture Program Since 1972." In *Art and the Performance of Memory: Sounds and Gestures of Recollection*, edited by Richard Candida Smith, 250–65. New York: Routledge, 2002.

Seppi, Lisa Ann. "Metaphysics and Materiality: Landscape Painting and the Art of Kay WalkingStick." Ph.D. diss., University of Illinois at Urbana-Champaign, 2005.

Seppi, Lisa Roberts. "The Artist in Italy: Desire, The Body, and the Divine." In Ash-Milby and Penney, *Kay WalkingStick*, 127–43.

Shapiro, Gary. *Earthwards: Robert Smithson and Art after Babel*. Berkeley: University of California Press, 1995.

Simpson, Audra. *Mohawk Interruptus: Political Life across the Borders of Settler States*. Durham, NC: Duke University Press, 2014.

Singleton, Sara. "Not Our Borders: Indigenous People and the Struggle to Maintain Shared Lives and Cultures in Post-9/11 North America." Border Policy Research Institute Working Paper No. 4 (January 2009): 1–20.

Sky, Alison. "Entropy Made Visible: Interview with Robert Smithson." *On-Site* 4 (1973). Reprinted in *The Writings of Robert Smithson: Essays with Illustrations*, edited by Nancy Holt, 189–96. New York: New York University Press, 1979.

Smallwood, Lyn. "Review: James Lavadour at Cliff Michel." *ARTNews* 90, vol. 1 (January 1991): 168.

Smith, Jaune Quick-to-See. "Curator's Statement." In *Our Land/Ourselves: American Indian Contemporary Artists*, edited by Deborah Ward, v–vi. Albany: State University of New York, 1990.

——. *The Submuloc Show/Columbus Wohs: A Visual Commentary on the Columbus Quincentennial from the Perspective of America's First People*. Phoenix, AZ: Atlatl, 1992.

Smith, Jonathan. "The Lie That Blinds: Destabilizing the Text of Landscape." In *Place/Culture/Representation*, edited by James Duncan and David Ley, 78–92. New York: Routledge, 1993.

Smithson, Robert. "Earth: Symposium at White Museum, Cornell University, 1970." In *The Writings of Robert Smithson: Essays with Illustrations*, edited by Nancy Holt, 160–67. New York: New York University Press, 1979.

——. "The Monuments of Passaic." *Artforum* (December 1967): 48–51.

Snyder, Joel. "Territorial Photography." In Mitchell, *Landscape and Power*, 175–201.

Solnit, Rebecca. *Storming the Gates of Paradise: Landscape for Politics*. Berkeley: University of California Press, 2007.

Spang, Bentley, and Marla Redcorn, eds. *Indian Time: Art in the New Millennium*. Santa Fe: Institute of American Indian Arts, 2000.

Spruhan, Paul. "The Canadian Indian Free Passage Right: The Last Stronghold of Explicit Race Restriction in United States Immigration Law." *North Dakota Law Review* 85 (2009): 310–28.

Tennant, John A., ed. "The Work of E. S. Curtis Among the Indians." *The Photo-Miniature* 6, no. 72 (September 1905): 662–64.

Theriault, Michele, ed. *Interpellations: Three Essays on Kent Monkman*. Montreal, Quebec: Concordia University, 2012.

Thiel, Mark. "Origins of the Jingle Dress Dance." *Whispering Wind* 36, no. 5 (2007): 14–18.

Thoreau, Henry David. *Walden, or Life in the Woods.* Boston: Ticknor and Fields, 1854.

"Thresholds along the Frontier: Contemporary U.S. Border Stations." General Services Administration Press Release 10206, January 23, 2006.

Timm, Jordan. "Landscape with Sexy Transvestite." *Maclean's* 120, no. 51/52 (December 2007–January 2008): 94–95.

Toedtemeier, Terry, and John Laursen. *Wild Beauty: Photographs of the Columbia River Gorge, 1867–1957*. Corvallis: Oregon State Press, 2008.

Townsend-Gault, Charlotte. "Being There, or Not: Native Performance Art—A Perspective." In Passalacqua and Morris, *Native Art Now*, 336–45.

——. "Northwest Coast Art: The Culture of the Land Claims." *American Indian Quarterly* 18, no. 4 (Fall 1994): 445–67.

——. "Rebecca Belmore and James Luna on Location in Venice: The Allegorical Indian Redux." *Art History* 29, no. 4 (2006): 721–55.

Tuan, Yi-Fu. *Space and Place: The Perspective of Experience*. Minneapolis: University of Minnesota Press, 2001.

Urrea, Luis Alberto. *The Devil's Highway: A True Story*. New York: Back Bay Books, 2004.

Valentino, Erin. "'Mistaken Identity': Between Death and Pleasure in the Art of Kay WalkingStick." *Third Text* 8, no. 26 (Spring 1994): 61–73.

Vartanian, Hrag. "The Violent History of Kent Monkman." *Hyperallergic*, June 14, 2014.

Vigil, Jennifer. "Will Wilson: Fellowship Artist." In *Diversity and Dialogue: The Eiteljorg Fellowship for Native American Art 2007*, edited by James Nottage, 95–107. Indianapolis, IN: Eiteljorg Museum of American Indians and Western Art, 2007.Vizenor, Gerald. *Manifest Manners: Narratives on Postindian Survivance*. Lincoln: University of Nebraska Press, 1999.

Vizenor, Gerald. *Manifest Manners: Narratives on Postindian Survivance*. Lincoln: University of Nebraska Press, 1999.

WalkingStick, Kay. "Native American Art in the Postmodern Era." In "Recent Native American Art," edited by Kay WalkingStick and W. Jackson Rushing, special issue, *Art Journal* 51, no. 3 (Fall 1992):15–17.

Wallach, Alan P. "Cole, Byron, and *The Course of Empire*." *The Art Bulletin* 50, no. 4 (December 1968): 375–79.

Waller, Sydney. *Homage to the American Elm: Photography, Painting, Sculpture, Drawings and Installations by Contemporary New York Artists*. Cooperstown, NY: Arts Communications, 1985.

Waltemath, Joan. "Native American Iconography Meets Modernist Aesthetic and Material." *Hyperallergic*, December 11, 2012.

Warrior, Robert Allen. *Tribal Secrets: Recovering American Indian Intellectual Traditions.* Minneapolis: University of Minnesota Press, 1994.

Watson, Mark. "Centering the Indigenous: Postcommodity's Trans-Indigenous Relational Art." *Third Text* 29, no. 3 (2015): 141–54.

Welish, Marjorie. "Susan Hoeltzel, Kay WalkingStick, and David Frumer at Bertha Urdang." *Art in America* 66, no. 5 (September–October 1978): 128.

Wells, Liz. *Land Matters: Landscape Photography, Culture and Identity*. New York: I. B. Tauris Press, 2011.

Wilson, Cheryl, ed. *This Path We Travel: Celebrations of Contemporary Native American Creativity*. Washington, DC: Smithsonian National Museum of the American Indian, 1994.

INDEX

Page numbers in *italic* refer to illustrations.

abstract expressionism, 2, 57, 151n23, 154n28
Abyss, The (WalkingStick), 13, 28, 43, 61, 157n84
Adams, Ann Jensen, 16
aerial views, 67, 77–78, 160n64
aesthetics, relational. *See* relational aesthetics
American Indian Movement, 37, 59, 60
Among the Sierra Nevada Mountains, California (Bierstadt), 131, 132
amplification of sound, 143–45, *144*, 146–47
Anthes, Bill, 58–60, 158n5
anti-invitational aspects, 4–6, 46, *54*, 55, 63, 64, 68, 70, 96–101, *97*, *98*, *99*, 103, 119, 131, 133; Harrison view, 18
April Contemplating May (WalkingStick), 116
Art as Illusion (Morrison), 58, 59
Art in Architecture Program. *See* General Services Administration Art in Architecture Program.
Artist and Model (Monkman), 130–31, 133
Art Seminar (DeLue and Elkins roundtable), 20–21, 152n48
Ash-Milby, Kathleen, 30
Asphalt Rundown (Smithson), 91
Atanarjuat: The Fast Runner (Kunuk), 25
audio devices. *See* listening funnels; megaphones
audio in installations, 88–89, 95, 125, 146, 147–48
Australia, 24. *See also* Sydney Biennale
Australian Aborigines, 88, 146
Auto-Immune Response (Wilson), 143
Autumn Dusk, Red Rock Variation: Lake Superior Landscape (Morrison), 61
Ayum-ee-aawach Oomama-mowan, Speaking to Their Mother (Rebecca Belmore), 143–45, *144*, 147, 170n93, 170n97

Banff Center for the Arts, 143
barbed wire, *98*, 99–100, *99*, 101
Beam, Carl, 57
Belmore, Michael: *Coalescence*, 83, 147; *Flux*, 82–83, *85*, 88; *Upland*, 83
Belmore, Rebecca: *Ayum-ee-aawach Oomama-mowan, Speaking to Their Mother*, 143–45, *144*, 147, 170n93, 170n97; *Fountain*, 143, 169n85; *Wave Sound*, 147–48, *147*, 170n97
Berlo, Janet Catherine, 142–43
Bermingham, Ann, 15
Bête Noire (Monkman), 138–39, *138*, 140
Bierstadt, Albert, 130, 134, 140; *Among the Sierra Nevada Mountains, California*, 131, 132; *Mount Corcoran*, 168nn60–61; *Sunrise on the Matterhorn*, 140; *Yosemite Winter Scene*, 133
billboards, 96–100, *98*, *99*
Birk, Sandow: *The Rise and Fall of Los Angeles*, 165n72
bison. *See* buffalo
Bitterroot Mountains I (WalkingStick), 53
Blame the Mountains III (WalkingStick), 116, *117*
Blanket (Lavadour), 12, 66, 70, *71*, 72, 73
blocking of access. *See* anti-invitational devices and aspects

Border Crossing (Haozous), 100
borders, national, 92–103, 162n34, 164n54, 164n57. *See also* U.S.-Canada border; U.S.-Mexico border
borders, reservation, 94–95, 96, *97*, 100–101
Bourriard, Nicholas, 170n95
Brown, Dee: *Bury My Heart at Wounded Knee*, 37
Buell, Lawrence, 133
buffalo, 129–30, 135–36, 138–39, *138*, 142, 143, 169n80
Buffalo Boy, Seize the Space (Thomas). See *Seize the Space, Buffalo Boy* (Thomas)
Bunn, David, 16–17
Bury My Heart at Wounded Knee (Brown), 37

Cache (Lavadour), 12, 66
Camouflage (Gibson), 119
camp (aesthetic), 128, 130, 132, 140
Canada, 24, 109, 136, 139, 143–46, 161n9, 169n85, 170n90; Border Services Agency, 162n34; national parks, 83, 161n9, 147–48, *147*, 170n97
Canada-U.S. border. *See* U.S.-Canada border
Capital Square Park, Richmond, Virginia, 111–13, *112*
Cardinal Points (WalkingStick), 33–34, 48, 49
Castle, Frederick, 39
Catlin, George, 129–30, 134, 168nn44–45
Ceci n'est pas une pipe (Monkman), 128–29
Charged Particles in Motion (Monkman), 133
Chase, The (Monkman), 135–36
Cher, 128, 130, 167n40
Chief Joseph series (WalkingStick), 33–34, 37–38, 53, 154n32
Christian iconography, 43, 44, 48, 49, 50
Church, Frederick, 29
Close Encounters: The Next 500 Years (Plug In Institute of Contemporary Art), 165n82
Closer View, A (Michelson), 161n13
Coalescence (Michael Belmore), 83, 147
Cole, Thomas, 29, 33, 111, 131, 151n26; *The Course of Empire*, 107–8, 165n72, 165n83; *A View of Fort Putnam*, 15
collages, wood. *See* wood collages
Collapsing of Time and Space in an Ever-Expanding Universe, The (Monkman), 140, 142, 143
Columbian quincentennial (1992), 22, 25, 46–47, 48, 81–82, 161n4
Columbia River, 27, 30, 31, 154n12
Confederated Tribes of the Umatilla Indian Reservation. *See* Umatilla Indian Reservation
Continuum: 12 Artists (National Museum of the American Indian), 53, 157n87
"Contradictions in Indian Territory" (Longfish and Randall), 11
copper, 50, 83, 156n70
copying of paintings, 130–33
Corn Blue Room (Jolene Rickard), 101
Cornwall Island (Kawehno:ke), 92, 102, 162n34
Cosgrove, Denis, 15
Course of Empire, The (Cole), 107–8, 165n72, 166n83
Coyotaje (Postcommodity), 164n60
Creation and Destruction of an Indian Reservation: An American Dilemma (Luna), 100, 161n4
cruciform motif, 48–49, *49*, 50, 69, 100
cubism, 64, 135
Cult of Memory (Michelson), 86, 87, 88
Cultural Crossroads of the Americas (Haozous), 96–98, *98*
Cultural Graffiti: A Tahltan Indian Declares War on the British Monarchy (Morin), 145, *146*
Curtis, Edward, 108, 111, 132, 165n76
Cryptochroma I (WalkingStick), 48, 49

Dakota Access oil pipeline, 1, 78, 143, 149n1, 160n63
Death of the Elm (WalkingStick), 33–35, *34*, 40, 41–42, 46, 51, 62
Death of the Female (Monkman), 136, *137*
Decade Show: Frameworks of Identity in the 1980s, The, 46, 156n68
Declaration on the Rights of Indigenous Peoples (UNDRIP). *See* United Nations Declaration on the Rights of Indigenous Peoples (UNDRIP)
decline, decay, and ruin: Cole and, 108, 111, 165n83; Michelson and, 90, 105, 108, 109, 111; Smithson and, 91, 105, 108, 109, 162n29
"decolonial" (word), 150n13
decolonialism, 5, 6, 109; strategies in art, 4, 21, 22, 25, 104–13, 109
Deep Blue Day (Gibson), 122–25, *124*
Deep Moon (Lavadour), 11–12, *12*, 66–67, 68, 70, 73, 76
Deloria, Philip: *Indians in Unexpected Places*, 135
DeLue, Rachael Ziady, 20
Devine, Bonnie: *Letters from Home*, 83, 88, 143
dioramas, 138–39, *138*, 140, 142, 143, 167n38
Dobkins, Rebecca, 71, 159n39, 159n42, 159n47
Do You Remember When? (Postcommodity), 3, 4, 81–83, *82*, 88, 111, 146–47, 161n17
drone technology, 1, 2, 78, 160n63
Dubow, Jessica, 20
Durham, Jimmie, 120, 143, 167n21, 169n84
Dying Day (Michelson), 108, 111

Eakins, Thomas, 134
Earth's Eye (Michelson), 86, *87*, 88, 113
earthworks, 3, 91, 111–13, *112*. See also *Mantle* (Michelson); *Do You Remember When?* (Postcommodity); *Repellent Fence* (Postcommodity); *Spiral Jetty* (Smithson)

Elkins, James, 20, 21
Ellegood, Anne, 125
ellipse (shape), 44, 45, 156n61
Entering Zig's Indian Reservation (Zig Jackson), 4
entropy. *See* decline, decay, and ruin
equilateral cross motif, 48–49, *49*, 50, 52
Escarpment paintings (Smith), 63–64
European landscape tradition, 2, 4–5, 15–18, 21, 29, 45–46, 129–35, 140; human figure in, 115; parody of, 130, 133; perspective in, 62
Everett, Caroline, 125, 128
Everett, Deborah, 87, 90
Expelling the Vices (Monkman), 168n61

Fast Runner, The (Kunuk). See *Atanarjuat: The Fast Runner* (Kunuk)
Fear of Non-Beings (WalkingStick), 156n56
Ferguson, Walter: *Geronimo at the Wheel*, 135, 136
films, 25, 95. *See also* video
First Principle, The (Gibson), 119
Flag 1 (Lavadour), 73
Flag 2 (Lavadour), 11
Flux (Michael Belmore), 82–83, *85*, 88
Flying Dutchman, The (Ryder), 118
For Those Who Cannot Speak: The Land, the Water, the Animals and the Future Generations (Myre), 93–94, *94*
Foucault, Michel, 16, 19,
Fountain (Rebecca Belmore), 143, 169n85
Four Directions series (WalkingStick), 156n74
Four Directions: Spirit Center (WalkingStick), 47, 48, 49, 50, 63
Friedrich, Caspar David: *Wanderer above the Sea of Mist*, 62
Frozen River (film), 95
Furnish, David, 133–34

gashes in canvases, 51, *52*, 123, 125, *126*
Gate/Negate (Haozous), 163n51
General Services Administration Art in Architecture Program, 92, 98, 99
Geronimo at the Wheel (Ferguson), 135, 136
Gibson, Jeffrey, 119–25, 166n20; *Camouflage*, 119; *Deep Blue Day*, 122–23, *124*; *The First Principle*, 119; *Infinite Sampling*, 122; *Natura Non Facit Saltum*, 120, *121*; *Promise*, 122, 167n27; *Realms of Fin, Feet, and Wing*, 120; *Red Black White* series, 120, 167n21; *Shields*, 122, 167n30; *Singular*, 120; *Submerge*, 120; *Surveillance*, 120
Gioioso, Variation I and Variation II (WalkingStick), 116
Glowen, Ron, 75
gold leaf, 52, 53, 83
Grappling with Chaos (WalkingStick), 28, 43
Greenberg, Clement: "Modernist Painting," 155n38, 157n90, 166n8
Grey Art Gallery, New York University, 86
grids, 155n53; Gibson, 120; Lavadour, 71–76, 160n53, 160n55; in modernism, 76, 155n47; in U.S. land partitioning, 75; WalkingStick, 35, 37–38, 39, 40–41, 48, 51
"Grids" (Krauss), 38, 39, 40–41, 73, 155n47, 155n53
Guswenta (Two Row Wampum) Treaty, 93, 95, 101

Haldimand Proclamation, 94–95, 162n37
Halper, Vicki, 159n34
Harrison, Charles, 18, 115
Haudenosaunee, 92–95, 162n37, 164n54, 164n57. *See also* Mohawk Nation
Haozous, Bob: *Border Crossing*, 100; *Cultural Crossroads of the Americas*, 96–98, *98*; *Gate/Negate*, 163n51; *Spirit of the Earth*, 98–100, *99*
Heard Museum: *Shared Visions: Native American Painters and Sculptors in the Twentieth Century*, 161n4
helium balloons, 102–3, *103*
History Is Painted by the Victors (Monkman), 134, *135*
Homage to Chief Joseph (WalkingStick), 154n32
Homage to the American Elm (Gallery 53, Cooperstown, New York), 33
homoeroticism. *See* queer identity and sexuality
horizon lines: Lavadour, 67, 77; Morrison, 57, 58–59, *59*, 61, 158n5; Myre, 125, *126*; Quick-to-See Smith, 64; WalkingStick, 39, 40, 45, 48, 52, 58, 63
Horizon Paintings series (Morrison), 60, 61
Horton, Jessica, 142–43, 160n63
Houle, Robert, 47, 83, 110–11
Hudson River, 104–7, *106*, 111, 165n66, 165n71
Hudson River School, 15, 105, 107
Human Condition, The (Magritte), 40

Ice (Lavadour), 71, 159n47
Idle No More (Broken Treaty Movement), 4, 93–94
Il Sogno, II (WalkingStick), 116
imperialism, 4, 17, 18, 115, 132, 151n34
"Imperial Landscape" (Mitchell), 17–18, 21, 151n37
inaccessibility. *See* anti-invitational devices and aspects
Indian Defense League of America (IDLA), 24, 101
Indian Man in San Francisco (Zig Jackson), 24
Indian Point, Twilight (Michelson). See *Twilight, Indian Point* (Michelson)
Indians in Unexpected Places (Deloria), 135
Indigena: Contemporary Native Perspectives in Canadian Art (Canadian Museum of Civilization), 22

Indigenous visual sovereignty. *See* visual sovereignty
Infinite Sampling (Gibson), 122
inscription on paintings, 47
installation art, 2–3, 81–95, 143, 161n4, 161n9; Jolene Rickard, 101; Luna, 100–101; Michael Belmore, 82–83, *85*, 88, 89–95; Michelson, 86–87, *87*, 88, 112–13, *112*, 161n13; Monkman, 125, *127*, 128, 138–39, *138*, 140, 142, 143; Postcommodity, 81–83, *82*, 88, 102–3, *103*, 111, 146, 164n60; Smithson, 87–88, 91; voice in, 146. *See also* video: installations
interventions, 96, 102–3, *103*, 109–10, *110*, 131, 144–45, *144*, *145*. *See also* anti-invitational aspects
"invitational" artwork, 4, 15–16, 21, 50–51, *52*, 102–3, *103*, *112*, 113, 131, 133. *See also* anti-invitational aspects
ironing boards, painted, 122, 167n30
Iroquois. *See* Haudenosaunee
Is That You? (WalkingStick), 43

Jackson, John Brinkerhoff, 75, 77
Jackson, Zig, 96; *Entering Zig's Indian Reservation*, 4, 96, *97*; *Indian Man in San Francisco*, 24
Jay Treaty, 101, 164n57
jingle dresses, 123, *124*, 125
Joseph (Nez Perce chief), 37, 53, 154n32
Judd, Donald, 81

Kane, Paul, 129, 130; *Scene from the Northwest: Portrait of John Henry Lefroy*, 133, 168n56
Kastner, Carolyn, 63–64
Katz, Jonathan, 139–40
Kawehno:ke. *See* Cornwall Island (Kawehno:ke)
Kay WalkingStick: An American Artist, 154n23
Keye, Amos, Jr., 95
kinesis, 1, 10, 28, 31, 123
kitsch, 119, 128, 167n38
Krauss, Rosalind: "Grids," 38, 39, 40–41, 76, 155n47, 155n53; on sacred-secular divide, 49–50; "Sculpture in the Expanded Field," 3, 81, 164n65

labyrinths, 113
Lake Superior, 58, 60, 61
Lake Superior Landscape series (Morrison), 57, 58, 59, *59*, 60, 61, 77
LaMarr, Jean, 101; *Some Kind of Buckaroo*, 101
Lamentation (Monkman), 140
land art movement, 2, 113. See also *Spiral Jetty* (Smithson)
LandMarks 2017, 83, 147–48, 161n9, 170n97
Landscape and Power (Mitchell), 4, 5, 9, 11, 14–20, 150n23
Landscape of Sorrow (Myre), 125, *126*, 143
Landscape Theory (Olwig), 66
Land, Spirit, Power: First Nations at the National Gallery of Canada, 22, 47, 82
Late Summer on the Ramapo (WalkingStick), 41–42, 53
Lavadour, James, 4, 9–13, 19, 20, 23, 28–32, 66–79, 160n57; *Blanket*, 12, 66, 70, *71*, 72, 73; *Cache*, 12, 66; *Deep Moon*, 11–12, *12*, 66–67, 68, 70, 73, 76; grids, 71–76, 160n53, 160n55; human figures, 118–19; *Naming Tanager*, 118; *Nest of Suns*, 67, 69; *North Bank*, 77; *Red River*, 78–79; *River* series, 30–32, *31*, 71; *Ruby Lift (I, II, III)*, 78–79; *Salamander*, 9, *10*, 67–68, 70; *Sunflower*, 69; *Spring*, 72; *Straight Ahead*, 12; *Tiicham*, 12, 66, *74*, 76; *Totem*, 76; *Tremor III*, 72; *Wash*, 12
Letters from Home (Devine), 83, 88, 143
Letting Go from Chaos to Calm (WalkingStick), 28, 44, 62
Lewis and Clark expedition, 27, 132
Light after Darkness (Michelson). See *Of Light after Darkness* (Michelson)
Lippard, Lucy, 101
listening funnels, 147–48, *147*
Lives of the Hudson (Tang Art Museum), 104, 105
Lone Dog (Lakota artist), 132
Longfish, George, 11
Loss (WalkingStick), 28, 43, 44, 46, 156n59
Lot's Wife (Monkman), 125, *127*, 128, 140, 143
Lowe, Truman, 23, 157n87; *Ottawa*, 82, *84*, 88, 161n5
Luger, Cannupa Hanska: *Mirror Shield Project: Water Serpent Action*, 1, *2*, 3, 5, 149n2
Luna, James, 100–101, 156n68, 161n4; *Creation and Destruction of an Indian Reservation: An American Dilemma*, 100, 161n4

Madill, Shirley, 131
Magritte, René: *The Human Condition*, 40
mandorla (shape), 44, 51
Manifest Destiny, 29, 134
Mantegna, Andrea: *Lamentation of Christ*, 43
Mantle (Michelson), 111–13, *112*
Martin, Lee-Ann, 22
McMaster, Gerald, 22, 133, 145–46
Me and My Neon Box (WalkingStick), 116
megaphones, 143–45, *144*, 170n93
Mespat (Michelson), 86, 89–92, *90*, 105, 109
metals: use in painting, 50, 51, 52, 53; use in sculpture and installations, 78, 83, 96, *98*, *99*, 147–48, *147*
Metropolis (Gibson), 120
Mexico-U.S. border. *See* U.S.-Mexico border
mica, 73, 159n47
Michelson, Alan, 5, 86–87, 88, 89–95, 101, 122, 161n13; *A Closer View*, 161n13; *Cult of Memory*, 86, 87, 88; *Dying Day*, 108, 111; *Earth's Eye*, 86,

87, 88, 113; *Mantle*, 111–13, *112*; *Mespat*, 86, 89–92, *90*, 105, 109; *Of Light after Darkness*, 107, 108, 111; *Permanent Title*, 86, 87, 88; *Shattemuc*, 104–7, *106*, 109, 111; *Third Bank of the River*, 92–93, *93*, 98, 101, 103–4, 109, 111, 164n58; *Twilight, Indian Point*, 165n71; *TwoRow II*, 94–95, 104, 107
Mignolo, Walter, 150n13
minimalism: land art roots in, 2, 113, 161n14; Postcommodity, 81, 146; WalkingStick, 13, 33, 35, 37, 45, 48, 49, 58, 117
Mirror Shield Project: Water Serpent Action (Luger), 1, *2*, 3, 5, 78, 149n2
Miss, Mary, 3
Miss Chief (Monkman alter ego), 128–35, *129*, *135*, 138–40, *138*, *141*, 142, 143, 168n61
Mitchell, W. J. T.: "Imperial Landscape," 17–18, 21, 151n37; *Landscape and Power*, 4, 5, 9, 11, 14–20, 150n23
modernism: dystopia in, 91–92; flatness in, 48; Greenberg on, 155n38; grids in, 39, 76, 155n47; Jaune Quick-to-See Smith, 64; Mitchell views, 15, 150n53; Ruth Phillips view, 165n80; WalkingStick, 35, 39, 42–43, 154n28
"Modernist Painting" (Greenberg), 155n38, 157n90, 166n8
Mohawk Interruptus: Political Life across the Borders of Settler States (Simpson), 164n57
Mohawk Nation, 92, 143, 162n34, 162n37
Mondrian, Piet, 76, 132, 134, 140, 155n53
Monet, Claude, 60
Monkman, Kent, 125–42, 143; *Artist and Model*, 130–31; *Bête Noire*, 138–19, *138*, 140; *Charged Particles in Motion*, 133; *The Chase*, 135–36; *The Collapsing of Time and Space in an Ever-Expanding Universe*, 140, 143; *Death of the Female*, 136, *137*; *Expelling the Vices*, 168n61; *History Is Painted by the Victors*, 134, *135*; *Lot's Wife*, 125, *127*, 140, 143; *Pity*, 140, *141*; *Portrait of the Artist as Hunter*, 128, 129–30, 133; *The Rise and Fall of Civilization*, 142; *Struggle for Balance*, 137, 143; *Trappers of Men*, 128, *129*, 130, 131, 132, 133, 140
Montauk I (WalkingStick), 34–35, *36*, 39, 42
Montauk II (Dusk) (WalkingStick), 39
Montauk series (WalkingStick), 34–35, *36*, 39–40, 42, 58
monuments, 104, 105, 109–13, *110*, 145, 164n65
"Monuments of Passaic, The" (Smithson), 91, 105, 107
Morin, Peter, *Cultural Graffiti: A Tahltan Indian Declares War on the British*
Monarchy, 145, *146*, 170n90
Morrison, George, 57–61, 77, 158n10, 158nn12–13, 158n19, 158n23; Art as Illusion, 58, 59; *Autumn Dusk, Red Rock Variation: Lake Superior Landscape*, 61; *Horizon Paintings* series, 60, 61; *New England Landscape II*, 58, 59, 60; *Provincetown, Sky—Seascape*, 58; *Quiet Light towards Evening*, 60, 61; *Spirit Path, New Day, Red Rock Variation: Lake Superior Landscape*, 57, 58, *59*, 60, 61
Mount Corcoran (Bierstadt), 168nn60–61
multipaneled paintings, 9, *10*, 11, *12*, 19, 66–71, *71*, 73–77, *74*
music and songs, 11, 88, 120, 140, 145, 146
Myre, Nadia: *For Those Who Cannot Speak: The Land, the Water, the Animals and the Future Generations*, 93–94, *94*; *Landscape of Sorrow*, 125, *126*, 143; *The Scar Project*, 3, 123

Naming Tanager (Lavadour), 118
Nanook of the North (film), 25
National Academy Museum: *Said the Pigeon to the Squirrel*, 121
national borders. *See* borders, national
National Gallery of Canada: *Land, Spirit, Power*, 22, 47, 82
National Museum of the American Indian, 83, 89, 94, 119; *Continuum: 12 Artists*, 53, 154n23; *Kay WalkingStick: An American Artist*, 154n23; *Off the Map: Landscape in the Native Imagination*, 119, 120
Natura Non Facit Saltum (Gibson), 120, *121*
Nest of Suns (Lavadour), 67, 69
Nevelson, Louise, 58
New England Landscape II (Morrison), 58, 59, 60
New Mexico Arroyos (WalkingStick), 54–55
New Mexico Desert (WalkingStick), 54, *54*
Nez Perce, 27, 37, 52–53, 154n32
Night (WalkingStick), 44
Night Café, The (Van Gogh), 45
"non-sites," 87–88, 161n14, 161n16, 166n88
North Bank (Lavadour), 77
nudes, 116–17, *117*, *129*, 134, *135*, 136, *137*, *141*

Off the Map: Landscape in the Native Imagination (National Museum of the American Indian), 119, 120
Of Light after Darkness (Michelson), 107, 108, 111
Olwig, Kenneth, 66
On the Edge (WalkingStick), 13, *14*, 28, 40, 43, 62
Orilla Verde at Rio Grande (WalkingStick), 54–55
Ortel, Jo, 161n5
Otay Mesa Crossing (Haozous). See *Spirit of the Earth* (Haozous)
Ottawa (Lowe), 82, *84*, 88, 161n5
Our Land (WalkingStick), 52–53
Our Land/Ourselves: American Indian Contemporary Artists (exhibition) 22, 46, 57, 60, 63
Our Selves, Our Land (WalkingStick), 47, 50
Owens, Craig, 88, 91, 108–9, 161n16

painting, Native: Gibson, 119–22; Jaune Quick-to-See Smith, 63–66; Lavadour, 9–13, 19, 28–32, 66–79, 118–19, 159n42; modernist, 38, 40, 76, 155n38, 166n8; Monkman, 125–42, 143; Morrison, 57–58, *59*, 60–61, 77; WalkingStick, 13–14, 19, 28, 29, 30, 32–55, 116–19
painting, non-Native, 4, 16; Bierstadt, 130–34, 140, 168nn60–61; Catlin, 129–30, 134, 168nn44–45; Eakins, 134; Friedrich, 62; Kane, 129, 130, 133, 168n56; Magritte, 40; Mantegna, 43; Monet, 60; parody, 129–40, *129*, *135*, *137*, *141*; Ryder, 118; Van Gogh, 45
paintings, copying of. *See* copying of paintings
paintings, devotional. *See* devotional paintings
paintings, inscription on. *See* inscription on paintings
paintings, multipaneled. *See* multipaneled paintings
paintings, repurposed. *See* repurposed paintings
panopticon, 16, 151n28
panoramas, 89, 92, 104, 105
parfleche and parfleches, 52, 122, 167n24, 167n30
parody, 25, 130, 133
Partially Buried Woodshed (Smithson), 91
Pecos, The (WalkingStick), 54–55
Penney, David, 61, 158n5, 159n23
performance art, 100, 143, 169n85
performative interventions. *See* interventions
Permanent Title (Michelson), 86, 87, 88
perspective, 2, 66, 78, 151n36; Bermingham view, 15; Jaune Quick-to-See Smith, 64; Lavadour, 66, 68, 73, 78; Morrison, 77; in video pieces, 95, 102, 104; WalkingStick, 38, 41, 45, 62–63. *See also* aerial views
"perspective" (word), 162n33
Petroglyph Park series (Smith), 63, 64
phenomenology, 5, 14, 19, 20–21
Phillips, Deborah, 38–39
Phillips, Ruth, 109–11, 165n80
photography, 24, 91; *Geronimo at the Wheel*, 135, 136; Thomas, 109, *110*; Jolene Rickard, 101; Michelson, 92–93, *93*; "The Monuments of Passaic" (Smithson), 91, 105, 107; Red Star, 167n38; Wilson, 143; Zig Jackson, 4, 24, 96, *97*
Picasso, Pablo, 136
Pity (Monkman), 140, *141*
Plug In Institute of Contemporary Art: *Close Encounters: The Next 500 Years*, 165n82
point of view. *See* perspective
Pollock, Jackson, 57, 132, 134, 140
Portrait of the Artist as Hunter (Monkman), 128, 129–30, 133
Positive Field (WalkingStick), 48, 49
Postcommodity: *Coyotaje*, 164n60; *Do You Remember When?*, 4, 81–83, *82*, 88, 111, 146–47, 161n17; *Repellent Fence*, 102–3, *103*; *A Very Long Line*, 102–3
postmodernism, 15, 21–22, 46–47, 50, 55, 62, 63, 66, 73, 108–9; dystopia in, 91–92
Powhatan (Algonquian chief), 111
printmaking, 9, 69, 159n40, 160n57
Promise (Gibson), 122, 167n27
protest art, 93, 143, 144–45; NoDAPL, 1–2, *2*, 78, 143, 149n2, 149n5, 160n63
Provincetown, Sky—Seascape (Morrison), 58
punching bag sculptures, 122–25, *124*

queer identity and sexuality, 120, 128–31, 134
Quick-to-See Smith, Jaune. *See* Smith, Jaune Quick-to-See
Quiet Light towards Evening (Morrison), 60, 61

Raheja, Michelle, 25, 29, 153n76
Ramapo River Early Spring (WalkingStick), 53
Ramapo River series (WalkingStick), 41–42, 53, 54, 61
Randall, Joan, 11
razor wire. *See* concertina wire
Realms of Fin, Feet, and Wing (Gibson), 120
Red Black White series (Gibson), 120, 167n21
Red River (Lavadour), 78–79
Red River of the North, 125
Red Star, Wendy: *Four Seasons* series, 167n38
relational aesthetics, 146, 170n95
Remnant of Cataclysm (WalkingStick), 45
Repellent Fence (Postcommodity), 102–3, *103*
reproduction of paintings. *See* copying of paintings
repurposed paintings, *124*, 125
Requiem (WalkingStick), 52, 53
reservation borders. *See* borders, reservation
Reservation X: The Power of Place in Contemporary Indigenous Art (Canadian Museum of Civilization), 101
Richmond, Virginia: Capital Square Park. *See* Capital Square Park, Richmond, Virginia
Rickard, Clinton, 101
Rickard, Jolene, 3, 24, 25, 101, 153n77, 164n54, 164n58; *Corn Blue Room*, 101
Rikers Island, New York, 89–90
Rio Grande Gorge (WalkingStick), 52, 54–55
Rise and Fall of Civilization, The (Monkman), 142
Rise and Fall of Los Angeles, The (Birk), 165n72
rivers, 28, 31–32, 42, 79, 83, 91, 125; in sculpture and installation art, 82, 83, *84*, 92–93, 101–2; stones, 83, *85*; in video installations, 89–92, 94–95. *See also* Columbia River; Hudson River; Red River of the North
River series (Lavadour), 30–32, *31*, 71
River (10) (Lavadour), 30–31, *31*
Robinson, Dylan, 5, 144, 145

romanticism, 62, 89, 105, 107, 109, 115, 139; Monkman, 130, 139; WalkingStick, 55, 63, 116
Royal Ontario Museum, 107
Ruby Lift (I, II, III) (Lavadour), 78–79
ruination. *See* decline, decay, and ruin
Rushing, W. Jackson, 14, 61, 77
Ryder, Albert Pinkham: *The Flying Dutchman*, 118

Said, Edward, 151n34
Said the Pigeon to the Squirrel (National Academy Museum), 121
Salamander (Lavadour), 9, *10*, 67–68, 70
Scaffold (Lavadour), 11, 70, 73, 76
Scar Project, The (Myre), 3, 123, 125
Scene from the Northwest: Portrait of John Henry Lefroy (Kane), 133, 168n56
sculpture, 3, 81–84; Devine, 83; Gibson, 122–25, *124*; Haozous, 96–100, *98*, *99*; Lavadour, 78–79; Lowe, 82, *84*; Michael Belmore, 82–83, *85*; Morrison, 58–59; Rebecca Belmore, 143–45, *144*, 147–48, *147*; Smithson, 91; WalkingStick, 156n70
"Sculpture in the Expanded Field" (Krauss), 3, 81, 164n65
Seize the Space, Buffalo Boy (Thomas), *110*, 165n78
Seppi, Lisa, 47, 48, 49
settler colonialism, 109, 131, 142
"Settler Monuments, Indigenous Memory" (Phillips), 109–11
sexuality, 117, 120, 123, 128–31, 130, 132, 134
Shared Visions: Native American Painters and Sculptors in the Twentieth Century (Heard Museum), 161n4
Shattemuc (Michelson), 104–7, *106*, 109, 111
Shields (Gibson), 122, 167n30
Silence of Glacier, The (WalkingStick), 52, 54–55
Simpson, Audra, 164n57
Singular (Gibson), 120
site-specific works, 1–3, 5, 81–113, 145–47
skin, 122–25. *See also* nudes; parfleche and parfleches
Smallwood, Lyn, 69, 118
Smith, Jaune Quick-to-See, 23, 57, 63–66, 156n68; *Sunset on the Escarpment*, 63, *65*
Smith, Jonathan, 62
Smithson, Robert, 87–88, 108–9, 161n14; "The Monuments of Passaic," 91, 105, 107; *Spiral Jetty*, 2, 91, 113, 166n88
songs and music. *See* music and songs
sound amplification. *See* amplification of sound
sound in installations. *See* audio in installations
sovereignty, 1, 5, 11, 21, 23–5, 75, 92–5, 96, 101–3, 109, 143, 145. *See also* visual sovereignty
Speaking to Their Mother (Rebecca Belmore). See *Ayum-ee-aawach Oomama-mowan, Speaking to Their Mother* (Rebecca Belmore)
Spiral Jetty (Smithson), 2, 91, 113, 166n88
spiral motif, 111–13, *112*
Spirit Center II (WalkingStick), 44, 48
Spirit Center series (WalkingStick), 44, 47, 48, *49*, 50
Spirit of the Earth (Haozous), 98–100, *99*
Spirit Path, New Day, Red Rock Variation: Lake Superior Landscape (Morrison), 57, 58, *59*, 60, 61
spray paint, 120
Spring (Lavadour), 72
square format, 38, 39, 42, 49, 76, 123
squeegee use, 9, 70, 72–73
Standing Rock Sioux reservation, 149n1. See also *Mirror Shield Project: Water Serpent Action*
Stanley, John Mix, 129, 130
St. Mary's Mountain (WalkingStick), 54–55
Straight Ahead (Lavadour), 12
Struggle for Balance (Monkman), 137, 143
Submerge (Gibson), 120
Submuloc Show/Columbus Wohs, 22, 46–47, 156n70
Sunflower (Lavadour), 69
Sunrise on the Matterhorn (Bierstadt), 140, *141*
Sunset on the Escarpment (Smith), 63, *65*
Surveillance (Gibson), 120
"survivance" (Vizenor), 138, 149n8
Sydney Biennale, 81, *82*, 83, 88

Tang Art Museum: *Lives of the Hudson*, 104, 105
Tears (WalkingStick), 156n70
text on paintings. *See* inscription of paintings
Third Bank of the River (Michelson), 92–93, *93*, 98, 101, 103–4, 109, 111, 164n58
Thomas, Jeffrey, 109–11, *110*, 165n78, 165n80; *Seize the Space, Buffalo Boy*, *110*, 165n78
Thoreau, Henry David, 30, 86, 161n9
three-dimensionality, 81; Greenberg on, 157n90, 166n8; illusion of, 35; of paintings, 32–33, 38, 44, 67, 70, 73, 128
Tiicham (Lavadour), 12, 66, *74*, 76
Totem (Lavadour), 76
tourism, 96, 104, 105, 164n66
Trappers of Men (Monkman), 128, *129*, 130, 131, 132, 133, 140
trauma, 6, 123, 140; Monkman, 140; Morin, 170n90; Myre, 123, 125; WalkingStick, 48, 50, 116
treaties, 95, 101, 164n57. *See also* Idle No More (Broken Treaty Movement)
treaty belts. *See* wampum belts
Tremor III (Lavadour), 72
Triumph of Mischief, The (Monkman), 168n45
Twilight, Indian Point (Michelson), 165n71
TwoRow II (Michelson), 94–95, 104, 107
Two Row Wampum Treaty. *See* Guswenta (Two Row Wampum) Treaty
two-spirit people, 128, 130

Umatilla Indian Reservation, 10, 27, 75, 160n57
Uncontrolled Destiny (WalkingStick), 28, 43, 46
United Nations Declaration on the Rights of Indigenous Peoples (UNDRIP), 11, 23, 24, 152–53nn66–68
University of Minnesota, 60
University of New Mexico, 96, 100
Upland (Michael Belmore), 83
Urban Res (Sargent's Daughters, New York), 136–37, 139
U.S.-Canada border, 92, *93*, 95, 101–2
U.S.-Mexico border, 96–100, *98*, *99*, 102–3, *103*, 164n60

Vancouver, 169n85
Van Gogh, Vincent: *The Night Café*, 45
"vanishing Indian," 108, 129–30, 165n76, 168n44
Venere Alpina (WalkingStick), 50–51, *52*, 116, 123, 125
Very Long Line, A (Postcommodity), 102–3
video, as medium, 3, 5; installations, 89–91, 94–95, 104–7, 111, 125, 127, 128, 164n60; Luger, 1, *2*, 78, 149n2; Michelson, 94–95, 104–7, *106*, 107–8, 111; Monkman, 125, *127*; Postcommodity, 102–3; stills, *90*, *106*, *127*
View of Fort Putnam, A (Cole), 15
visual sovereignty, 3, 11, 21, 23, 25, 29, 66, 75, 149n9, 164n58
Vizenor, Gerald, 138, 149n8
voice and voices, 88, 145, 146. See also *Ayum-ee-aawach Oomama-mowan, Speaking to Their Mother* (Rebecca Belmore); *Cultural Graffiti: A Tahltan Indian Declares War on the British Monarchy* (Morin); *Do You Remember When?* (Postcommodity)
vortices, 68–73

Wakemup, Rory: *Mirror Shield Project: Water Serpent Action*, 1, *2*, 3, 5, 149n2
WalkingStick, Kay, 5–6, 20, 29, 30, 32–55, 62–63, 76, 78; *The Abyss*, 28, 43, 61, 157n84; *Bitterroot Mountains I*, 53; *Blame the Mountains III*, 116, *117*; *Cardinal Points*, 33–34, 48, 49; *Chief Joseph* series, 33–34, 37–38, 53, 155n32; *Cryptochroma I*; diptychs, 13–14, *14*, 28, 35, 40, 41–46, 63, 76, 116; *Fear of Non-Beings*, 156n56; *Four Directions* series, 156n74; *Four Directions: Spirit Center*, 47, 48, 49, 50, 63; *Grappling with Chaos*, 28, 43; grids, 35, 37–38, 39, 40–41, 48, 51; human figures, 116–18, 119; *Letting Go from Chaos to Calm*, 28, 44, 62; *Loss*, 28, 43, 44, 46, 156n59; modernism, 154n28; *Montauk* series, 34–35, *36*, 39–40, 42, 58; *New Mexico Arroyos*, 54–55; *New Mexico Desert*, 54, *54*; *Night*, 44; *On the Edge*, 13, *14*, 28, 62; *Orilla Verde at Rio Grande*, 54–55; *Our Land*, 52–53; *Our Selves, Our Land*, 47, 50; *The Pecos*, 54–55; *Positive Field*, 48, 49; public recognition, 154n30; *Ramapo River* series, 41–42, 53, 54, 61; *Remnant of Cataclysm*, 45; *Requiem*, 52, 53; *The Silence of Glacier*, 52, 54–55; *Spirit Center* series, 44, 47, 48, *49*, 50; *St. Mary's Mountain*, 54–55; *Tears*, 156n70; *Uncontrolled Destiny*, 28, 43, 46; *Venere Alpina*, 50–51, *52*, 116, 123, 125; *Where Are the Generations?*, 47, 50
Walla Walla Foundry, 78, 160n65
wampum belts, 92, *93*, 94, 102, 125
Wanderer above the Sea of Mist (Friedrich), 62
Warrior, Robert Allen, 24
Wash (Lavadour), 12
Washington Square Park, New York City, 86
Watson, Mark, 161n20
Wave Sound (Rebecca Belmore), 147–48, *147*, 170n97
Welish, Marjorie, 37
Where Are the Generations? (WalkingStick), 47, 50
Wilson, Will, 143; *Auto-Immune Response*, 143
Winnipeg, 136, 139, 165n82
wood collages, 58–59, 158n10
words and writing on paintings. *See* inscription on paintings

Yosemite Winter Scene (Bierstadt), 133

Zabusky, Norman, 69